FOR THE LOVE OF FIRE

Colin Kirkham

Grosvenor House
Publishing Limited

This book is published by
Grosvenor House Publishing Ltd
Link House
140 The Broadway, Tolworth, Surrey, KT6 7HT.
www.grosvenorhousepublishing.co.uk

A CIP record for this book
is available from the British Library

ISBN 978-1-83975-636-8

CONTENTS

PREFACE

Having had a fascination with fire from as far back as I can remember, I strongly believe that I was born to be an **Arsonist** or a **Firefighter**. As luck would have it, I stuck to the right side of the law and ended up having a full and eventful Fire Service career, with an added experience of being a Police Constable for two years!

My career was also unique in the sense that my Fire Service role was spread across two completely different Brigades, each with its own regional issues and challenges. This, along with my Police Constable role, shaped me into a more rounded firefighter, being able to see incidents from both the fire and police perspectives. This allowed me to deal with incidents safely, but to also have the awareness of what the Police required with regard to evidence gathering and scene protection.

The nature of a firefighter's role enthralled me, from my first day on duty as a Probationary Firefighter in Tyne and Wear Metropolitan Fire Brigade until my last day served as a Station Officer in the Isle of Man Fire and Rescue Service. The incidents I have attended over the years have created a mind full of memories – some good, some bad – but have also allowed me to look back with fondness on all the personnel that I have served with, who without a doubt helped facilitate so many laughs and humorous moments along the way. I respect you all for your courage, and especially your dedication in doing a job that isn't always for the faint-hearted.

ACKNOWLEDGEMENTS

The thought of writing a book never occurred to me until my son, Kai, joined my old Brigade – Tyne and Wear Fire and Rescue Service. He discovered that at every station he went to, someone told a story about me. Considering that I had moved to the Isle of Man over twenty years before, I had obviously left an impression.

Kai suggested that I should write a book so that the family could read about what I really got up to during my time in the Service. My girls, Gemma and Zoe, totally agreed, stating they had no idea what I did in either the Fire Service or the Police, and that they had heard bits and pieces of stories over the years but none from the horse's mouth.

COVID-19 had hit the island and we were in lockdown. So, sat in my boredom, I began jotting down a few notes about my fire and police career, and I found reminiscing on old incidents quite therapeutic, while I laughed at some of the things I got up to. However, other incidents like the Grieveson murders left me having sleepless nights, as I still felt anger and frustration. I have clear memories of every one of the fatalities that I dealt with over the years, and my sincere condolences go out to each and every one of their respective families. I haven't written down every fatal that I came across, as a lot were accidental or the result of RTC's, but I emphasise that I have not forgotten any of them.

The stories told are there to give you a sense of what life for me was like, in both my fire and police roles. But no matter how clearly I describe an incident, a pen cannot relay the smells or sounds that occur at the scene. Those are memories for those who were there.

My wife, Lorna, has been witness to the frustrations and sadness that some jobs have brought me, and for her love and support I am eternally grateful. But I am also sure that she doesn't miss my alerter going off at silly o'clock in the middle of the night, or even the Control Room phoning to inform me of an ongoing incident. I have missed birthdays, anniversaries, Christmas meals, and numerous parties over the years, so I also thank all my family and friends for their patience and understanding.

I would also like to thank Catherine Traynor, Alan Gash, Billy Forster, Alan Gawne, Peter Killey, Justin McMullin, and Eric Hudson, for their assistance and encouragement during the writing of this book.

I didn't want to write the book as all doom and gloom. There were many good times and successful rescues, along with the heartache and despair. I hope I have managed to balance both, to give a good overall view of life at its best and worst. The job of a firefighter is challenging but very rewarding, and despite budgetary cutbacks and at times bad leadership, it is still the best job in the world. I respect all the Emergency Services who live day and night to help others around them. God bless you all.

FOR THE LOVE OF FIRE

A FIREFIGHTER'S PRAYER

When I am called to duty, God,
Wherever flames may rage,
Give me the strength to save some life
Whatever be its age.

Help me embrace a little child
Before it is too late,
Or save an older person from
The horror of the fate.

Enable me to be alert and
Hear the weakest shout,
And quickly and efficiently
To put the fire out.

I want to fill my calling and
To give the best in me,
To guard my every neighbour
And protect their property.

And if according to your will
I have to lose my life,
Please bless with your protecting hand
My children and my wife.

CHAPTER ONE

THE EARLY YEARS

Born in April 1963, I am the middle child of seven, with two brothers and a sister older and two brothers and a sister younger. Created by my father James Francis and mother Hilda, I was brought into this world at the home address of 207 High Street, Jarrow – delivered by my mum's sister, my Auntie Mary, because Mum always left it too late to get to the hospital when her waters broke, mainly due to the fact that she didn't want to cause a fuss with anyone. This was true of all the kids, who were born at home except the youngest, Terence, who managed to get delivered at hospital. After all, he is the 'bairn' of the family.

Jarrow, for those who do not know, is a small, working-class town in the North East of England, on the banks of the River Tyne. It is known for 'The Jarrow Crusade' when, in 1936, all the unemployed from Jarrow and the surrounding areas marched from there to Parliament, to protest about the lack of jobs in the North East following the great depression. This event showed the real meaning of being a 'Jarrovian'. With true grit and determination, they walked the length of the country, with little food and money, but with a sense of pride in their heritage. Jarrow is also known for the Venerable Bede, the scholar and Saint who lived at Jarrow Monastery in 731AD. The monastery was raided by Vikings in 794AD, but their leader was captured and killed by the locals, and to this date there is a statue of two Viking warriors standing in the town centre. This sort of history makes 'Jarrovians' proud of where they come from, and instils attributes that can be used to face any situation in life.

I have fond memories of being brought up in a house full of kids. Dad had a great sense of humour, which certainly got passed onto all his children. He spent a lot of years working as a merchant seaman, and showed his sense of humour by bringing all sorts of wild and weird things home from his trips abroad. Once, he even brought a live monkey home, which Mum steadfastly refused to have in the house, so he ended up giving it to a local pub landlord. Unfortunately, the landlord allowed the monkey the run of the bar, and it started to steal all the customers' beer, therefore even the pub had to get rid of it. Dad thought that was hilarious and loved to tell that story. Meal times in the house were always a source of laughter, and at times it seemed that everyone living there just wanted to be a comedian. Jokes were told and stories divulged of pranks that had been committed (normally to each other, but often against others), causing laughter amongst us – and sometimes even tears. This upbringing obviously stuck with me during my adult years, as mischief seemed to follow me around. If something happened on the fire station, you could guarantee I was the one who got the initial blame. Admittedly, many of the pranks or jokes that were played either involved me or were set up by me. I do like to have a good laugh!

DANCING ANGELS

My childhood at High Street also gave me my first memories of 'Dancing Angels' – flames that flickered from the fire. Every year on the lead up to Guy Fawkes' night, the local kids would go on the search for 'Bonty Wood', looking to get as much wood or combustible materials to help build the biggest bonfire in the area, before eventually setting it alight on the 5th November. Unfortunately for my gang, we had rivals living across the road, led by Steven and Danny Fenwick. Such was the rivalry, we had to leave guards at the bonfire being built, in fear that they would either steal our wood or, worse still, set fire to our bonfire before the 5th. The Fenwicks, of course, had to do the same, so generally both bonfires were left to burn at the correct time. The sight of two bonfires, approximately 100ft apart, was a sight to behold. The fires illuminated the cold winter's night, with flames soaring 30ft high, and fireworks flying high into the sky before bursting into an array of colours. I would stand with the rest of my family, mesmerised by the flickering flames dancing around like angels in the evening sky, throwing out colours of red, amber, orange, and blue, with the occasional green coming into play, depending on what was being burnt. The feeling of heat on my face was immense, yet my back was cold with the winter breeze. That only added to the evening, along with the strong smell of smoke which engulfed everything around, leaving my clothing impregnated and needing to be washed the next day.

Then came the industrial actions in the early 1970s, leading to three-day working weeks, which then resulted in power strikes. When the power was off, it was bizarre to look outside and not see the street lighting illuminating the roads, leaving a darkness that I had not witnessed before. At these times, as a family, we would sit around the coal fire, toasting crumpets on the end of our forks. I would sit there for hours watching the flames dance around the fire, whilst candles, illuminating parts of the room, cast shadows that seemed to move on their own free will. Meanwhile, the flames danced their unique dance, twisting and turning, throwing out their warmth into the room. The movement of the flames fascinated me then, as it still does today.

DEADLY FORCE

At the age of ten, the family moved to a new house on the outskirts of Jarrow – to Hadrian Road, which is in the suburb of Primrose. It was here that I first came across what a deadly force fire can be. A candle, left unattended, set fire to a house around the corner from mine. The resulting blaze took the lives of two young children, leaving a lasting impression on everyone in the surrounding area. A sadness seemed to engulf the area, and questions of why and how could be heard being asked.

The fire happened in the middle of the night, so I only heard about it the next morning when a friend came knocking and told us the news. I gathered with others on the playing fields, opposite the severely burned house, to watch the comings and goings of the Police Forensic Teams and Fire Service personnel, who were trying to establish the sequence of events leading to the tragedy. I heard stories of how the firefighters fought through the flames to locate the children and carry them from the building. Unfortunately, despite their best efforts, it was too late.

On reflection, I think this was the first time that I had thought about becoming a firefighter on leaving school. I did not know at this time that it was to become a reality, with me facing tragedies of a similar nature to the one I was witnessing, or being the one trying to establish the facts when investigating fires.

CHAPTER TWO

PASSIONS

Although I left school in 1979, life for me took other twists and turns, so thoughts of becoming a firefighter were pushed to the back of my mind. The reason behind this was that I had achieved success in another passion I had. This passion was for the sport of basketball, which I had played throughout my school years, attaining international honours at all age groups. This had led me to become a semi-professional basketball player, playing in the top British National League with Sunderland Basketball Club. As well as playing for the club, I was also employed in the role of Basketball Development Officer, where I spent any spare time coaching the sport in schools, colleges, and youth clubs throughout the North East of England.

I had some fantastic times with Sunderland, and at times we were very successful, winning two play-off championships at Wembley, in 1981 and 1983. The people of Sunderland really got behind the team, and after we had won the second championship, the City of Sunderland bestowed the honour of Freedom of the City to all members of the team. As well as being a great honour, the Freedom allows me to walk my sheep through the streets of Sunderland without requiring permissions. I didn't, and probably will never have any sheep to take for a walk, but at the time it was nice to be appreciated.

I played for 15 seasons before the club was bought out by Sir John Hall, who at the time was the Chairman of Newcastle United Football Club. His vision was to have a sporting club to match the likes of Barcelona and Real Madrid, so as well as the basketball club, which he renamed Newcastle Comets, he also bought a rugby team (Newcastle Falcons) and an ice hockey team called Newcastle Cobras. However, the Sporting Club concept just didn't seem to work, and in a short space of time the different sports were off-loaded by Sir John to become independent again. The Comets were renamed Newcastle Eagles by the new management team, and went on to become one of the most successful teams in the UK.

Realising that my basketball career wasn't going to make me my fortune, and was hardly a secure employment, my father kept telling me to get a proper job! He added that all my basketball training sessions were being held in the evenings, so I could, as other players were doing, have a separate career and still play my sport. He was right, of course. So I started to look around for another means of employment which would still allow me to compete at the highest level of my sport. It was then that I came across an advert that would change my direction in life, and give me an opportunity to dance with the angels!!

RECRUITMENT

Tyne and Wear Metropolitan Fire Brigade (now Tyne and Wear Fire and Rescue Service) were recruiting, so I threw my hat into the ring to see how far I could get in the selection process. I was certainly fit enough with the amount of training I had done for basketball over the years, but did I have the rest of the attributes required for a firefighter? I also had to compete with a couple of thousand other applicants who were vying for the limited places available, but I had faith in my ability to compete with the best.

One thing that did concern me, though, was that I had a slight fear of heights, so I knew I had to sort this out before going any further. To try and resolve this irrational fear, I went about town, leaning over any tall bridges or buildings that I came across – to the extent that I am sure some people watching were convinced I was going to throw myself off. Slowly, my confidence grew, and I accepted I was not going to fall every time I came upon a height. Dad, having worked as a scaffolder for many years, gave me a piece of advice that rang so true, when he said, 'It's not the height that kills you, it's the landing.' He added, 'You could fall off a kerb, bang your head, and be gone; and equally, you could fall from a great height and still survive.' Anyway, by the time I reached training school, I had conquered my fear.

The recruitment process for the Fire Service at this time consisted of the following.

- Initial Application
- Written Exam Papers
- Dexterity Tests
- Claustrophobia (fear of confined spaces) and Acrophobia (fear of heights) Tests
- Formal Interview
- Medical – including eye test

It was at the written exam stage of the process that I first met another potential recruit called Jimmy McCabe. Jim was a character from the word go, and we stuck together through all the stages including the full training course, helping each other whilst also enjoying some great laughs in between.

It so happened that all the applicants were processed by the Brigade in alphabetical order, so that was how Jimmy and I ended up attending all the process stages at the same time. This helped to bond the friendship which lasted well past the passing out parade. I no longer live in the North East, but I know I could call at Jimmy's house at any time and be welcomed with laughter and memories. This can be said of numerous people I worked with over the years, which is why it is said that once you join the Fire Service, you not only start a career but join one big family.

Now, Jim had a sight issue with one of his eyes, and knowing that, at that time, the Brigade only allowed glasses to be worn for driving and routine station work, he wasn't very confident of achieving his dream job. He was particularly concerned with the medical stage, as he knew a basic eye test was part of this process. (Nowadays, breathing apparatus masks can be adapted to take prescription glasses, relieving some of the eyesight issues, although there are set standards still to be met). But first the acrophobia part of the test needed to be completed.

To test if you had any signs of being acrophobic, the potential recruits were lined up in the drill yard of South Shields Fire Station (Station Kilo). One by one, we were asked to climb a ladder that had been pitched to the fourth floor of the training tower. The fourth floor of this tower had a balcony which protruded out a good few feet, so if you looked directly down from there, you could not see the floors below – just open space to the ground. The instructors watched carefully to see if you appeared confident climbing the ladder, and not hugging it like a long-lost friend. Once at the top, you had to step off the ladder, onto a ten-inch windowsill, and turn around to face out towards the drill ground. Once in this position, the instructor would ask you some basic questions: (i) What is the time on the town hall clock (situated half a mile away)? (ii) What is the registration of the car parked in the station yard? (iii) What is in the doorway of the tower on the ground floor? In this case, it was a butane gas cylinder. To see the doorway, you really had to lean over, and with nothing to hang onto, it really put the frighteners on some of the candidates who automatically failed at this stage. In reality, you were quite safe, as the instructor standing behind you on the balcony was watching very carefully with one hand on your tunic, ready to pull you back if you showed any signs of panicking or falling.

I completed my turn successfully and came back down the ladder to line up next to Jim, who was discreetly asking me what the instructors were asking for. I told him just before he got called to ascend the ladder. Jim quickly looked over his shoulder at the car registration number, observed the cylinder in the doorway, and glanced at his watch before heading up. Needless to say, Jim passed this stage with ease, although he said tongue in cheek that he struggled to see the town hall, never mind the town hall clock.

MEDICAL

As had been the pattern on the other stages, Jim was scheduled to have his medical directly after me, so we arranged to travel together to the venue. At that time, Dr Douglas was the Brigade Medical Specialist. He was a lovely man who had a keen interest in a number of sports, but especially a passion for rugby union. He loved rugby so much he also served Newcastle Rugby Club as their Medical Officer. I knew this prior to going into my medical, and Dr Douglas made me so relaxed that we sat talking about sport, mainly basketball and rugby, to the extent that my medical overran by twenty minutes.

Jim, sitting outside in the waiting room, was panicking, thinking Dr Douglas was being extremely thorough and that he had no chance of passing the eye test. When I eventually came out to the waiting room, he was on the verge of just leaving and giving up. He asked me what had gone on and I told him, "Jim, just relax. When you go in, just talk about sport, especially rugby, and the doc will get distracted."

Twenty minutes later, Jim came out with a big smile on his face and ushered me out of the building. Once outside, he confessed that during the eye test, where you cover one eye with your hand and read the examination board then repeat with the other eye, he had started talking to the doc about Newcastle Rugby Club. At this stage, Jim covered his weak eye with his left hand and read the chart with his strong eye, passing with ease. Whilst still talking rugby, Dr Douglas asked Jim to do the other eye. Jim, being alert that the doctor was distracted, merely put his right hand over his weak eye and therefore got his strong eye tested again. The movement of the hands was enough to convince the doctor that both eyes had been tested, and Jim passed with flying colours. His theory was that in the Fire Brigade you would spend most your time in smoke-filled, dark places, so did you really need perfect eyesight? And he went on to have a full 30-year distinguished career with Tyne and Wear Fire and Rescue Service.

CHAPTER THREE

CLASS OF '87

About ten days after the medical, I received a letter through the post with the news that I had passed all the stages, and with an offer to start the recruit course on Monday, 7th September, 1987. I was elated, and felt that the dream was almost within grasping distance. But I had also heard a few horror stories of how hard and intense the training school could be, and was well aware of the fact that even at this stage one could easily fail and be dismissed from the Service at short notice. I was determined to take nothing for granted, and looked to face the 15 weeks on a day-to-day basis. Survive that, and there would only be the four-year probation period to complete!

KIT ISSUE

A few days prior to the start of the course, all the recruits were summoned to the Brigade Stores, where we were kitted out with uniform and fire kit. It was like Christmas come early, as the stores officer threw all sorts of things at us. We left with a number of bags, full of everything we needed to get straight down to business on the first day at training school. The kit issued included shirts, trousers, shoes (both steel-cap work shoes and smart undress shoes), socks, t/shirts, shorts, tracksuit, cap, fire tunics, fire leggings, helmet, steel-capped fire boots, gloves (both firefighting and general purpose); the list seemed endless. This kit, of course, had to be meticulously cleaned, ironed, and polished to the extent that the creases in clothing were razor sharp and the polish on shoes and boots mirror-like, all ready for inspection on that first training day.

Getting the shoes bulled up to a glaze is an art in itself, and it took me weeks to get anywhere near to the standard that was required. A couple of ex-servicemen tried their best to show the rest of us how to achieve the shine by using cotton wool with polish and water, but no matter how long I spent on the shoes, I struggled to get the result required. In the end, I paid one of the ex-soldiers to get my shoes up to standard, and once there, I was able to keep on top of them.

FIRST DAY NERVES

I turned up on that first day, anxious and excited at the same time. It felt like my first day at secondary school, even down to the fact that I had been to WH Smith's to buy new pens, pencils, Post-It notes, folders, and other bits of stationery that I thought I would need/use. Like any first day in a job, we waited for instructions of what to do, and the instructors didn't let us down. They stepped out of their office and proceeded to holler and shout at anything and everyone, until we were all dressed in the right uniform and lined up ready for inspection. Once lined up, they continued to yell and bawl, even though we were standing right in front of them and could hear them perfectly well. You could tell that some of the recruits were intimidated by all this shouting, and some were getting their backs up about it. I had to control a smile coming onto my face as I thought to myself, *Yes, my first day. I am finally here in the Fire Brigade.*

CFO's PEP TALK

As was tradition, we, the class of '87, were informed that the Chief Fire Officer was coming to the Training School to welcome us all to the Brigade. We were warned by the instructors to be on our best behaviour or face the consequences.

Chief Fire Officer Fred Elton entered the classroom and, as instructed, the 20 recruits immediately stood to attention behind their individual desks. The Chief then stood us down and asked us to take a seat. We had been informed prior to his arrival that the CFO liked to have a word with everyone and that, when requested, we were to stand to attention, give our name, and answer the

CFO's questions with the utmost respect. The Chief started down the rows of recruits, asking each person their name, and usually what the person had done for a living before joining the Brigade. Each recruit answered politely, and the instructors seemed reasonably happy and relaxed.

When the CFO got to me, I immediately stood to attention and called my name out loud and clear. The Chief looked at me and said, "My, you're a big lad! How tall are you?" "Six foot six, sir," I replied. He added, "And what were you before you joined the Brigade?" To which I replied, "Six foot six, sir." The Chief laughed; the rest of the recruits laughed; but the instructors looked at me with daggers. *This was going to be a long 15 weeks!* I thought, as I struggled to keep a smile off my face.

FAILURE NOT AN OPTION

It certainly was the hardest 15 weeks of my working life. I never realised how much work a firefighter recruit has to go through before getting anywhere near a fire station. We covered a variety of subjects, ranging from the science behind fire (including fire behaviour) to firefighting media, trauma care and first aid, Brigade policies and procedures, knots and lines, pumps and primers, hydraulics, all the equipment carried on the appliances, and so much more. Added to this list was a detached two-week breathing apparatus course, held at the Brigade's Breathing Apparatus Complexes, for those who made it to week 10. We worked hard, but also realised that we needed to study even harder.

At the end of each week on the Friday afternoon, we sat a written exam covering everything that we had been taught up to that point. On the following Monday morning, we were given our exam result. If you failed one exam, you were automatically given a written warning. If you failed a second exam, you were immediately dismissed. It was ruthless, and not altogether fair, as one recruit called Diamond – a plumber by trade – was excellent practically but failed two written exams and was dismissed. To this day, I still think he would have made an excellent firefighter.

On top of the written exams, we also had practical exams that covered all aspects of what we had learned on the drill ground, from being a pump operator to being in charge of a ladder drill. There were also exams covering first aid and trauma care, as well as weekly tests on your skills with knots and lines. The testing was continuous, bringing with it stress levels which allowed the instructors to assess how you coped under pressure.

JANKERS

Our working days were long and tiresome, and designed to be as packed as possible. We started each day at 0715hrs and were expected to be on parade in full undress uniform, ready for inspection, bang on 0730hrs. This was the first opportunity for the instructors/inspecting officers to issue out jankers (extra work duties – normally some cleaning of equipment, during your lunch hour). If there was a crease out of place or a bit of fluff on your uniform, you got jankers. If your shoes didn't shine enough, you got jankers. If you hadn't shaved close enough, you got jankers. You even got jankers if the recruit next to you had a hair on his uniform (you got the jankers for not telling him before inspection). Standards were set high, and you were expected to respond to those standards.

Following inspection, you were dismissed to quickly change into PT uniform and get back out onto the yard for a keep fit session that normally lasted about an hour. This could consist of a run around South Shields, or circuit training in the yard. Then it was a quick change into working uniform for some classroom work, before changing into fire kit for practical drills in the drill yard.

Lunch came next, and you soon learned to be very careful of how much you ate, as you knew that after lunch you would be on the drill yard again in full fire kit. The instructors ran the sessions hard, pushing you towards exhaustion. It wasn't uncommon for a recruit to vomit and collapse in a heap, only to be told to get their act together and carry on. As I have already stated, we had a couple of guys on the course who were ex-military, and they stated that their Army basic training was nowhere near as tough as what we were going through.

After the physical beasting on the drill yard, we would retreat into the classroom for another session of lectures and classroom-based practical tutoring, designed to stretch your thinking capacity to the maximum, especially when being so tired. I am sure the instructors used to turn the heating up in the room for those afternoon sessions, as it was always a struggle to keep your eyes open, especially if the subject being taught was a bit mundane. As soon as someone yawned or the instructor noticed your eyes closing, they would rant and rave with great haughtiness, as if they were just waiting for someone to let their guard down. It was at these times that I often wished I were back outside on the drill ground, where no matter how tired you were, you at least had the fresh air to keep you awake.

Every day always ended the same, with everyone being allocated cleaning duties. All the equipment we had used throughout that day had to be meticulously cleaned and serviced, as well as cleaning of the centre's facilities, such as the toilets, shower block, kitchen, classroom, and kit room, etc, which all needed to be spotlessly clean for the instructors to scrutinise. Only when the inspection party considered that the cleaning had been done to an acceptable level, would we be dismissed. This could happen at any time between 1900hrs and 2000hrs, where we would then go home, eat, and prepare uniform, only to do it all again the very next day. How I looked forward to the weekends!!

SWIM LIKE A BRICK

Once a week, instead of the normal PT session, we would run a mile to the local swimming baths and do training exercises in the water. Unfortunately for me, due to an ear operation as a child, I hadn't learned to swim when the rest of my peers had, and subsequently had never got around to it as an adult.

The question of whether one could swim or not had never been brought up in any of the recruitment stages, so I hadn't given it much thought, and just assumed that I could do the training in the shallow end of the pool. But as we ran to the pool for the first session, I decided that I needed to inform the instructors before we got into the water.

Once lined up alongside the pool, I stuck my hand up and was given permission to speak. "Sir, I think you should know that I can't swim," I declared. Station Officer Herbert, the Second in Command of the Training School, looked annoyed and stepped in front of me and said, "What do you mean, you can't bloody swim?" But before I could explain, he told me to follow him to the deep end of the pool. The rest of the recruits stood there wondering what was going to happen.

Once at the deep end, Station Officer Herbert ordered me to jump in. "But, sir," I said, "I can't swim". Getting really annoyed now, he shouted, "Get in that pool now!" He continued, "Unless you want to face a discipline charge."

Reluctantly, I jumped into the water, but luckily for me the depth of the water in the deep end was only 6 foot 6 inches, and being just over 6 foot 6 inches tall, I managed to get on my tip toes and still be able to get my mouth above water. "GET YOUR FEET OFF THE BOTTOM!" he roared, to which the rest of the recruits and the other instructors who were watching burst out laughing.

Station Officer Herbert let me get out of the water, and by good fortune another recruit, Ash Howard, had been a swimming instructor before joining the Fire Service, so he was allocated the job of teaching me to swim before the end of the course. However, I never forgot the embarrassment Station Officer Herbert had dealt me that day, and looked forward to the day when I could get some payback.

THE DUNK

Ash was a really good teacher, and by the end of the course he had me swimming two lengths without stopping, which I thought was respectable, considering I had started from scratch. This ability to swim came in handy on our last visit to the pool, when the instructors joined us for a game of water polo.

I hadn't forgotten how Station Officer Herbert had treated me that first week, so I shadowed him to prevent him from excelling in the game. However, almost as soon as the game started, the ball came in our direction and, being directly behind Herbert, the mischievous devil inside me took over. As he rose to get the ball, I placed my hand on top of his head and pushed, then held him under the water. It was only for about five seconds, but he came up spluttering away and demanding to know who had dunked him. By then, I had swum away, and although another instructor had seen the whole thing, he had grasped the humour in it and played along that he hadn't seen the incident. Revenge is sweet!

CHAPTER FOUR

TEAMWORK

Not all the instructors were pains in our butts, but all had the same objective. Their aim was to turn this class of individuals into a team that could fit onto any Watch within the Brigade, without being a danger or hindrance to themselves or others. The 15 weeks was just the start of the road to being a competent firefighter, and the instructors had their own reputations to protect, so they needed us to be ready for that first day on a live station. Any failing by any of us, in those first weeks on a Watch, would reflect badly on the instructors so they weren't going to let that happen. Discipline was harsh and the learning intense, but by the end of the 15 weeks, those of us that were left had bonded into a team which had taken away so much knowledge from all the staff at the Training School.

One of the instructors 'Dusty Ashman' went above and beyond to help, encourage, and to teach us in a way that was appreciated by all. He had had a distinguished career in the Brigade, carrying with him an immense amount of experience from years spent on busy stations, before moving to the Training School to pass on his knowledge. He was also ex-military so knew all about discipline, but he also had this gentle manner which brought out the best in people. I learned a lot from Dusty, not just on the theory or practical sides of the job, but also on how to manage a group of firefighters.

In one of Dusty's first lectures, he commenced by saying, "To put a fire out is a simple thing, you just put the wet stuff on the hot stuff! But to do it safely and efficiently requires training, planning, leadership, and most importantly TEAMWORK! Add a little courage now and again, and there isn't anything that can't be overcome." Little did I know at that stage how true his words were. But over the years I have reflected on them, and could see the importance of what he was telling us.

TOILET HUMOUR

It took me until the second week of training to realise that being given jankers for some inane reason was just a tool used by the instructors to encourage discipline and teamwork. Being aggrieved at what we thought were trivial punishments, helped the class bond together against the instructors, which was exactly what they wanted to happen.

Even so, at times the instructors were ridiculous and relentless at dishing out the punishment. One afternoon, I was given the job of cleaning the toilets. By the time I was finished, everything was gleaming, so I stood to attention outside the door to await the inspection party. Two minutes before they were due, Sub Officer Youll, a ginger-haired instructor decided, to my dismay, to use the loo. I waited patiently for him to finish, and once he came out, I rushed back in to check everything was still okay. I squirted more cleaner down the toilet and quickly ran a paper hand towel round the sink. Everything seemed in order, so again I lined up outside to await inspection.

The inspection that day was being taken by Sub Officer Curry, who entered the toilet with notepad in hand. Within the space of a minute, I was summoned to join him. "Kirkham!" he said. "What's that lying in the sink?" I looked to see something that hadn't been there two minutes earlier. "Well?" he demanded. "It looks like a ginger pubic hair, sir," I replied. "And how on earth did it get there?" he inquired. "It must be Sub Officer Youll's, sir," I cringed. "Are you telling me that Sub Officer Youll has ginger pubes, and he left it there in the sink?" he asked.

I tried to explain about Sub Officer Youll's toilet visit prior to inspection, but by then Sub Officer Curry was shouting along the corridor for Sub Officer Youll to join us. Sub Officer Youll obviously denied all knowledge of the pubic hair, and gave me jankers for having the nerve to accuse him. I then got double jankers from Sub Officer Curry for failing the inspection. I could hear them chuckling about it as they strolled away down the corridor.

The following day, as part of my punishment, I was given the toilets to clean again, and despite meticulously cleaning and checking them, the inspection party managed to pull a fine fishing line, complete with hook, from out of the plughole of the sink. They asked why it was there, so I just replied, "JANKERS." Enough said!

MIKHAIL GORBACHEV

Although being tall does occasionally brings its advantages, it does mean that you stand out from a crowd and can easily be recognised. Also being follicly-challenged means I have little protection if I do bang my head.

One day, prior to starting duty, myself and Jim McCabe were having a right old natter at the end of the corridor, not realising it was almost time for Parade. Just then, the instructors came out of their office, saw me, and screamed for me to get to the drill yard at the double. I jumped and started running past the instructors, when one asked who had I been talking to. It was then, as I turned around to check, that I realised that Jim, being the slippery goat he is, had quickly exited out of the back door without being seen. Unfortunately for me, I was in mid-stride as I turned to look, and didn't register that I was going through a doorway. Now normally, when I go through an average doorway, I have to duck slightly to avoid banging my head. This time I didn't duck, and I hit the head of the door frame with such force it almost knocked me unconscious. Blood started trickling down my face, and when I looked up, I could see a two-inch piece of skin hanging from the framework where my head had hit. I got little sympathy from the instructors, who merely gave me a cloth to stem the bleeding and ordered me out on Parade. Standing on Parade, the instructors pointed out to everyone that the injury had been caused because 'Kirkham' couldn't adhere to the rules. Due to having a bang on the head, I claimed I couldn't remember who I had been talking to, so Jim yet again escaped getting jankers.

The laceration on my head took ages to heal, made worse by the fact that that my fire helmet would rub the wound when doing practical drills. This meant that I had a semi-permanent scab/scar for weeks on my head, which enabled one of the instructors to nickname me 'GORBACHEV', after the Soviet Union President Mikhail Gorbachev, who happened to have a large birthmark in the same place as my wound. I have been called worse things in my life, so accepted the nickname with the humour that was intended.

Following instruction from the Training Centre Staff, the two-inch piece of skin was left on the door frame, dangling there for all to see. The instructors used it as a reminder to all new recruits of what happens when you disobey orders. The following year, I returned to the Training School for my twelve-month assessment... and yes, like a dried-up crisp, the skin was still hanging from where I had left it.

NO PAIN NO GAIN

The cut to my head wasn't the only injury I picked up at Training School. A more serious injury threatened to derail my plans of completing the course. During week seven, I accidentally banged my knee on the ground whilst doing hose running drills. The knee swelled up like a balloon and I was terrified that I was going to be back coursed, meaning I would have to start training all over again. After a couple of days, things had not improved with the knee, so I was sent to the local hospital to get it checked out. I was there for almost three hours being examined, as well as having an X-ray. The doctor eventually came to the conclusion that I had torn my meniscus cartilage. He stated that the initial treatment should be rest and elevation, with an ice pack to reduce the swelling, along with anti-inflammatory medication to help.

The ice pack I could do, but the rest would have to wait. I returned to the Training School and informed the staff that it was just a bruise and would settle down. I wore an elasticated knee support and hobbled on through the next couple of weeks on painkillers and ice packs until eventually the knee started to improve. Suffering the pain was so much better than suffering the heartache of being back coursed.

CHAPTER FIVE

B.A. SCHOOL

My knee just managed to settle down in time for the breathing apparatus (BA) part of the course, commencing on week ten. It was a two-week course held at the Brigade's BA complex, situated behind Tynemouth Fire Station (Station Juliet), with a couple of visits to the Brigade's Marine Firefighting Complex based on the banks of the Tyne at South Shields, thrown in for good measure. The feeling amongst the recruits was that this would be our biggest test yet, and if we got through this fortnight, we should survive to complete the full course.

I enjoyed every minute of these two weeks, and excelled in all the scenarios that we faced. Searching for casualties in a pitch black, smoke-filled, hot environment requires great focus and concentration, and I took to it like a duck to water. Various situations were set up which included firefighting and search and rescue. Fourteen stone dummies – along with smaller child and baby dummies – were hidden within the complex, and teams were sent in to retrieve them. The importance of working together as a team is never more important than when wearing BA and entering the unknown, and this is drilled into you from day one of the course. Having been a team player all my life, it was easy for me to work with others and adjust to the different situations, so I looked forward to anything the instructors would throw at us. Each scenario we faced, we tackled as a team, and worked together as a team, and within these conditions I excelled.

SHIP FIREFIGHTING

The visits to the Marine Firefighting Complex proved to be a real challenge. Scenarios were set up to simulate incidents on board ships, normally with a fire in the engine room to contend with and rescues to be fulfilled. You entered the structure from the roof, hauling charged hose through hatchways while descending down vertical ladders to the decks below. Once at the source of the fire, you would extinguish the flames before hauling out any casualties back up the ladders and through the extreme heat barrier to the safety of outside. The temperatures inside the complex were recorded as being in excess of 1000-degrees Fahrenheit, which understandably drained the energy from you. A number of recruits struggled with heat exhaustion, and on one occasion, having completed the drill of carrying a fourteen stone dummy up the vertical ladder to the outside, I began to feel light-headed and noticed that my legs had turned to jelly. These are typical symptoms of having been exposed to excessive heat for a period of time, so I needed to cool myself down as soon as I reached the safe area. In doing so, I immediately stripped off my helmet and my tunic, and sat down whilst rehydrating myself with water until I finally recovered enough to carry on.

A couple of years later, after a series of near misses, Health and Safety stepped in to monitor the temperatures. This resulted in thermometers being strategically placed throughout the complex, and a limit on what temperatures firefighters were expected to work in. If the temperatures got too hot, the instructors were obliged to open doors to vent the complex until it was cool enough to work in. This seems reasonable enough, but in a real live situation, on a real ship, there will be a need to work in those extreme temperatures, so why not practise in them? The debate on this goes on.

LONGTAIL

Part of the BA training included search and rescue in the confined space of a sewer complex. Lucky for us recruits, the Brigade had built its own simulated sewer complex, so we could crawl through without getting covered in the delights of a real sewer. Nevertheless, for me, this complex became a source of a few nightmares following one exercise.

Although reasonably tight to crawl and drag dummies through, it wasn't the claustrophobia element of the drill that sent shivers down my spine; it was something much more alive and sinister. The drill started by being put into BA teams of two, with each team being timed on completing the same exercise. Throughout the course, the instructors had loved to set competitive challenges amongst the recruits, and probably set friendly wagers with each other as to the results. Being the tallest recruit on the course, I didn't hold out much hope of being in the fastest team, but I was always up for the challenge.

We were instructed to crawl into the sewer and recover a casualty that had been reported as being trapped and unconscious. My team leader and I crawled into the sewer, and traversed through a few pipes until we finally found the casualty at a junction. This junction came in handy, as we managed to manoeuvre the dummy so that my partner could get to the other side of him and turn around. We placed an oxygen mask over the dummy's head and strapped the O2 cylinder onto his chest. Now was the hard part – getting him out as fast as we could, in the hope that we would not be the slowest team. I shuffled backwards, dragging the shoulders of the dummy, while my team leader pushed the feet and legs towards the entrance. The sweat dripped from my body with the exertion required in doing this task, but we moved along the pipe inch by inch, methodically keeping to a rhythm which seemed to be working well for us.

The exercise was proving to be an energy draining one, but I was happy with how we were proceeding, when all of a sudden, out of the corner of my eye, a movement caught my attention. A rat, approximately 18 inches long, was scuttling over the dummy and was heading straight for me. I swear it looked me straight in the eye before scurrying across my shoulder into the darkness behind. All that sweat turned to ice, as my mind visualised the rat doing a U-turn and heading straight up my leggings. Because the pipe wasn't big enough to turn around in, I was left with no option but to reverse out of that pipe as fast as my toes and elbows could shuffle me (although we still didn't get anywhere near the fastest time). My BA partner struggled to keep pace, as he wondered where I had suddenly got that burst of energy from. I reported the rat to the instructor, and all he could say was that the rat probably got the biggest fright looking at my mush (face) in the torchlight!

I am not embarrassed to say that for a few nights after this incident, all I could dream of was rats chewing various parts of my body, whilst I couldn't move to do anything about it. At least twice I awoke in a cold sweat. But despite this trauma, as I have already said, I thoroughly enjoyed the BA course. There was, however, a price to pay. With all the crawling around and the physical side of the exercises, my knee took another hammering. So much so, that I was left to ice down the balloon every night, right up to passing out on week 15.

PASSING OUT

The Pass Out Parade went like a dream. Family and friends were invited to watch the 15 remaining recruits march around the drill yard in synchronised movements, and also to put on demonstrations of their skills that had been learned over the previous months. Everything went according to plan, and even the instructors looked impressed for once. The Chief and Leader of the Fire Authority congratulated us and wished us all luck as we started a new chapter working on our new Watches, at our designated station.

It was a very emotional day for me, as my parents had come to watch me passing out to start the next phase of my new career. At that time, my dad was going through a tough time with terminal cancer, and I had thought it would be best for him to stay at home in the warmth. But Dad, being an ex-seaman, was as tough as old boots, and despite the cold December day, he turned up determined to watch the whole thing. I looked across at him a few times during the day and he looked chilled through to the bone as he sat watching with the other families, but I could also see a sense of pride in his face as he watched intently. When it was over, he told me that he wouldn't have missed it for the world and 'how proud he was of me'. Those words alone made the whole 15 weeks totally worthwhile.

CHAPTER SIX

BRIGADE LAYOUT

Tyne and Wear Metropolitan Fire Brigade, at that time, covered an area of approximately 208 square miles. Within its area was a wide-ranging variety of fire risks, ranging from shipyards and heavy engineering industries to rural areas and industrial estates. It's an area that covers two cities, Newcastle and Sunderland, and has a population of approximately 1.2 million. The Brigade had 19 stations split between three Divisions:

North Division consisted of eight stations:

- Alpha – West Denton
- Bravo – Newcastle West
- Delta – Newcastle Central
- Echo – Gosforth
- Foxtrot – Newcastle East
- Golf – Wallsend
- Hotel – Whitley Bay
- Juliet – Tynemouth

East Division consisted of five stations:

- Kilo – South Shields
- Mike – Sunderland North (Fulwell)
- November – Sunderland Central
- Oscar – Sunderland West
- Romeo – Sunderland South

South Division consisted of six stations:

- Sierra – Washington
- Tango – Hebburn

- Victor – Gateshead
- Yankee – Swalwell
- Whiskey – Birtley
- Zulu – Chopwell

VICTOR GREEN

We had been told by the instructors that we would be allocated our new stations on the day before the Pass Out Parade. That day arrived, and we all sat impatiently in the classroom waiting for the instructors to arrive to deliver the news. Rumours of how good or how bad certain Watches on different stations were, floated around the classroom as we awaited our fate. Each recruit was just hoping to get a good Watch that they would be happy on, but I was sure that no matter where they sent me, I was going to be in my element and enjoy every moment.

The instructors arrived and began the distribution. Starting in alphabetical order, they progressed around the classroom, leaving some happy and some disgruntled recruits in their wake. Finally, they got to me and said, "Kirkham, Green Watch Victor." I hadn't heard much about Victor except that it was a busy station, so I was quite happy with what I had got and just sat there with a huge grin on my face. The instructors finished and left the room, leaving us to discuss and debate who had been lucky and who had got a raw deal. Some of the other recruits told me that they knew a few people on Victor, and assured me that I was going to a great station and that I was lucky to be going there. This made me even more excited just to get there and get started.

FIRST SHIFT

My first shift on duty was allocated to be the 31st December, which was the Green Watch second nightshift. (The work rota at this time was two dayshifts, 0900hrs-1700hrs, followed by two nightshifts, 1700hrs-0900hrs, followed by four days off.) This meant that I would only do the one night before having a few days off, which disappointed me; I just wanted to do a full two

26

days and two nights to settle in. But I thought that at least a nightshift would give me a good taster of what the Watch was like, and hopefully I would get a few shouts to ease any nerves I may have.

The 31st arrived, and I was so excited that I arrived on station, ready to start, well before any other members of Green Watch had turned up – much to the amusement of the Blue Watch dayshift crew. I had hardly slept the night before, with thoughts whizzing around my head of what my first job would be, and praying that I wouldn't let the Watch down in any way at all. After talking to some members of Blue Watch, I had a walk around all the appliances, which looked fantastic all parked up in a row and ready to respond to the bells going down. *What a way to spend New Year's Eve*, I kept thinking excitedly to myself, as I awaited joining my Watch on parade to start my first nightshift.

Parade came, and I was allocated to ride the Category 1 (Cat 1) appliance, call sign V01, as BA entry control officer. The officer in charge (OIC) of the Watch, Station Officer Tommy Sidaway, always rode V01 when he was on duty, leaving his second-in command, Sub Officer Jimmy Thompson, to be OIC of the Category 2 (Cat 2) appliance, call sign V02. After checks were completed, the Station Officer summoned me to his office and went through how he thought my training was to go. He said that I would be riding the Cat 1 with him until he was satisfied that I was competent enough to move onto the Cat 2. He said that he would be overseeing all of my training, and that if I had any issues, to go straight to him. He added that whilst out in the public, or at an incident, I was to address him as Station or Station Officer, but on station I could call him Tommy. He made me feel at ease and assured me that I was going to enjoy my time at Victor, and said I should just relax as I wasn't expected to know everything straight off, but would learn through experience and time.

We then joined the Watch in the canteen for a cup of tea, where the rest of the lads took their first opportunity to try and suss me out. Even at this early stage I could see who the dominant members of the Watch were, and I also started to figure out who would be helpful to me and who would be a pain. After tea, Sub

Officer Thompson took me to one side and basically told me that he didn't like probationers, and that I was to have very little to do with him. He said that I was to address him as Sub or Sub Officer, and that I was not to use his first name whatever the circumstances, even though the rest of the Watch could because they had earned the right! I stood there wondering what charm school Sub O Thompson had been to, and thinking perhaps it was time he had a refresher. I also ticked him off my list in my head of who would be helpful!

As things worked out, Tommy did oversee all of my training during the time I spent at Victor, and for his support I am forever grateful. As expected, I cannot recall any time that Sub O Thompson encouraged, taught, or advised me. I knew which management style I thought was more useful, and swore that if I ever climbed the promotion ladder, I would treat probationary (proby) firefighters with the respect they deserve.

FIRST CALLOUT

Things started out really quietly, and two hours into the shift all we had done was a bit of cleaning of equipment. I felt that after Sub O Thompson's inspirational welcome to the Watch, the New Year's Eve shift was going to be a total disappointment. Just then, the bells went down, and I nearly jumped out of my skin as I grabbed my fire boots and leggings to start getting dressed. V02 'car fire' was called out, and I felt deflated as I watched the crew of V02 climb onto their appliance and start getting into their fire kit. I put my boots back on the truck and turned to watch, just as the appliance pulled out of its bay, with blue lights rolling and sirens blaring, leaving me to continue cleaning. V02 came back after about 40 minutes, and the Watch sat down to eat dinner, leaving me slightly disillusioned. I had hoped to have seen flames by then.

At around 2200hrs, the bells went down again and V01, V02 and V03 (turntable ladder) were called out. I jumped onto the truck, and in my excitement got ready into fire kit so quickly that I was fully dressed before the driver had started the engine. Alarms at the Nurses' Home was the call; it was part of the Queen

Elizabeth Hospital in Gateshead, and was the accommodation block for nurses. We proceeded at speed – my first experience of a blue light run, thrillingly weaving in and out of the traffic with the siren wailing. I sat there watching as we progressed along the road, with a huge grin on my face, as I helped the other lads sitting next to me into their fire kit and BA sets. We arrived a few minutes later at the hospital, where we were met by one of the hospital porters, who told us there was no panic. He stated that some of the off-duty nurses were having a New Year's Eve party and had accidentally set off the alarms. A decision was made that I should stay with the appliances and man the radio, while the rest of the crews went into the party to ensure all was okay. I guess this was the downside of being the proby!

I sat on the appliance listening to the radio, as other stations mobilised to other jobs, and I just wished that we would turn out to something that would be a bit more exciting than sitting by myself. Time seemed to tick by so slowly, and I knew the lads were not going to be in a rush to return to home station – not when they were surrounded by a load of nurses. I was in no doubt that they were having a great time but, as luck would have it, their fun was soon short-lived, as 20 minutes later a call came through for us to attend the Swallow Hotel in Gateshead. A water tank had burst, causing flooding to the rooms below, which, in turn, had set off the fire alarms. The lads came running back to the trucks and we swiftly mobilised to the Swallow Hotel. We pulled up at the front of the hotel to be greeted by a crowd of party-goers, all dressed up to celebrate the New Year but having to be evacuated from the building as the alarms sounded. They cheered as we pulled up, and a few of the boys received drunken kisses from ladies who were obviously having a great time. The hotel maintenance staff had already stopped the flow of water, so all that was left to do was a small amount of salvage work to prevent further damage. I proceeded with a couple of others, with salvage sheets under arm, to the affected rooms. It didn't take us long to do what was asked of us, and before I knew it, we were all back on the trucks ready for our next job. The Station Officer advised the hotel manager on how to reset the fire alarm system, which had to be done before he could allow the party back into the premises, where they could continue their countdown to New Year. Although I hadn't seen any flames yet, I had thoroughly enjoyed just being part of the team, and felt good about being able to help the hotel in their time of need.

BLACK SHEEP

We had just made it back to station before the bells went down again, and as V02 had already been diverted to their second car fire of the night, it was left to V01 to pick up the call. It was to a reported chimney fire at a property on Sunderland Road, Felling. Once again, I dressed quickly as the other two lads, sat in the back of the truck with me, casually put their fire kit on. It was only a chimney fire, after all, but it was still enough to give me an adrenalin rush as we sped along the road. The other guys, though, looked uninterested with the whole thing, as all they wanted to do was to get back to station to climb into their beds.

As we approached the address, we could see a large amount of smoke coming from a chimney stack. The lads sitting next to me moaned that this might take a while, but I just smiled with satisfaction that we were going to be fighting fire – not the big one that I hoped for, but at least I would see flames, I thought to myself.

Tommy and I approached the house to knock on the door, but as I lifted the letter box to knock, a load of grey smoke came billowing out. The house was on fire! Station Officer Sidaway immediately shouted out orders. "Make pumps 3, possible persons reported!" he called to the driver, who then passed his radio message to Control (due to the time of night, Tommy had assumed the possibility of people being in the building, hence the 'possible persons reported' call). He told the two nominated BA wearers to get their sets on, and for me to break down the door. My adrenalin levels shot through the roof, and with one kick the door flew open, where I could see that the smoke was thick and had come down to about a foot from the floor. Station Officer Sidaway told me to crawl into the hallway to see if I could see anyone, but not to go too far in, as the BA team would be nearly ready.

I got down on my belly and crawled along the carpet, where I observed two seats of fire in what appeared to be the living room. I keenly scanned everywhere, looking intently for any casualties, but couldn't see any in the immediate area. My eyes were starting to sting with the smoke, and I was fighting to quell a cough that wanted to escape my throat, so I concentrated on only breathing through my nose. I had been in the property for no more than a minute when, as expected, I received a tap on the heels from the BA team who were moving forward with hose-reel in hand. That was my cue to crawl back out to report what I had seen to the Station Officer, which I did, as my stinging eyes watered, leaving streaks on my smoke-blackened face. I found the whole incident an immense adrenalin rush as I darted around doing whatever was asked of me, making me feel that I was finally part of the Fire Brigade team.

Once the fire had been extinguished and the smoke vented, it became obvious that the house had been broken into while the occupants were out. Unfortunately for me, the burglar had decided to take a number two in the hallway, and I had crawled right through the human faeces. My tunic stunk and had to be put into the pump bay locker of the truck until we got back to home station, where I could scrub it and change into clean kit. I felt as if I had well and truly been christened! It was disgusting, but something like that wasn't going to take the shine off what I was feeling inside; in fact, it just added to a memorable job.

As I cleaned my tunic, the rest of the Watch cleaned the equipment that had been used at the fire. They were twittering away, complaining that they were knackered, and blaming me for the fact that they hadn't had any sleep that night. They said that I was a black sheep (a probationer who attracts incidents). The Watch had hoped to get a white sheep as a probationer (someone who doesn't seem to get their fair share of incidents), as they felt they were busy enough without having extra work to do. I, of course, was relatively happy to get as many jobs as possible, even if the rest of the watch wanted an easy life, so I happily carried the mantle of Black Sheep and they would just have to get used to being busy!

But it was getting late into the night, and even I was starting to feel a bit tired. So when the cleaning was done, I headed up to the dormitory along with the rest of the lads, to try and get some sleep. I lay down on my bed, but my body was restless, as my mind went over the jobs that we had been to so far. There was no way I was going to get to sleep, and was just considering getting up to watch some television, when lo and behold the bells went down again. Black Sheep strikes again, I figured, as I jumped up with a smirk on my face.

A SIGHT TO BEHOLD

The call was to a reported house on fire in the Benham area of Gateshead. The bay doors of the appliance room rolled open as I climbed onto V01 and started to dress into my nice, clean fire kit. Once dressed, I helped the BA wearers into their sets, in preparation of what lay ahead, as V01 and V02 drove into the early morning darkness.

All dressed and ready for action, I looked out of the cab window to see the blue lights reflecting back as we passed a few shop windows. "Just around the next corner," the lad sitting next to me said, which made the hairs on my neck stand up in anticipation. We turned into the street to see a slight haze of smoke coming from a house on our left, so I knew straight away it was going to be a working job. I couldn't wait to get off the appliance to get stuck into another fire, but what I hadn't noticed was a lady standing on the right side of the road.

Station Officer Sidaway turned to me, sitting wide-eyed in the back of the cab, and said, "That's your job, Colin. Get her sorted out." I looked to where Tommy was pointing, and saw a lady, probably in her mid-60s, totally naked, crying, and waving her arms around. My heart sank, because I wanted to be with the rest of the lads dealing with the fire, but I guessed that being the proby, I was the obvious choice to deal with the lady. When the appliance came to a stop, the BA wearers got to work while I grabbed a blanket and approached the woman. All of a sudden, just before I got to her, she took off like an Olympic sprinter straight down the street, with me chasing her as fast as I could. She dodged in and out between parked cars, bawling her eyes out, until finally she tripped on the kerb and landed in an unsightly heap. I quickly wrapped the blanket around her and tried my best to console her, as I checked over my shoulder to see if any of the other lads had seen the big chase. If they had, I was sure I would be in for some stick when we got back to station, and that they would say that I had been outrun by a pensioner. But I would have to wait and see if anyone noticed, as for now I had a job to do with this unusual casualty. So I started chatting to her as if she were my best friend, while checking with her that she wasn't injured in any way.

It came to light that she had had an argument with her daughter, who had told her to 'go to hell' before leaving the house. So, taking her daughter's words to heart, in her drunken state, she had stripped off her clothing and set fire to the house. When the flames and smoke started to become unbearable for her, she had started to panic, eventually staggering out into the street where a neighbour heard her screams and called the Fire Brigade.

After a little while, an ambulance arrived to assist with the lady, and the paramedic decided that it would be best if she was taken to hospital, due to her suffering from slight smoke inhalation from when she had been in the property. By now the fire was out, and all that was left to do was to clear some burnt debris out into the back yard of the house, which I did while the BA wearers serviced their sets. We finished at the incident and returned to station with the lads trying to tell me that this night was not a normal night, and that they had not been this busy in a long time. I thought nobody had seen me chasing the woman and that I had gotten away with the embarrassment, until the driver of V02 announced to all that he thought he was at the pantomime watching *Beauty and the Beast,* as he heavily exaggerated a description of my chase up the street. I cockily asked him which one was the Beast, which made the lads laugh and deflected some of the heat. He assured me that any woman seeing my face approaching them in the middle of the night would do exactly the same as she had, and run for their life, to which everyone rolled around laughing.

33

It certainly was a baptism of fire for a probationer on his first night shift, and soon enough, 0900hrs came and we were dismissed to allow White Watch to take up the reins of the station, while we began our first of four days off. Instead of heading straight home, one of the lads invited all the Watch round to his house for a drink to celebrate the New Year. Not wanting to appear unfriendly, I gratefully accepted the offer, and a good few of us proceeded to his house. We sat and discussed the jobs of the previous night, and some told stories of other incidents that they had attended over the years. A few drinks were consumed and those that were there got to know me a little better in a more relaxed atmosphere. I had a great time and called my dad to pick me up at around noon. When he arrived, he took one look at me in my slightly inebriated state and said, "If this is the modern-day Fire Service, God help us all." To which I laughed and giggled all the way home.

SHORT STAY

My time at Victor was to be short-lived, as a decision by senior management to relocate specialist appliances meant that each Watch on Victor had to lose two men. Being the last man to join the Watch, I was an obvious choice to be one of the two to go, but that didn't ease the disappointment that I felt inside. I was just starting to settle into my new surroundings and felt that the Watch were just starting to warm to me. But as expected, I received orders that I was to leave Victor at the end of April and join the Green Watch on Station Mike, which was in East Division. The Watch seemed genuinely disappointed that I was leaving them, and had decided that we should at least have a leaving drink in Newcastle before I went.

Sadly, as my father passed away on April 23rd, the last thing I wanted was to socialise, so the leaving drink was postponed. And I left Victor, gloomily saying goodbye to good colleagues that had treated me so well during my short period on Watch. I had had a good time at Victor with some interesting incidents to add to my experience. All the lads had accepted me as part of the Watch from day one and helped me settle into station life. Although we never had another nightshift as busy as my first shift, there were other jobs of note that still stick in my mind.

One rain-drenched night, we turned out to flooding on the Team Valley Industrial Estate, and when we got there, we realised that the flooding was due to a blocked culvert not allowing the heavy rainfall to flow away freely. The blockage was created by a tree trunk that had been washed along the stream into the mouth of the culvert. The only way to free the blockage was for someone to tie a rope around the stump so that it could be pulled free. Being the proby, I got the job, and a safety line was quickly tied round my waist as I climbed into the freezing water. Boy, it was so cold I shivered from head to toe, and even the exertion of pulling on the tree trunk failed to warm me up. I couldn't wait to get back to station to thaw out, but I figured it was a good learning experience at a different type of incident, and at least I was able to do something useful in the eyes of the Watch.

Another incident which I recall was a shop fire, in the middle of the night, on the Gateshead High Street. The actual fire wasn't the greatest that I had come across, but I still learned something from the event. The job was done and dusted, and we made up all the equipment used, placing everything back in their correct lockers and the ladders back on their mountings on the top of the appliance before we finally left the scene to head up the hill towards home station. We were all looking forward to having a nice cup of hot tea.

Halfway up the hill, as we eased to a stop at some red traffic lights, a Post Office van pulled up alongside and beeped his horn. Our driver wound down his window and the postman asked if we had realised that we had left our ladder behind. The driver said, "Yeah whatever," but when we got off to check the roof, right enough, the 13.5m ladder was missing. The boss was furious as we did a U-turn in search of the ladder. Right at the bottom of the hill lay the ladder, in the middle of the road. Somehow, it had slipped its mountings and rolled off the top of the appliance. Fortunately, as it was the early hours of the morning, there wasn't much traffic around and we were feeling extremely lucky that the ladder hadn't caused an accident. We sheepishly put the ladder back onto the roof, ensuring all the safety catches were holding the ladder before continuing on our way again. I was so glad that I hadn't been part of the crew that had initially placed the ladder back on the appliance at the job, but I still kept my head down while the boss ranted and raved all the way back to station. Once there, he made us fully test the ladder to ensure no damage had been done. They say you always learn from mistakes made and this was no different; from that day, I always double-checked ladder security on leaving incidents, especially if I was the nominated driver.

CHAPTER SEVEN

STATION MIKE

Station Mike, at the time, was probably the busiest station in the Brigade. Based at Fulwell, it had a mixture of risks within its station area, which covered the north side of the River Wear in Sunderland. It was a mixture of urban and rural areas that contained major road links (including single and dual carriageways), a major river, coastal areas with cliffs, farms (some with livestock and others growing crops), local housing estates, a football stadium (Roker Park), and industrial estates that predominantly focused on light engineering.

The station consisted of three bays which were filled with two pumping appliances, call signs M01 and M02, and a turntable ladder (later to be replaced with an Aerial Ladder Platform (ALP)), call sign M03. Along with the customary rooms, such as offices, kitchen, kit room, lecture room, recreational room, sleeping quarters, etc, the building also housed the East Division Social Club. This club was used by outside patrons as well as station personnel and retired members.

My first shift at Mike arrived, and although I had already dropped off all my kit and met some of the Watch, I still felt that I was starting all over again. I arrived at the station and the first question that was asked of me was which football team I supported. The looks on some of the lads' faces were amusing to see as I proudly stated I was a Newcastle United fan. As expected, being on a station that had Roker Park within its area, I found that I was going to be the only Newcastle supporter on the Watch. In fact, there was only one other Newcastle supporter on the station, and that was a firefighter on Blue Watch called Martin Connolly. The others were all Sunderland AFC supporters, along with a couple of 'not interested in football' firefighters thrown into the mix. Although I always thought that if you supported Sunderland, you clearly also had no interest in football! Knowing the rivalry between Newcastle United and Sunderland supporters, I expected to get a lot of stick and was quite prepared to give some back, so I looked forward for the banter to begin. But I was also aware that the Watch knew that I had history with Sunderland, as a few of them used to attend the basketball matches I played in, so I suppose that helped with them partially accepting me as part of the Watch. To get fully accepted, I figured I would just have to rely on my quick wit and lovable nature to bring them all around!

Green Watch at this time had a decent mix of firefighters, some young, some older, all with a reasonable amount of experience for me to tap into. They were friendly enough, despite my allegiance to Newcastle, and I got on well with each of them as I settled in to my new surroundings. The Station Officer, called Reggie Thompson, was old school who liked things done his way and his way only. I found that he was totally different to Tommy Sidaway at Victor, who had always been there to answer any questions that I had. I found Reggie to be a bit standoffish; he came across as neither friendly nor unfriendly, but was often in a world of his own. He had some strange ways which the Watch had learned to adjust to, so they gave me a few pointers on how to keep on the right side of him. One of the first things they told me was that Reggie would challenge me to a game of snooker and that I must let him win, or he would be a right old grump. The snooker table was in the recreational room and could be used during your stand down periods, such as lunch breaks, or after all the station work routines had been completed on night shifts. It took up to my first nightshift duty for Reggie to come upstairs and challenge me to a game. It felt more like an order than a request, so I agreed to play him. I set the balls up and the game started. Now, I am no snooker player, but straight from the off I could tell that Reggie was rubbish. After going a few points ahead, I sensed the Station Officer wasn't very happy and his general chit chat became less and less. It was then that I decided to look out of the window every time it was Reggie's turn to play. In the reflection of the glass, I could see Reggie placing balls over pockets, so that he had an easy pot. I would hear the ball drop into the pocket, and I would occasionally congratulate him on the shot. Slowly, he regained the lead, and the chit chat recommenced. He ended up winning and left the room feeling as proud as punch. *Strange man,* I thought!

FIRE AT MILL

One quiet Sunday evening, we were on nightshift and just starting to relax around the television set, when the front doorbell rang. Now normally, being the proby, I would have jumped up and gone straight down, but I knew Reggie was downstairs in his office, so figured that he would answer it. I thought to myself, *if it rings a second time, I will go down.* It didn't ring again, so I thought that was that. A couple of minutes later, the station alarms went off and we all slid down the pole shaft to find Reggie at the bottom, fully dressed in fire kit, including his fire helmet and gloves, shouting, "FIRE AT MILL!" He stood almost to attention and pointed towards the front of the station, where he had already opened the three appliance room bay doors. We looked to where he was pointing and instantly saw the smoke drifting past the station, looking just like a sea mist that was rolling in, but coming from the wrong direction.

Apparently, the doorbell had been a taxi driver reporting the fire in the old mill just along from the station, and instead of Reggie setting the alarms off straight away, he decided to dress himself first. *How bizarre,* I thought, but pretty normal behaviour from Reggie, the rest of the Watch assured me.

The Fulwell Windmill was built in the early 1800s and was one of the last working mills of its type left in the North East. It had been restored a number of times over the years, and is an easily recognised landmark in the Fulwell area. It is situated on Newcastle Road, which was less than a quarter of a mile from the station.

We rapidly jumped into our fire kit, as Reggie shouted out orders to hurry up, which slightly annoyed me, as I thought that he shouldn't have delayed setting the station alarms off.

39

Nonetheless, we proceeded up the road, and on arrival it was quickly established that it wasn't the mill that was alight, but the buildings that sat to the front of it. The flames were impressive against the night sky, but we couldn't lose any more time admiring the scene, as rapid intervention was needed to prevent damage to this historical building.

Reggie quickly radioed control and requested extra pumps to tackle the job in hand, while the rest of us promptly got to work, putting water onto the fire in a battle to try and stop the blaze from spreading any further.

Within a short period of time, the reinforcements started to arrive to help tackle the blaze. However, it wasn't only extra pumping appliances that had turned up, but also senior management in the form of the Assistant Chief Officer (ACO) Jimmy Bremner. He had been monitoring the job on his radio and had decided to come for a look. But having turned up and gotten himself dressed into his fire kit, he wasn't just content to stand and observe the incident; he wanted to be part of the action. So, within minutes of receiving an update from Reggie, the ACO had grabbed a hose-reel from a surprised firefighter and got stuck into the job, leaving Reggie standing with a look of bewilderment on his face. At one point, the ACO ordered me to foot a ladder while he climbed it to put a jet through a window. I would have rather been the one putting the hose through the window, but I thought, *Respect to you, sir, for getting your management hands dirty.* Soon enough, the job was sorted, and we returned to the station to start cleaning all the lengths of hose that had been used.

As a footnote, ACO Bremner was another character that only the Fire Brigade seems to produce. He would do yearly inspections of all stations, and God help anyone who crossed him. He was feared by all ranking officers, but loved by the firefighters for the way he handled the inspections. If something was not quite right during the inspection, it was the officers that took the rollicking, not the firefighters. His theory was that if the officers ran their stations correctly, mistakes amongst the men wouldn't happen.

A SOOTY END

But, as you know, mistakes happen all the time in all aspects of life, even in the Fire Brigade. One sunny afternoon, M02 turned out to a reported chimney fire at a house in Castletown, on the western border of station Mike's area. We arrived to see plenty of smoke coming out of the chimney pots above the address we had been called to. The homeowner came out to greet us, stating that some embers had dropped down from his chimney into his fire, so he thought it best to call us out.

Now, the normal procedure we had for tackling chimney fires was to place salvage sheets around the fire and try to attack it from the grate. This was done by squirting water onto the fire to create steam to go up the flue, hopefully extinguishing anything that was burning. It can be an effective method, and a lot of appliances carried empty washing-up bottles, used to fill up and squirt into the fire. This kept the use of water to a minimum, reducing the chance of any soot dropping down into the grate. If this method failed to work, then we would attack the fire by putting firefighters on the roof to squirt water down the affected chimney – again limiting the amount of water used.

We tried attacking the problem from the grate, but hadn't had any success by the time the coal fire had lost all its heat. A decision was then made to get the roof ladders off and put a firefighter on the roof to resolve the issue. While this was happening, I got told to cover the front of the fire with a chimney sheet, and report as soon as any water came down the chimney. The firefighter on the roof started to use the hose-reel in short bursts and I was asked if I could see anything. "Not yet," I replied. He tried again and asked again, but still nothing. He tried a third time; this time giving it a longer burst of water, and that's when all hell broke loose. Not for me, may I add, as I was still sitting patiently for the first sign of water, but outside, where the next-door neighbour had come out of his house screaming and swearing and covered from head to toe in soot. The firefighter on the roof had put the water down the wrong chimney! The Leading Firefighter in charge of the appliance apparently went white, as he could see his career disappearing into the distance.

I went outside to see what was happening, and when I saw the soot-covered, angry man, I struggled to contain my laughter and had to walk swiftly away. I looked up to the firefighter on the roof who, I could tell by his jiggling shoulders, was also struggling to contain his laughter, even though he knew he was in for a rollicking. This made me laugh out loud, much to the annoyance of the Leading Firefighter. Things settled down and, after cleaning up as best we could, we left the irate gentleman reasonably happy with the knowledge that the Fire Brigade insurers would be in touch to sort out any damage caused. The Leading Firefighter returned to station to a mass of paperwork and an ear-bending off Reggie.

Reggie Thompson retired not too long after this incident, and we eagerly awaited to see who our next boss would be. Before long, it was announced that Alan (Gashy) Gash was to become our new leader. Alan was reasonably young for a Station Officer, and I was looking forward to his arrival, as he had a reputation of being really keen on keeping the watch on their toes, with regular drill sessions and a good work ethic. *Just what I needed at this stage of my probation period*, I thought. The older hands on the Watch weren't so keen, though, as they had had an easy life with Reggie as he wound down to retirement, and were comfortable just doing enough. Over the next few months there would be some unhappy faces and some serious whingeing amongst the older hands, as Gashy got to work, laying down the rules of how he wanted the Watch to be run, and taking every opportunity to drill us out on the yard. There was a twinkle in his eye as he deliberately targeted the lazy members of the Watch, to make sure they pulled their weight. This was a refreshing change, as we had a few members of the Watch who had taken Reggie's winding down to retirement as a means of sticking all the jobs to be done onto the younger lads. There was no doubt who was the boss, and despite the whingeing, the lads adjusted to the new regime and we soon became a solid group.

KEEN GREEN DRILL MACHINE

Gashy had knocked us into shape, and as a probationary firefighter I felt confident in all the equipment we carried. The drills we did on the drill ground were diverse, and very often original. Scenarios were set up and we were left to figure out the most efficient way to achieve our objectives. This was so much better than just being told to do this and that without any input. The older hands brought their experiences to the forefront, relaying ideas that they had used at particular jobs, and the younger element of the Watch suggested new ways to achieve the same objective. We all learned from each other and it made us stronger as a team.

Every tour of duty was different, with the variety of drills being planned, not only using every room on the station including the roof, but also at off-station venues such as scrapyards and disused properties. The other Watches on station thought it was excessive and nicknamed us the Keen Green Drill Machine, but I can honestly say that all the drilling brought an assurance within the group which meant that any incidents coming our way would never be feared by those attending. Everyone had the utmost trust in each other and of their ability to use any of the equipment assigned to them, making most incidents run as smoothly as a drill on the station yard. I thrived in this learning environment, and can honestly say that I loved every minute, both at jobs and on the drill ground!

CHAPTER EIGHT

THE 'GASHY' YEARS

Life at Mike was really enjoyable, mainly due to the fact that it was a really busy station and the Watch were a good set of lads. From the day I arrived in 1988 until I left in September 2000, I remained on Green Watch, never once feeling the urge to ask for a transfer, or change things by taking that step onto the promotion ladder. The core of the Watch remained relatively unchanged in all the years I was there, apart from the occasional movement of someone getting promoted, or one or two of the older, senior hands retiring. This in itself is testament to how everyone who served on Green really enjoyed being there. Also, the old sweats who retired were generally replaced with probationers, due to Gashy's reputation for training up new firefighters, which had the effect of keeping the Watch on their toes whilst bringing a freshness to the group. The way I looked at it was that I was on a good Watch, working on a busy station, and managed by a fantastic Station Officer, so why on earth would I want to go to any other Watch or station in the Brigade?

Gashy was my boss in 1988 and he was still there in 2000, although he did take a couple of temporary promotions before always returning to Mike. During these missing periods, the Watch was run by either Station Officers Graeme Bowser, Tommy Taylor, or Colin Powell – all three great personalities in their own right, but I always regarded Alan as the Gaffer. He could be a stubborn character at times, and his doggedness at fires would always show through. He just hated leaving any fire without finding the cause; even the smallest rubbish fire would be prodded and probed and theories talked about until Gashy was happy. This used to get the backs up of some of the more senior members of the Watch, who just wanted to put the fire out and head back for a cup of tea. It annoyed them even more when it was in the middle of the night and they had their sleepy heads on. I, however, had the same mindset as Gashy, and found it fascinating to watch him working out what the cause of the fire could be. I learned a lot from him during these years, and went on to put all I had learned to good use when I became a fully qualified Fire Investigator in my own right, during my time serving in the Isle of Man Fire and Rescue Service.

Being able to read how a fire has started, and how it has spread, is an art form that takes years of experience and understanding. Every fire is unique in its own way, and the investigation into how it started carries with it so many factors that need to be considered. Knowledge of an array of subjects, such as melting points of materials, explosive limits, and ignition temperatures of common gases, as well as an awareness of how electrics work, are just a few aspects to be looked at. An in-depth understanding of the nature of fire and fire behaviour, along with good scene management, will also help an investigator to get to that point of origin and probable cause. External issues, such as weather conditions and fire-fighting methods, also have to be considered, as investigators can go down the wrong path if they don't have all the correct information prior to starting their investigation. So, all those hours spent poking around in the ashes with Gashy was just time spent learning my trade, helping me to develop my knowledge and understanding of fire, for which I sincerely thank him for sharing all he knew. This helped me to become a better firefighter, as well as a more competent Fire Investigator.

STRANGE JOB

We had plenty of opportunity to prod around in the ashes, as we seemed to get more than our fair share of jobs, which of course made me as happy as a pig in muck. Apart from the run of the mill fires, such as car fires and grass fires that seemed to happen every other day, we also attended a variety of different jobs that would stick in my memory for one reason or another. One such incident was a fatal house fire just around the corner from the station. It was a strange one, as the call came in as a running call (someone who reports a job directly to the station rather than dialling 999 to Control). A family member had called on an elderly gentleman, to find the windows blackened and a strong smell of smoke. They immediately ran round to the station and rang the doorbell so vigorously that we knew something was amiss. We responded, and quickly broke into the house to find that there had been a fire in the living room, but it had burnt itself out, probably due to lack of oxygen. The elderly gent was lying on the floor of the fire-damaged living room, but nothing could be done for him, so we requested the attendance of the Police.

A Constable arrived, and when he entered the room, he was immediately taken aback by the fact that the deceased had been burnt so badly that his leg had burnt off. However, instead of just observing the scene and leaving the job to experienced fire investigators, he started to make assumptions. He boldly stated that the fire had obviously started on the side where the leg had burnt away. Wrong! It was local knowledge that the gent had a false leg, and this had burnt with ease. The fire had actually started on the other side of the body, and when this was pointed out to the Constable, he quickly backtracked on his theory and decided to leave the job to the experts, with an embarrassed glow to his face and a wry smile on mine.

WHAT A STAR

Not all fires required a full fire investigation to be held, but those deemed to be suspicious or those that had fatalities certainly did. One nightshift in 1998, we turned out to a flat fire in the Roker area of Sunderland. We arrived to find a small fire in a bedsit, which we easily dealt with, but the circumstances surrounding the fire were certainly dodgy and the Police seemed more than interested in the flat's occupier. At this time, a new member had been added to the Brigade's Fire Investigation Team; 'Star the fire dog' had been trained, with his owner Bob Foster, to detect accelerants used in starting fires. Gashy decided to call him onto the job, and we waited patiently for his arrival while Gashy explained to the Police Officer in attendance that he would be impressed with this dog and that he should be able to pinpoint the origin of the fire.

Star, a beautiful golden Labrador, turned up and Bob, his handler, led him straight into the bedsit while Gashy and the Constable followed behind with a look of interest on the Constable's face. Having never seen a fire dog in action, I also hastily trailed behind them; being a nosey bugger, I didn't want to miss anything. I was intrigued as to how a dog could save hours of digging around the ashes for answers, and stood in the bedsit doorway to watch this expert in action. I was wanting to see something impressive, and sure enough I wasn't disappointed.

Star had a quick sniff around, before suddenly stopping, then squatted and proceeded to have a number 2 right in the middle of the floor – much to the horror of Gashy and Bob. They stood there looking stunned at what had just happened as the Policeman laughed out loud, which in turn set me off laughing, especially when Bob tried to apologise by stating that it wasn't Star's fault as he always did his business at this time of night. I excitedly rushed off to tell the rest of the lads of what had happened, as Bob commenced his clean-up operation. Needless to say, Gashy never requested the use of Star's services again – at least, not at jobs that occurred at that time of night!

DANGEROUS BROTHERS

Towards the end of 1988, a gangly, strange-looking chap turned up on station with kit bag in tow. If grasshoppers were to look like humans, then this man would fit the description. At six foot 4 inches, he had a long, skinny body, with even longer arms and legs. Placed on top of this torso was an abnormally shaped head with two bulging eyes. This specimen was the new probationer called Billy Forster. Now Billy came to Mike brimming with confidence and with a bounce in his step that disturbed the older members of the Watch. What made it worse for them was the fact that Billy was a Geordie (born on the Tyne), and that meant two non-Mackems (born in Sunderland) were now having to be tolerated. His accent was strong and his wit as sharp as anything. And we bonded from day one.

At last, there was someone else with a great sense of humour and devilish streak. Billy had been a plumber before joining the Brigade, so was used to taking stick as well as giving it back in abundance, from his time working on building sites. He was hyperactive, so if there were any quiet periods on station, he would go stir crazy and look to wind up the older members of the Watch. Being his best buddy, of course, I had to assist him in whatever jape was being planned. It wasn't long before we were given the nickname of 'The Dangerous Brothers', and anyone coming onto the station was pre-warned to keep well away from us or risk getting into trouble. At least now with Billy onboard, I had someone to share the blame with if something happened on station or at a job. Looking back, I wonder how we got away with so much joviality, but I guess we were lucky to have a boss who also had a good sense of humour and allowed us to get away with most things. Gashy very often had to turn a blind eye to some of the things we got up to, but I guess he thought laughter helped to build morale on the Watch. I will return to some of the things 'The Dangerous Brothers' got up to in later chapters, but felt it necessary to mention the arrival of Billy, as he changed the dynamics of the Watch and brought my mischievous nature out to play.

BUM DEAL

It was shortly after the arrival of Billy that the station started to go through a really busy period of jobs. All types of incidents rolled in, and we on Green Watch were certainly getting our fair share. One dark nightshift, M01 and M02 turned out to a house fire on the Red House Estate. I was wearing BA on M02, and as we pulled up, we could see flames leaping from a downstairs window that had blown out. We jumped off the appliance, and as we prepared to start up our sets, word came that it was possible persons reported with kids trapped inside. These are the words any firefighter hates to hear, making the adrenalin rush round your body, pushing you to move as quickly as you can. My BA partner and I donned our masks as the hose-reel was pulled from the appliance for us to go in with. It was then that I noticed the other BA team were struggling to make an entry through the locked front door, so I decided that our best course of action was to climb through the broken window into the lounge that was on fire. While my partner held the hose-reel, I cocked my leg over the sill, only to be met with an excruciating pain in my left buttock. I had sat on the window latch peg, which due to the fire was red hot. The peg had instantly burned straight through the yellow PVC leggings that we wore, as well as the work trousers underneath. It hurt that bad that I jumped off the sill straight into the middle of the room, which was still well alight. So now my feet were on fire! My partner saw that I was in a bit of trouble, so turned the hose-reel on the fire in the room. Unfortunately, this created a massive amount of steam, which duly started to scald my ears (this was pre-flash hood days, where your ears were open to the elements). I must have looked ridiculous dancing around the room in pain, and the Watch made certain I was the butt of all jokes for the following few days!

As it happened, the kids had already escaped through the back entrance prior to our arrival, so relief spread across us all and the incident was wrapped up. On arrival back on home station, I went to see Gashy to show him my injuries. "Hold it there," he said. "I am not getting caught out with you in the room and your trousers round your ankles." So he went onto the station tannoy system and called the whole Watch down to his office, for them all to inspect the damage. The peg had fused some of my leggings into the skin, and after picking out what I could, I got sent to A&E for a tetanus injection – a second jab in the backside in one night!

DEAF NOT DUMB

Another evening, at around 2000hrs, we turned out to alarms at Dame Dorothy Crescent, a set of high-rise flats close to the River Wear. We arrived and proceeded to the 7th floor, where the alarms were ringing loud and clear. On looking through a letterbox of one of the flats, we could see a slight hazy smoke beginning to drift into the hallway. The Gaffer told us to start up our sets, as he broke down the door, and within seconds we were in and starting to search. The first door I came to was a bedroom, where I came across an elderly lady fast asleep in her bed and unconscious to the noise from the alarms. When I shook her shoulder, she woke to see me in my face mask, screamed, and sat bolt upright. This give me such a shock that I stumbled backwards, landing in a big heap in a corner. Once recovered, I tried to explain who I was and led her out of the flat. It turned out that the smoke was from a pan that had boiled dry, and that the lady was deaf so hadn't heard the alarm or understood anything that I had said to her. In follow up, we managed to get her a vibrating pillow linked to the alarm system, to try and prevent her from scaring the life out of some other poor unsuspecting firefighter!

SPINE-TINGLING

The deaf lady wasn't the only incident I attended that sent shivers down my spine. On another shift, on a cold autumn night, we found ourselves turned out to an alarm actuating at a Funeral Directors in Whitburn, a coastal town about a mile from the station. As was quite common at this time of year, a sea mist had rolled in, leaving a strange silence in the air. We arrived at the destination, where the blue flashing lights of the appliances seemed to hold in the air as we approached the front door of the premises. Everything was locked up, but as we lifted the letter box to the door of the building, the distinctive whiff of smoke could be detected. The OIC, Station Officer Bowser, instructed us to don our sets immediately as he ordered another crew member to break in.

For some unknown reason, I felt as jumpy as hell, and all my senses seemed to be totally stimulated. I don't know if it was a combination of the swirling mist and the fact that it was a funeral home that was making me nervous, but I just wanted to get in and out of this job as quickly as possible. Having gained entry through the front door, I and another wearer entered the building to advance through the smoke in search of a fire. I was fully alert, and my mind was playing all sorts of games with me, when all of a sudden, my progress was halted by a solid object blocking my path. I initially thought it was a large piece of furniture, but when my hand moved over the top, there was the discernible feel of a body. My heart jumped into my mouth and a shiver ran down my spine, but before I reacted too abruptly and dragged the casualty out of the building, I quickly realised that the furniture was a coffin and the casualty had been deceased well before we got there. I composed myself as best I could, and continued with the search for the source of the smoke, knowing in my mind that I would probably have a nightmare or two when remembering this job in the future.

Eventually, the source of the smoke was located by using a thermal imaging camera, which showed a defective starter motor in a light fitting. As damage was very limited, the job was wound up pretty swiftly, and I couldn't have been happier as I climbed onto the appliance to head back to a warm, well lit station, where I could finally relax. However, the Watch were not going to let me off the hook that easy, and as we headed back to the station there was some serious dark humour going on in the appliance. The boys took great pleasure in giving me some stick for being frightened of a dead body, and they teased me on how funny it would have been if I had dragged the corpse out and started CPR (Cardiopulmonary Resuscitation).

PEELING HANDS, DRIPPING EARS

It was busy times, and not a tour of duty seemed to go by where we didn't have a decent job to tackle. It was unusual if we went a couple of days without seeing flames and car fires became part of the normal routine, with the station dealing with 4-6 vehicles each week. Weekends were the worst time for these fires, as the car thieves seemed to be more active, and once they were finished joyriding or doing some other illegal activity, they would park the car up and torch it, all in the hope of getting rid of any evidence against them. Derelict properties also seemed to be a big attraction to youths, who broke in and again set fire to the property – sometimes for the thrill, and sometimes to hide what they had been up to. As a Watch, we enjoyed being busy, but too much of the same thing begins to drain the energy, so we looked forward to any incident that wasn't the norm, and those weren't always in our station area.

One night we mobilised to station Sierra's area (Washington), following a make-up of pumps to fight a large fire in premises run by Mailcom. The company specialised in sending large quantities of mail on behalf of a number of companies, such as advertising leaflets and promotional offers that some people would call junk mail. It was a large warehouse-type building, with pallet upon pallet of burnable material lined up row after row. The fire was going well inside and BA crews were committed, using guidelines to help lead you to the seat of the fire. Visibility wasn't great due to the smoke layer that had come down to near floor level, and the heat was baking. Teams would go in and fight the fire until their set was nearly exhausted, come out and have a quick break, before going straight back in wearing another set. I wore a set three times in quick succession at that job, and was loving every minute of facing the Beast.

Billy was partnered up with John Adamson, another young lad on our Watch who had joined the service a year before me. He was a fabulous fireman, who later in his career went on to become the Assistant Chief Fire Officer of Durham and Darlington Fire and Rescue Service. Billy and John also wore a BA set three times at that job, and when they came out after the third wear, John took off his leather fire gloves, as they were soaking wet from the hose-lines used. Unfortunately, as the gloves came off, so did a lot of skin from John's hands. It had been so hot inside the building that the wet gloves had literally steamed his skin. Yet he never complained once, and even wanted to go back in for another wear. Eventually the fire was brought under control hours later, and we returned to home station to talk of our roles at the incident. John had the best boasting rights due to his hands, which looked a right mess, but fortunately in time healed really well.

It is an accepted fact that, despite health and safety and Brigade procedures to try and eliminate injuries, every firefighter recognises the nature of the job will create circumstances where unfortunately you can get hurt. Most firefighters pick up small injuries throughout their career, and some suffer life-changing injuries, with a number giving the ultimate sacrifice in dedication to their profession.

Often small injuries suffered in the line of duty became learning points that just added to your experience in becoming a better firefighter. One such instance involved a lad on the Watch called Neil Harrison. He was just a probationer at the time, and clearly very keen to impress. We had turned up to a fire in an upstairs flat in Boldon Colliery, and being a bit too keen, Neil had his BA set on and started before we had pulled up to the job. As soon as we hauled the hose-reel off, he dashed up the stairs straight into the heat layer. Now this was at the time before flash hoods were issued as part of your fire kit, so no sooner had Neil reached the heat layer than he did an about turn and scuttled down the stairs holding his exposed ears, much to the amusement of the rest of the crew. He had badly blistered both his ears, and the blisters oozed serum for days afterwards, but it taught him a valuable lesson not to go dashing in without assessing what you are dealing with. Had he kept low and steadily progressed up the stairs, he would have realised how hot it was and cooled the gases before advancing. Needless to say, he took some ribbing back on station and had the nickname 'Drippy' for quite a while!

CHAPTER NINE

DARK HUMOUR

Every firefighter throughout their career will come across horrific incidents, often with tragic and fatal consequences. These incidents leave a lasting impression on individuals, and I can say, in my case, that I can easily recall every one of the incidents that I have attended which ended with a death or serious injury. The effects on firefighters can be life-changing, and mental health is a subject that the Fire Services across the country now take very seriously. Most Fire Services nowadays train Specialist Trauma Counsellors to debrief staff that have attended any incidents of a serious nature. However, during my career, especially in the early years, trauma counselling was in its infancy, with very few Brigades investing in any training in this department. Back then, firefighters were expected to cope with any traumatic incidents themselves and just literally dust themselves down ready to attend the next incident. You were left at these times to heavily rely on the support of your fellow Watch members, and it would be those colleagues around you that would help to manage any stress related issues that may have been caused by what had been encountered.

You can walk into any station in the country and be able to tell if a serious incident had occurred. The life seems to get sucked out of the atmosphere on a station after any fatal house fire, or even a death at a road traffic collision (RTC). Every incident of this kind that I have attended has followed the same pattern. All the personnel on Watch seem to isolate themselves with their own thoughts of what happened and why we couldn't have done more to help the victim. The dark cloud is even thicker when a child has been involved, and Watch morale is understandably at its lowest level. One or two would sit chatting quietly, trying to make sense of it all. Then, after a period of time, things on station begin to heal.

This healing process normally starts with some dark humour relevant to the incident; it may be a simple joke on somebody's performance at the job, or even an untimely thoughtless comment about the casualty. No offence towards the deceased or injured is meant, and the words are for the Watch only – as only they understand the true relevance. The ice is broken, and before long more comments are made, and the dark cloud begins to lift. Smiles can be seen again, but it doesn't mean we hadn't cared about the casualty. It's just that we realise we have to recover quickly, as you never know when the next job will be.

Some people take massive offence with dark humour and see the comments as being insensitive, tasteless, and unacceptable, especially when someone's life has been lost. This is especially so in today's climate of political correctness, where everything has to be prim and proper, and everyone wants to be a do-gooder. A lot of these people who object have never seen the aftermath of a serious house fire, or heard the screams of a trapped casualty as you fight to save their lives. They should realise that dark humour is a coping mechanism used to try and ease the stress and trauma caused by the incidents we have attended. The words spoken are meant to heal scars with humour, to hopefully allow you and your buddies to push the sights you have witnessed and the smells you have tasted to the back of your mind (but never forgotten). This is essential in bringing a sense of normality back into their lives.

I always found the best counsellors are those from a background of having served as a firefighter, or someone who has been there and witnessed and experienced the same sort of things. This wasn't the case of the first trauma counsellor that attended Mike for a debrief of a nasty RTC that we had attended. The job involved a poor 14-year-old child who had been run over by a bus in the Southwick area of the town. We arrived to find panic in the street and the girl fully trapped in the wheel arch of the bus. I lay down and shuffled under the bus to see if she could be freed, but it wasn't going to be easy. A paramedic turned up to assess the casualty and insisted that we had no time to lose; the girl had to come out straight away as she had lost a pulse. I physically had to use all my strength to release her out of the wheel arch, but it was to no avail as she passed away (God bless her). The memory of the job stayed with me a long time, especially the screams of the mother who turned up at the scene.

As this was our second dayshift, a debrief with a newly-formed Trauma Counselling Team was to be conducted at the station on the following nightshift. We sat in the lecture room to await the counsellor, and soon enough a pleasant lady – obviously a civilian – turned up to start the debrief. This was our first dealing with this department, so we were all very unsure on how it was going to go. She began by stating that she would be saying very little, and that we should start by going round the room, one by one, telling everyone what we had seen or heard – from arriving at the incident to the end, or mentioning any other point that we thought might be noteworthy. By now the incident was over 24 hours old, and as a Watch we had reached the dark humour stage of recovery from the fatal. Some of the things that were said in the debrief, in hindsight, were probably inappropriate, ill-timed, and slightly insensitive, which resulted in the counsellor stopping halfway through. She had realised that she was wasting her time, so she stood up, bade us farewell and left the station, never to be seen again. We all laughed and joked about her leaving so abruptly, and felt that maybe she was in the wrong profession. But at least some good came out of it, as the Brigade started to train up firefighters to become Trauma Counsellors, so at least in the future we had people who understood us and our use of dark humour.

A GRAVE REMINDER

One of the saddest RTCs that I ever attended involved a car and a van. The collision took place just off the roundabout on Newcastle Road, Sunderland. The van had one male occupant who, although badly injured, was easily released from his van. The occupants of the car were a young couple who, by chance, had just gotten engaged to be married and had just popped out to collect a Chinese takeaway to celebrate. Their happiness had been cut short by this horrific incident, and as soon as we arrived on scene, we could tell that we were in a fight to save their lives. We battled as fast as we could to free them from the twisted metal that was once their car, and managed to free the female passenger reasonably swiftly, removing her from the wreckage to be dispatched by ambulance to hospital. Sadly, she later died as a result of her injuries. Her fiancé looked even more seriously hurt, and as we cut away at the metal, Gashy, who was keeping a close eye on him, checked for a pulse only to find that there was none. There was no time to lose, so we dragged him out as quick as we could and commenced CPR on the roadside. As hard as we tried, we were unable to save his young life, and as the incident concluded we returned to home station to face the dark cloud that was to be over Station Mike again.

The healing process commenced on the station, but for me this job had a longer lasting effect, and I found that I had to work harder than at any other time to push the sadness of the fatalities to the back of my mind.

As a demonstration of the love that the couple had for each other, their parents sadly buried them together in Jarrow Cemetery. For me, it became a permanent reminder of a very tragic incident, as the couple are buried in a grave adjacent to my parents, leaving me to sadly reflect on their untimely deaths every time I visit my parents' grave. May they rest in peace.

CHAPTER TEN

MEADOW WELL RIOTS

On September 9th, 1991 a stolen car fleeing from police crashed, killing the two youths inside. This incited a riot of a scale never seen before on the council-owned housing estate on which they had lived. The Meadow Well Estate, North Shields, had already become a no-go area for police, but on this night both police and fire crews faced the brunt of their anger. At the height of the riot more than 400 people were involved and over 50 people were arrested. Numerous buildings were set alight, including a Youth Club, an electricity sub-station, and a Health Centre, as well as a number of derelict and lived-in houses. Cars were set ablaze, and road blocks set up to try and trap and stone any vehicle carrying police or fire personnel. It was a HELL of a night, well remembered by those who had been involved.

That night, I was riding M02 and came on duty at 1700hrs, to be turned out almost immediately to cover Station Tango's area (Hebburn). Their appliances had already been dispatched to the north side of the River Tyne, and we could hear on the appliance radio how busy it was starting to get over there. The way things were progressing I just had a gut feeling that we would end up on the north side, and right enough, just as we got into Tango's area, we were redirected to go through the Tyne Tunnel to cover Wallsend. From then, we seemed to go from job to job, fighting car fires, small fires, fires in buildings, and anything else that would burn. We were out all night, and returned to home station as the sun came up the following morning, feeling totally knackered.

As I have stated, I love a good fire, but what happened that night was totally unacceptable. I couldn't get my head around that so much damage had been done in one night, by people who obviously had no respect for the law and didn't care less for others living in their community. I had never spent so much time at jobs looking over my shoulder, just waiting to be hit by a rock or other type of missile, and all for just doing my job. I sincerely hope that something like the Meadow Well riots never happen again.

When people read up on the Meadow Well riots, they assume that the only fires that night were contained within the Estate. In truth, copycat fires and smaller scale disturbances were being instigated throughout North Tyneside that night. Also, as the riots in the Meadow Well area settled down, other areas such as Newcastle's West End (in deprived areas such as Scotswood and Benwell) and council estates in Sunderland decided it was their turn to join in the disorder, and began their own period of destruction.

However, a lot of the disorder was just a diversion for organised crime, and seemed pretty well organised. As we turned up to fires, you would see the same faces as part of the crowd that you had seen at previous jobs. The Police would be requested to attend for our protection, and as soon as they did, we would witness the familiar faces go on their mobile phones and disappear, leaving the rest of the crowd all hyped-up and causing chaos. Meanwhile, ram-raiding of shops and businesses would occur in an area away from our incident, with the crooks knowing that the Police resources had already been tied up with us. The Police were aware that this was happening, but were really struggling to cope with the number of incidents that were occurring.

The unrest continued for a few weeks, and we faced many incidents in Mike's area, including derelict house fires in the Southwick area where we would have to request police escorts into streets before committing to the fire. This had come about following an incident where we had driven to the top of a cul-de-sac to fight a house fire, only to realise that the local yobs were building a blockade behind us, blocking our exit. We dumped our hose and made a hasty retreat under a hail of stones. From then on, we always waited for police attendance before committing up dead-ends, and once they arrived, we would then slowly reverse towards the job in a manner where we would be prepared for a quick getaway if required.

The other favourite trick of the local gangs was to set traps within the houses they had set alight. This could be by tying fishing line across doorways to either trip or tangle the BA wearers, or cover floorboards, that had been ripped up, with thin board or cardboard. This one actually caught me out at one job. We had made entry into the derelict flat through the first-floor window, as the ground floor steel security doors were causing us issues and delaying our ingress. I stepped off the 10.5 m ladder into the room and, apart from heavy smoke-logging, everything seemed in order, so I started dragging the hose-reel up as my BA partner climbed in to join me. We advanced as far as the landing, when all of a sudden the floor gave way beneath my feet. Luckily, or unluckily, I came to rest straddled across a floor joist, where I could see a small rubbish fire down on the ground floor beneath me. Although not seriously hurt, the shock was immense, and I had some nasty grazes to both my groin area and also to the inside of my thigh. It could have been a lot worse, and I felt fortunate that my crown jewels had avoided any damage. I blamed myself for not operating proper search patterns, shuffling to test the floors with my feet as I did the BA shuffle. I reflected that the fire below could have been an inferno and the fall a lot higher, which only served to scare me even more. I had gotten careless because the job had seemed like a straightforward routine event, so I hadn't been concentrating like I should have been. It became a lesson I never forgot, and going forward I treated every incident as if it were my first, and always expected the unexpected.

BEATEN

As well as the damage and destruction that the local yobs were causing to derelict properties and burnt-out stolen cars, we at Mike had another running battle with youths. This was a yearly event and involved youths setting fire to fields full of crops, such as wheat, barley, and rapeseed. It happened throughout our area, but was certainly a big problem for the farms around the Downhill and Red House housing estates.

The wheat and barley field fires were relatively straightforward jobs that could be tackled with hose-reels and fire beaters (a flexible rubber mat on a pole that can be used to beat or smother the fire with). The rapeseed was another case altogether, and if the fire within the crop was started just prior to the crop being harvested (normally around June/July), the blaze could be immense. That is because the rapeseed is harvested for rapeseed oil and animal feed, and it is the oil content which becomes more prevalent in the plant just prior to harvest, so burns with the same characteristics of so many other oils. These fires burn with an extreme heat whilst generating a huge amount of thick, almost black, smoke, which can hinder firefighting and create major headaches for any OIC.

Once the crops had been harvested, the threat of fire still remained, as the stubble and straw left in the fields seemed to be a great attraction to the youths of Downhill and Red House. Time and time again we would turn out to these fields, and no sooner had we put one fire out than we would turn out to another one. One night, we turned out to the same field on Downhill Lane three times in quick succession. It was clear that the youths were watching us put the fire out and then leave for home station, before they started another fire once we were out of sight. After the third time, we decided to park round the corner just out of sight and see if we could catch anyone in the act. Right enough, within minutes of us leaving, we could see a group of youths entering the field, and a minute or so later smoke could be seen. We quickly jumped on the truck and, with lights and wailers on, we scooted around the corner, cutting off the main escape route back into the housing estate. We were starting to lose natural daylight at this time, but we could see the youths darting in all directions. We grabbed the fire beaters and headed to where the fire was, but as we got close, I veered off to my right where I had spotted one of the youths lying down in the stubble/straw, trying in a feeble effort to hide from us. I crept up slowly and could see him keeping really low to the ground, and as I got really close, I swung the beater and smacked him right on the backside. He jumped up shouting and swearing and not a happy bunny, but just then one of my colleagues recognised the youth and told him he would be speaking to his mother, to which the kid meekly sloped off back into the estate. The smack on the backside didn't stop the fires occurring in the fields on the following nights – in fact, the station seemed to attend those fields more that year than in previous years – but it did give me some satisfaction knowing that I had distributed some punishment for all our sweat and toil.

A CLOSE CALL

One sunny dayshift afternoon, M01, M02, and M03 turned out to a reported silo on fire at a furniture-makers in Southwick. Homeworthy was an established company specialising in flat-pack furniture and office furniture, using the dust from their processes as fuel for their heating system. Any sawdust created in the manufacturing process was sucked out of the factory workplace into an exterior silo, to be forwarded on to fire the boilers when required. For some unknown reason, potentially spontaneous combustion, the sawdust in the silo had ignited and smoke was seen wafting from the top.

While figuring how best to tackle the issue, the gaffer asked me to climb to the top of the silo and report what I could see from there. The silo stood 30ft high and had a vertical ladder attached from bottom to top, so – as instructed – I started climbing up. What happened next took me totally by surprise and could have had catastrophic consequences. As my head came level with the top of the silo, there was an almighty bang and something smashed into the top of my helmet. The force almost knocked me off the ladder, but I regained my composure and managed to drag myself over the top railing. I took my helmet off and observed a two-inch-wide indentation to the top of it. *What the hell was that?* I thought, and when I looked over the side, I saw Billy standing next to the pump holding what looked like a round metal disc. It was then that I realised what had hit me. An inspection hatch, about fourteen inches in diameter, that had been fitted on the top of the silo, had blown off due to the pressure caused by the fire inside. Had I been two seconds faster climbing the ladder, the disc would have hit me directly in the face or body. It was certainly a close call, and one that still digs deep in the memory banks.

The fire ended up being a right pain to put out, because if we put too much water into the top of the silo, the contents inside would just become a solid mass of sawdust, plus the fact that there was no guarantee that the water would reach where the fire was burning. We therefore had to open an inspection hatch on the ground level and basically pull out the sawdust until we got to the fire, and then deal with it from there. It was a long, slow process, but we got there in the end.

Billy, not to lose an opportunity to have some fun at my expense, took the metal disc back to home station and when I came into work the following day, there it was hanging by an industrial-sized chain on my fire kit peg. My very own bravery medal presented with an inscription calling me 'The Almost Headless Bald-Headed Muppet'. I suppose it was the thought that counted!

CHAPTER ELEVEN

A NEW YEAR BLAST

On 31st December, 1991, we were nightshift when we responded to another job that remains planted in my memory bank as an incident I will never forget. The initial call was at approximately 23:45hrs to a reported house fire on the Red House Estate of Sunderland. M01 and M02 flashed through the nearly empty streets, fully expecting a working job. I was wearing BA on M01, and thought to myself that this was going to be my first BA job of the New Year.

We arrived and felt a bit deflated when we realised it was a malicious call and that there was no fire to deal with. Some of the residents had come out of their houses and started wishing us a Happy New Year, which was nice, and a female Police Constable worked her way around both crews, wishing everyone a Happy New Year whilst giving everyone a New Year kiss. As midnight arrived, we started to see fireworks being set off into the clear sky, but also heard a muffled bang which we assumed was a firework going off in the distance.

Just then, Control radioed up M01, which we assumed would be for their traditional New Year greeting. But no, it was for M01 and M02 to respond to reports of an explosion on Hylton Castle Road, which was literally just down the road from our location. We mobilised, and as we cleared the houses of Red House Estate, we could see the sky glowing when we looked across to Hylton Castle.

We arrived at the scene in under two minutes and were greeted by a site that would have been more at home in Beirut. Where there had been a block of flats, with a ground and first floor, there was now a single-storey pile of rubble. There seemed to be casualties everywhere we looked, and as we jumped off the trucks, people were grabbing at us to give them, or someone with them, first aid. Gashy rapidly made up pumps and requested an ambulance response that could deal with multiple casualties. To add to the chaos, Mark Linton, our driver/pump operator, was trying to engage the pump to supply water to the fire in the flats, when a man with severe head injuries grabbed him for assistance. Mark sat him on a garden wall, while he dragged off the hose-reel that would be needed, but when he turned back to the gentleman, he had disappeared. Mark quickly realised that the gentleman had collapsed backwards over the wall, where he had landed in a heap in the garden, leaving Mark with no option but to jump over the wall to administer first aid until he could get the attention of another firefighter to take over, allowing him to ultimately return to his pump operation duties.

Not aware of Mark's predicament, we quickly got to work trying to extinguish the intense fire that engulfed the ground floor flat, but as we stood with the hose-reels, Billy Forster realised that there was someone underneath the rubble on the first floor. He shouted to Gashy, and within seconds Gashy and Colin Powell, our Sub Officer, had dragged a 10.5m ladder off M02 and placed it against the rubble. It was done in such haste that the ladder was upside down and round the wrong way (*more ladder drills required for management*, I thought), but it still acted as a ladder, and Billy and I scuttled up to the first floor.

We could hear a woman pleading for help, but the roof had come down on top of her when the walls had been blasted out. There was just enough space for us to crawl under the roof, and we started to remove the rubble to uncover the lady. Straight away, we could see that she was seriously injured, with burns covering most of what we could see. She also had a four-inch piece of wood protruding from her eye, but she was conscious and able to speak with us. The fire was still raging below, and we could feel the heat penetrating up through the concrete floor, which was adding to her discomfort. We continued working away, endeavouring to remove as much of the rubble from her as possible, whilst trying to work out the best way to retrieve her from this challenging position. She told us that her name was Vera and Billy chatted away to her to try and keep her conscious until the ambulance personnel arrived.

At this time, in trying to control the fire in the flat below, the crews had inadvertently put out the fire coming from an exposed gas pipe, leaving gas to pour freely into the room below. A more senior officer had arrived on scene at this time, and tried to get Gashy to withdraw Billy and I from the rescue area due to the risk of a further gas explosion. We refused to budge, as we had promised Vera that we would stay with her. As luck would have it, the pipe reignited, and the crews were ordered to put a covering jet on it but not to extinguish it until the Gas Board arrived to isolate it.

Meanwhile, Vera was not in a good way, and we were happy to see the paramedic turn up. He clambered up next to us as we formulated how we were going to get her down from the rubble pile. A Ked stretcher was brought up, but before the paramedic was happy to move her, he wanted to get an intravenous drip into a vein. Unfortunately, Vera was so badly burned, he was struggling to find a vein through her badly blistered skin. I have never seen anyone so badly burned yet so conscious and aware of her surroundings. The sound of her screaming in pain, as he tried to get the drip in, will haunt me forever. Eventually, we got her strapped onto a stretcher and she was passed from firefighter to firefighter down the ladder and into the waiting ambulance. Hours later, Control contacted Gashy to tell him Vera had lost her fight to live, and had died in hospital. We were all gutted at the news, and the dark cloud settled over the station yet again. On reflection, the job could have produced more than one fatality, and a lot of people could count themselves as being remarkably lucky that night. The amount of devastation caused by the explosion is hard to describe in words, but it is sufficient to say that it is a job that will forever remain in my memory.

On investigation, it was discovered that a thief had broken into the flat below and had decided to steal the gas meter. In doing so, he had just cut through the pipe, allowing the gas to pour into the room. The Gas Board calculated that to do that amount of damage to a building, the gas must have been flowing for hours, giving the Police a timeframe to work with.

The source of ignition was also established. In the first floor flat, Vera's husband had gone out for the evening and planned to be back in time for New Year. He kept his promise, and arrived back a couple of minutes before midnight. Realising the time, he decided to wait outside their front door and be the first foot (a tradition where the first person through the front door of a house on New Year is supposed to be the bringer of good fortune). Whilst waiting, he decided to have a cigarette, and the lighter he had used to light it unfortunately became the ignition source that caused the gas to explode. The walls and windows blew out of the building, hitting neighbours who were also outside waiting to first foot, as well as other people passing by as they made their way to New Year's house parties. Following the blast, Vera's husband staggered down what remained of the communal stairs to the outside, where we found him lying on the pavement. It was one hell of a start to 1992, and we hoped against all hope that would be our only fatal of the year. In July of that year, CFO Dunlop wrote to us, saying that following our actions at the incident, we were to be presented with a commendation for bravery. I am sure all of us would have handed that back if it meant having a more successful outcome by saving Vera's life.

CHAPTER TWELVE

MONKWEARMOUTH PIT INCIDENT

The North East has a proud history of coal mining, with pits being operated throughout its region, covering Tyneside, Northumberland, Durham, and Wearside. At its peak in 1913, there were about 400 pits in the North East area, employing almost a quarter of a million men, whilst producing over 56 million tons of coal every year. North East ports were also kept busy shipping coal all over the UK and further afield, making coal a major asset to the region's commerce. The two world wars kept the need for coal high, and the mines flourished. Nevertheless, following the end of the Second World War, the need for coal diminished and pits in the North East began to close, causing shattering consequences for many of the small mining communities whose men had relied on the pits for work. Even nationalisation of the coal industry could not stem the flood of pits closing across the region, and many small pit villages fell into deprivation, with no other industry in the area able to cope with the number of men requiring work. Major strike action in 1972 followed, calling for better pay and conditions, which caused chaos in the industry, and although the Tory Government gave in to many of the strikers' demands, further closures soon occurred across the region. In 1984/85 a well-documented miners' strike was called to protest at pit closures that were happening all across the UK. This time, the Conservative Government, led by Prime Minister Margaret Thatcher, refused to budge, and eventually the strike ended with the miners defeated and the knowledge that the coal mining industry was just about destroyed.

However, one pit to survive was Monkwearmouth Colliery – it was a deep coal mining pit with a seam that ran 1700 feet below the surface, heading far out under the North Sea coast. Close to the banks of the River Wear, it had opened in 1835, and in 1846 was known to be the deepest pit in the country. It was a major employer for the city of Sunderland, employing over 2000 men, most of whom spent their whole shift underground.

THE INCIDENT

On Thursday, 13th February, 1992 we were on nightshift when the alarms sounded, and along with the other members of the Watch, I slid down the pole shaft to the appliance room. All three appliances – M01, M02, and M03 – were being mobilised to an incident at Monkwearmouth Colliery, but there was very little information on the turn-out sheet as to the nature of the call. The colliery was at the bottom end of Newcastle Road, less than a mile from the station, and we knew we would be there pretty sharpish. So we quickly mounted the appliances and hastily got into our fire kit, as the appliances rolled out the doors. Gashy asked Control on the radio if they had any further information about the call, and Control came back stating that there had been an incident underground at the pit, involving a derailment. The hairs on my neck stood up as the adrenalin started to pump through my body. *This was going to be a pig of a job*, I thought to myself, as we silently proceeded with only the blue lights on, as the roads were empty due to the time of night.

We had done familiarisation visits to the Monkwearmouth Colliery in the past, but that had just covered the areas above ground, so the thought of operating in an unfamiliar environment crossed everybody's mind as we got closer to the gates of the colliery. We knew that the laws covering mines were different from laws covering other industries, and were also aware that we had no real jurisdiction when it came to any incidents within the pit. But what we were also aware of was that following the introduction of the Coal Mines Act 1911, a section covering safety at mines meant that all mines were obliged to have a Mines Rescue Team within a certain distance of the pit, ready to respond to any incident underground. With that knowledge, we pulled up at the gates, thinking we were back-up for the Mines Rescue Team which had, without a doubt, been summoned from their base at Houghton-le-Spring, approximately 9 miles away from Monkwearmouth.

We pulled up to the gate with blue lights still rotating, and Gashy jumped off to get the Security Officer to open the gates. He refused, and seemed surprised that we had been called. Gashy insisted on seeing the person in charge, so the Security Officer called the Pit Manager to attend the gate. The manager arrived and confirmed that there had been an incident underground, but that he couldn't let us go down and that they were in the process of calling for Mines Rescue to attend. Gashy tried to compromise with the manager, and asked him to allow us to set up an equipment dump for any of his staff/miners to use; the manager, being under pressure, agreed to this.

Gashy told us to set up the equipment dump, with every tool and lighting that were intrinsically safe to be placed as close to the pit entrance as we could. The Security Officer opened the gates, and a salvage sheet was placed down, to where the trucks were stripped of all the equipment that we carried that wouldn't cause any issues in a flammable atmosphere. BA sets were laid down next to hand-operated hydraulic cutting equipment, as well as any hand tools and medical equipment we thought might help. All intrinsically safe lighting, including Wolf lamps and personal issue BA torches, were put down in the hope that they could be of some use to those working underground. In the meantime, Gashy pressed the Pit Manager for more information on what had happened. The manager stated that a train carrying miners had somehow derailed, causing it to crash, trapping some of the miners in the wreckage. Gashy asked how long it would be before Mines Rescue turned up, and it was then that the manager stated that he was having trouble getting through to them. Gashy immediately radioed Control for them to try and raise the rescue team. Control swiftly came back and stated that no-one at Mines Rescue appeared to be answering the phone, but they would keep on trying.

Minutes seemed like hours while we waited for news from below, and eventually a cage came up carrying a few miners, their faces covered in coal dust and sweat, and the look in their eyes showing they had witnessed something really horrific. They rapidly approached the manager and were highly irate, demanding to know how long Mines Rescue were going to be. Gashy asked if there were still men trapped, to which the men replied that there were and "they are in a bad way". The men asked why the Fire Service couldn't go down to help, while the manager replied that it was against regulations. Just then, one of the miners stepped forward and grabbed the manager, and in a menacing way told him that the Fire Service would be going down and that he (the manager) was going to authorise it. Gashy attempted to defuse the situation, but by then you could see that the manager was at the end of his tether, and he quickly told Gashy that he could take a small team down to see if they could assist.

Before the manager could change his mind, Gashy quickly put together a team of the smaller firefighters that were in attendance, and they, along with the miners, carried a lot of equipment down the pit to the incident. I was left on top to man the equipment dump, as Gashy thought my height would be a disadvantage in the tight space of the pit tunnels.

For a Fire Service to attend an incident down an active pit was a very rare occurrence, but with the Mines Rescue Team failing to respond, I think the Pit Manager was left with no option but to allow our attendance. The crew that went down did all they could to help save the men that were trapped, but unfortunately two men, Eric Evans and Gerard Sumby, lost their lives at the scene. Two others, Jeff Branson and Alan Curry, were left with severe spinal injuries that made them wheelchair-bound for life. The train had derailed and jack-knifed, trapping the miners against the roof of the tunnel, which made the rescues extremely difficult to carry out. Stories were told of miners trying to dig out their colleagues with their bare hands prior to the arrival of the Fire Service with their cutting gear, so the conditions down there must have been grim for all involved. A few other miners had been injured in the crash, but their injuries were not life-changing and, being a tough breed, they more or less rescued themselves to be ultimately treated above ground. It was a bad night for all involved, and as a station so close to the pit, everyone knew someone who worked there so the job became quite personal.

Monkwearmouth Colliery was the last of the North East pits to close. On December 10th, 1993, the final shift came up from the coal face, and the gates were locked for one last time. The pit and its associated buildings were demolished throughout 1994, with the land being left for redevelopment. By the end of 1995, the land that the colliery had stood on was acquired by Sunderland Association Football Club to house their new stadium, that would replace their home ground of Roker Park. £24million was spent on building a 49,000-seater stadium, which was opened in July of 1997. The Stadium of Light, as it is known, is named in reference to the area's coal mining heritage, with the 'light' referring to the Davy Lamp carried by all miners. A statue of a miner's Davy Lamp is located at the front of the stadium's ticket office as a permanent reminder to all who worked in those dark conditions.

CHAPTER THIRTEEN

A TRAGIC DAY

As part of my personal development during my four-year probation period, I sat my Leading Firefighter's tickets (exams needed at that time if you were to go for promotion). I had no real desire to join the promotion rat race, as life at Mike was agreeable with the station being so busy, as well as it being within easy walking distance of my home. Nevertheless, I thought it best to take the exam whilst I was still in the habit of studying. I had also figured that if I passed the exam, I would be allowed to act-up to the next rank at Mike whenever one of our Leading Firefighters was on leave or away from station on a Junior Officer Course.

Being an acting Leading Firefighter at Mike allowed you to either be the BA Team Leader, riding in the back of M01, or to be the OIC of M03, the station's Turntable Ladder (later to become the ALP). You were also expected to complete all the relevant paperwork that comes with working on a busy station, including – whenever required – sorting out the Watch's leave requests and detachments. It was a change from the norm, and although both roles came with different responsibilities, I enjoyed more being the OIC of M03, as you felt that you had more freedom to make essential decisions. That was because M03 was regularly mobilised to incidents within other station areas, and when you arrived at those incidents, the OIC of the job often looked for your advice on how best to use the aerial appliance, in the knowledge that you knew its capabilities and limitations.

The only downside to riding on M03 was that if there were flames to be fought, it was going to be from the outside of the premises and not at the pointy end, where I relished being. Of course, there were plenty of times when I acted up on the three (M03) that M01 would be mobilised to a job and I would jealously watch as the pump rolled out of the station with horns wailing and blue lights flashing. The boys would return to station and try and taunt me on how big the job had been, along with how much fun they had had. But I already knew how big the job had been, because I would monitor their radio messages from when they left the station until their return.

One sunny dayshift, I turned up for duty to be told I was acting up on M03 for the day. The other Leading Fireman on duty that day was Alan 'Kit' Carson, who was rostered to be the BA Team Leader on M01. Alan was a cracking lad who had a load of firefighting experience behind him. He had come to us after being a firefighter on November (Sunderland Central) Green Watch, so we all knew him well before he had even joined us. He was one of those blokes who had a wickedly dry sense of humour, which some people would take as Alan being a grumpy old sod. He had settled in nicely onto the Watch and seemed really happy with his move to Mike.

For reasons of fate, Alan asked me if I fancied swapping with him onto M01. He said that he hadn't rode M03 in a while, and fancied a change from M01. I agreed, as I felt in my guts that M01 was going to get a fire that day, and if I refused, I would have regretted missing the job. We swapped, and the day started out like any other normal dayshift, with drills on the drill yard in the morning, then lunch, followed by fire safety duties in the afternoon.

Late in the afternoon, the station alarms rang out. M02 and M03 were being turned out to a derelict bingo hall that was on fire in the Tyne Dock area of South Shields. K01 and K02 were also being dispatched from their home station in the centre of South Shields, and I listened in to the radio messages as K01 arrived on scene.

The first message made it pretty obvious that the job was a live one, and that flames could be seen coming from the building. The OIC of K01, due to the size of the building, made the decision to make pumps 4, which then mobilised M01 to the incident. We hurriedly mounted the appliance and booked mobile for the six to eight-minute run that it would take us to arrive at the incident.

M02 arrived at the bingo hall to join K01 and K02, and got straight to work. M03 was only a minute behind them, and drove up into the bingo hall car park, where Leading Firefighter Carson opened the door of the appliance and jumped down from the cab, intending to speak to the OIC of the incident to see where he required M03. Unfortunately, Kit hadn't waited for the appliance to come to a complete stop as he jumped down, and as he landed on the ground he stumbled and fell, with his leg becoming horrifically trapped under the wheel of M03 as it rolled to a halt. Having seen what had happened, one of the other firefighters at the scene shouted to the driver of M03, telling him to quickly reverse the appliance in order to free Kit's leg. The driver did so while firefighters rushed to Kit's aid, where they instantly discovered that he had sustained a serious leg injury.

We were still on our way to the incident when we heard the request for the ambulance with a firefighter down, and it sent shivers down my spine. I sat quietly in the back of M01, wondering what on earth had happened at the incident, whilst silently praying that the injury was not too serious. Soon enough, we arrived at scene, to be told that it was Kit who had been injured. We all automatically went to go over to where Kit was being attended to, but we were instantly stopped in our tracks by the OIC of Station Kilo, who assured us that Kit was being looked after and that we had to carry on fighting the fire.

We did as we were ordered and stuck to the job in hand of firefighting, whilst trying to keep a close eye on what was happening with Kit. Within a very short period of time, I glanced over to where he was lying, and I felt a sense of relief as I saw the ambulance arrive. I thought everything would be okay now that the paramedics had arrived. They quickly assessed him, and Kit was swiftly taken to hospital. But sadly, despite their best efforts, the surgeons were unable to save his leg.

Once the fire was out, we returned to home station, where I sat and reflected on the fact that I should have been the Leading Firefighter on M03 that day. Had I not swapped duties to go onto M01, Kit would not have received that horrendous life-changing injury. Regrettably, fate had dealt its hand that day, and there was nothing either Kit or I could do to change the outcome. This didn't stop me feeling extremely guilty for swapping with him, and that feeling remained with me for a very long time afterwards, until I learned to accept that it was just fate and nothing to do with me agreeing to swap duties. Due to the severity of injury, Kit was retired from the Service shortly afterwards, but I still to this day think of him and hope that he is coping with what he has been dealt.

CHAPTER FOURTEEN

ONE TO MISS AND TERROR ALERT

RED WATCH TANKER FIRE

Green Watch wasn't the only Watch on Station Mike who were getting jobs that were out of the ordinary. It was a bright sunny Wednesday, on August 26th, 1992, and Red Watch were the duty dayshift crew enjoying a reasonably quiet day, when the bells went down for a reported RTC causing a petrol spillage on Newcastle Road, which was just around the corner from the station. The crews mounted the appliances and dressed quickly, due to the close proximity of the job, and travelled up Station Road towards the traffic lights, where they would turn left onto Newcastle Road.

Nothing seemed unusual about their journey until that left turning, where they were faced with what can only be described as a scene from a disaster movie. There, before them, was a thick blanket of black smoke covering the whole of Newcastle Road, and it wasn't until they got closer that it registered what was burning.

A 38-tonne petrol tanker, carrying 33,000 litres of fuel, had collided with a minibus, causing the tanker to turn on its side and burst into flames. Luckily, the driver of the tanker escaped from his cab with only minor burns, and the minibus driver was left uninjured. However, the flames were rapidly spreading, and the OIC of the first appliance immediately requested further pumps and the foam tender to be dispatched.

Unfortunately, the road was on a slight slope, and a running fuel fire swiftly developed. This created further issues, as lined up in the direct line of the flowing fire were a number of parked cars. One by one, they burst into flames while the crews struggled to contain the blaze.

A decision was made to evacuate 200 people from their homes, as the flames continued to roar. In the end, 14 appliances were required to get the inferno under control, using 13,000 litres of foam. The tanker and 42 cars were totally destroyed, and the damage done to the road surface required extensive repair, but at least there were no serious casualties. Red Watch had fought the fire from Hell, which left them with at least one decent story to tell their grandchildren. Although used to dealing with car fires on a weekly basis, it must have been a shock to the system to have to fight a year's supply all in one incident, so it was definitely one to miss!

TERRORIST ALERT

On the 10th May, 1992, an incident occurred at the Metro Centre Shopping Centre, Gateshead (one of the largest shopping malls in Europe). Incendiary devices were detonated in a number of shops, and although causing little damage, the impact on those working in the Emergency Services was huge. After tackling the initial six devices that ignited, a thorough search of the premises revealed three other devices that were still intact, and one that was found burnt out. The Provisional IRA claimed responsibility for the attack, and stated that an active service unit had planted the devices and would continue to be active whilst British soldiers roamed the streets of Northern Ireland. Tyne and Wear Metropolitan Fire Brigade put all their fire stations on high alert, and procedures were put in place on how we were going to respond to such incidents.

For the next few weeks, we waited to see if the threat was going to escalate, and wondered if any of the shops in our area were to be targeted. Just when we thought the threat had passed, we were turned out to Joplings – a major clothing store based in Sunderland city centre. The caller to Control stated that there were explosive devices within the store, and gave a recognised IRA code word to prove its authenticity. We sat for hours outside the premises before the Police and bomb specialists completed a full interior search and came to the conclusion that it was a hoax call.

I found it extremely frustrating just sitting on the appliance waiting to get the all clear, especially when we heard K02 turn out to a couple of small fires within our station area that we should have been dealing with. But with the correct code words being passed, we couldn't take any chances, and had to adhere stringently to procedures put in place for incidents such as these.

There were a few similar calls over the next few days to a number of properties across the area, and each time the threat had to be taken seriously, all with the agreed pre-determined attendance (PDA) being dispatched. This not only tied up valuable resources, but was also a big drain on morale; sitting outside a property with adrenalin pumping through your body was not the reason why we joined the Service. This being the case, we all hoped that the hoax caller would be swiftly caught, if only to allow a sense of normality to return to stations.

No other incendiaries were found in this period, and the IRA activity seemed to cease until just over a year later. On 8th June, 1993, a large explosion at Dunston Gas Storage Plant, less than a mile from the MetroCentre, rocked the local area and sent flames shooting 30ft into the sky. The tank, containing 2 million cubic feet of natural gas, was burning away merrily, threatening other tanks that were in close proximity. Over 100 firefighters and 20 appliances battled to protect the surrounding tanks, as well as 250 nearby houses, which needed to be rapidly evacuated as a precaution. I turned up to the job on M02, to join a number of firefighters on jets and monitors, battling to contain the blaze and to help cool the surrounding tanks. I must admit that when the fire was at its height, it was an impressive sight which was mesmerising to look at, but we battled away until finally we had it under control.

This battle against the beast on that night was won, but we almost had to do a repeat performance the following evening, as three Semtex explosive devices were set off at the Esso Oil Refinery Plant in North Shields, approximately 12 miles away from the Dunston Gas Plant. The explosions severely damaged supply pipelines and blew a huge hole in the side of one of the oil tanks. But luckily, the tank was empty at the time and the residue of oil that was left failed to ignite. The relief on the face of the OIC of the pump that turned out to that job must have been immense, as the magnitude of the Esso site being ignited would have sent shivers down any experienced fire officers' spine. It was, nonetheless, a reminder that in our line of work we could be turned out to absolutely anything, whilst being expected to work in the most hazardous of conditions.

CHAPTER FIFTEEN

ANIMAL INCIDENTS

If you ask a member of the public to describe a firefighter's daily work routine, a high percentage would say that we turn out to fires when needed, attend car crashes, save cats from trees, and play snooker. All of which is very true, but what they don't realise is the amount of training required to do each of those activities safely, along with the variety of other incidents that we are expected to attend and train for. This, in truth, is probably why there has never been a world champion snooker player with a Fire Service background, as we have to plan and train for so many different scenarios that we just don't have time to improve our snooker game. As for the cats up trees, I have never seen a cat starve to death up a tree, as they will always come down when they are hungry. I have, nevertheless, rescued a number of cats in trees, but that has been done to pacify the owner or to stop someone from climbing the tree and putting themselves at risk. Throughout my career, I have also rescued a collection of other animals from all sorts of different circumstances – from hamsters and gerbils stuck under floorboards, to snakes and kittens stuck in machinery; from dogs in rabbit holes, to budgies in house fires. From small animals to large animals, each job has proved interesting and at times mind boggling, but each case is taken seriously, and all firefighters get great pleasure from doing the job right and getting a successful result.

A LOAD OF BULL

One dark night, we turned out to a report of a farm fire in Whitburn. On arrival, we could see that large bales of hay were on fire, which were in close proximity to a number of farm buildings.

There was a strong sea breeze gusting inland, and this was causing the heavy smoke to be blown into the buildings. A decision was made for two of my colleagues, Billy Forster and Gary Lowes, to don sets and enter the buildings to make sure they were empty. The BA team entered, and on getting to the rear of the barn, they realised they were not alone. Standing there in its pen was a huge bull, complete with nose ring, and getting slightly agitated by the smoke. Billy, being fearless, decided to take the bull by its horns and tried to get it to move towards the door. It wouldn't budge! He then decided to go to its back end, where he and Gary started to slap it on its behind in an attempt to make it head towards the door. It still wouldn't move, and the smoke was getting thicker.

I was on the outside, enjoying myself, putting water on the fire with a hose branch, when all of a sudden this irate gentleman turned up and started ranting at the OIC. I was standing close enough to work out that he was the farmer, and that it was his prize bull that was in the barn. The gaffer tried to pacify him, and told him if he really wanted to help then he should use his tractor to help spread the hay bales, which would make the firefighting easier.

He stomped off towards his tractor, with us all expecting him to get stuck into the bales, but what happened next was more like something out of a comedy sketch. He mounted the tractor and started it up with loads of revs, but instead of steering towards the hay bales, he drove the tractor straight at the barn. The building was constructed of single layer breeze block, so the wall was no match for the tractor as he ploughed straight through it. I have no idea what was going on in his mind, but he was unbelievably reckless, and his actions could have killed his bull along with the two BA wearers.

As he went through the wall, I dropped the branch and ran with the gaffer towards the barn, arriving just as the farmer reversed out of the hole. Seconds later, out came the bull, slowly striding out into the midnight air, followed by two heavily dust-covered firefighters. Billy said they were inches from getting crushed and wanted to have serious words with the farmer, but we managed to calm him down. The farmer claimed he didn't know that we had BA wearers in there and thought he was just helping. Gary being Gary, an ex-Para with a fear of nothing, took the whole thing in his stride and thought the whole thing was just a load of bull, as he stood laughing at their near miss!

PUT OFF PORK

Another farm fire in our station area ended up having an unforeseen effect on the whole Watch, which was to last for weeks. One late Sunday evening, the station got turned out to a reported fire in a pig farm in Cleadon Village, about a mile away from the station. As we approached, we could tell it was going well, so the OIC immediately made pumps 4. When we pulled up, I could see that it was a large barn building that was alight, so quickly got to work running out hose and getting a jet onto the fire as soon as possible. Hydrants were located and plumbed into, while BA wearers prepared themselves to go in. Now, fires in farm buildings can be extremely volatile and hazardous, due to the storage of fertilizer, poisons, and chemicals used by the farmers, so all necessary precautions have to be considered before risking crews. On this occasion, the farmer was on site to inform us that there were about 100 pigs in the barn, but no other really hazardous materials.

On getting the barn doors open, I could see that the fire was well developed and the pigs were squealing in fear. The BA teams entered and started to fight the fire from the inside, whilst opening pens to allow some of the pigs to escape into the farm yard. The noise made by the pigs was soul-destroying and some of the pigs escaping into the yard were obviously seriously injured. The fire was eventually brought under control, and crews started to dampen down various hot spots. The saddest part of the damping down was that a lot of the sows had been due to give birth to piglets, and those that had been badly burned in the fire were obviously not going to survive. Some of them, on getting hit with a jet of water, had burst open to reveal the dead piglets that were just days away from birth. The sight was horrendous, but the overall smell was even worse, with the deathly stench hanging heavily in the air. The injured pigs were rounded up and the farmer was asked if he wanted our Control to contact a veterinary practitioner to come and treat them. He declined the offer and stated that he would deal with the issue himself with his shotgun. He had decided the cost of the vet was not worth the money to him, so the pigs would be slaughtered instead.

We returned to home station and washed as much of our kit as we could, but for weeks afterwards there was always a strong smell of burnt pork on the station. This lingering smell was a constant reminder of that job and the poor pigs, which understandably put a lot of the lads off eating pork. The station cook at the time thought this was an ideal time to get some payback for all the japes and insults we had thrown his way over the years, and deliberately made pork his main choice of meat. Pork stir-fry, pork chops, pork sausages, pork casserole, roast pork, all made it onto the list, with Tony the chef smiling in delight as the boys turned their noses up at the meals, whilst throwing verbal insults at him for his sick choice of menu.

GASHY AND HIS CURRIED RABBIT

Talking of food, it would be a shame not to mention Gashy and his curried rabbit. Gashy's father-in-law just happened to be a gamekeeper on land up in Northumberland, where Alan would visit him on a regularly basis, if only to stock up his larder back in Sunderland with a few freshly caught rabbits. One Sunday nightshift, he had brought a few of these rabbits to the station to prepare and cook for the Watch. He had raved that although rabbit was known as a poor man's meat, it tasted absolutely beautiful when basted in curry sauce and baked in the oven. The Watch, just happy to have the Station Officer in the kitchen instead of drilling them on the drill ground, encouraged him to crack on, and left him to it. Now these rabbits that Alan had brought in had come straight from the fields, so needed skinning and butchering, but he wasn't exactly dressed for the occasion in his white Station Officer's shirt. Nevertheless, he was determined to show the Watch how nice rabbit could taste cooked this way, so just got the knives out and started preparing. He sliced and cut, and within a short period of time his shirt was covered in blood and guts, but Alan was in his element.

Just then the front door bell rang, and I slid down the pole to answer it to a man requesting to speak to the Officer in Charge. Normally I would have taken the gentleman into the downstairs office and used the station tannoy system to call the Station Officer, but I knew how busy Gashy was, so I decided to take the gentleman straight up to the kitchen. We arrived in the kitchen for the gentleman to witness a scene from a horror movie. Alan was in mid-strike of chopping the rabbit in half, with this demonic look on his blood-spattered face. His shirt was, as I have said, covered in blood, and when the gentleman saw this, he almost took a step back out of the kitchen. Gashy apologised for the mess he was in as he tried to explain what he was doing, but I could tell the man just wanted to leave as soon as he could. For some unknown reason, the man refused a cup of tea from this mad Station Officer standing in front of him, and just stated his business quickly before scuttling out of the building in haste. Gashy wasn't impressed with me for bringing the visitor directly upstairs without giving him prior notice, but I must say his curried rabbit was fantastic!!

CHAPTER SIXTEEN

THE GRIEVESON MURDERS

On 26th May, 1990, a request from the Police was made for assistance to gain entry to a property called Gillside House, in the Roker area of Sunderland. I was part of the crew that mobilised with M02 to assist the Police, and having pitched a ladder to a window, the Police informed us that the body of a young male had been found in one of the rooms and that only they would enter the building, in order to preserve the scene.

Simon Martin, a 14-year-old schoolboy, had gone missing from home a few days earlier, only to be found lying in a semi-naked state, having been strangled and murdered. Two young boys playing in the derelict house had come across this gruesome discovery, and had immediately left the building to report their horrific finding to the Police. It then took over 20 years before the culprit of this vicious act was brought to justice and made to pay.

MURDER ON THE FIREGROUND

On 26th November, 1993, Red Watch were on duty when they received a call to a fire in the allotments just off Newcastle Road, Fulwell. They turned out and located an abandoned allotment shed that was well alight, with flames stretching up into the dark evening sky. By the time they got into the allotment, the roof and side walls of the shed were fully engulfed, causing them to eventually collapse in on themselves due to the intensity of the blaze. The fire was quickly extinguished, but all that was left of the shed was the charred remains of timber, which would need turning over to douse any hot spots that remained. It was during this damping down stage of the incident that Red Watch made a disturbing discovery. At first, the firefighter thought he was moving charred timber to one side, but he soon realised that what he'd thought was wood, was in fact the arm of a body.

Police were called and the scene made secure for scenes of crime officers (SOCO) to arrive. The body was severely burnt, and forensic evidence must have been a nightmare to obtain, but from early on we had heard down the station that the Police were treating the incident as a glue sniffer who had set himself on fire while under the influence of inhaling aerosols. In the early 1990s, glue sniffing and aerosol sniffing had become pretty common amongst a number of youths, not only in the North East but throughout the UK. It wasn't unusual to see youths in the area as high as a kite, slumped in some state or other, whilst holding glue or aerosol containers, so the Police theory could have had some credence.

Shortly after the fire, it was released to the media that the body found was of an 18-year-old male called Thomas Kelly, who was local to the area. The local press confirmed from the Police that the incident was being treated as a glue sniffing session that had gone wrong, which I thought at the time would have been very hard on his family to read.

The naming of the youth and the theory of his demise became the talking point on the station. A lot of lads on the station had young sons who knew the deceased, and they reckoned that glue sniffing just wasn't his scene. Something just didn't sit right, but we figured the Police must have had more intel that they just weren't sharing.

DARK DAYS-DARKER NIGHTS

The dark winter nights continued, and soon a New Year was upon us as we moved into 1994. Green Watch were on nightshift on Tuesday 4th, February, when we responded to a fire in a derelict building overlooking the seafront. Roker Terrace was a block of terraced houses that faced out onto the North Sea, but also had access to the rear of the properties by means of a back lane that ran the full length of the Terrace. I was riding BA on M01, which turned into the lane at the rear of the property, as the caller had stated that access to the inside could be gained from there. It was a typical North East, dark, damp and cold winter's night, and with there being no street lights in the back lane, everything seemed that little bit darker.

Along with my BA partner, I entered the rear of the house, where we both began to start up our sets. Just then, due to a faulty seal, my set started to rapidly leak air. I was totally hacked off, as I had tested my set at the start of the shift and everything had been in order, but now it looked as if I was going to miss out on a live wear. I informed the Gaffer of the leak and that I was not able to proceed, so Gashy immediately ordered Garry Teasdale, who was a designated BA wearer on M02, to don his set and enter the building with my BA partner. Not wanting to miss out on anything else, I quickly dumped my BA set back on the appliance and followed Gashy and the BA wearers up the stairs, to the room on the first floor that contained the fire.

The fire didn't appear to be too big, allowing Gashy to lay on the floor next to the room door to get a situation report from the BA Wearers. I was just behind Gashy, asking if they needed anything and whether Gashy wanted more lighting brought in, when we heard Garry announce that he thought he had found a casualty. But he couldn't confirm it, as visibility wasn't great and there was a load of stuff in the room. We listened intently for an update, and within a minute, having found a window to ventilate the smoke from the room, Garry confirmed that it was indeed a person, who was past saving, that he had stumbled upon. The atmosphere around the whole job changed at that moment, and police were immediately requested to attend.

The BA team, having ensured the fire was totally out, returned to the appliances to service their sets, while more portable lighting was brought up to light up the stairway and room involved. While this was going on, I began a search of all the other rooms in the house to ensure that no-one else was in the building. The hairs on my neck were standing on end as I moved from one dark room to another, whilst silently praying that I wouldn't come across any other persons, either alive or dead. The tension within me increased as the Wolflite (BA Lamp) I was carrying cast shadows in each of the rooms, which occasionally made it look as if things were moving around me. To my relief, I cleared the rest of the building without finding anyone else, and quickly made my way back to the original room that contained the fire.

Whilst awaiting the arrival of the Police, Gashy and I walked into the room to assess the scene from a fire investigation view point. It was a bizarre scene: the room was packed with furniture, including a bed with mattress which was totally covered with fully filled boxes. There was also a ton of soft furnishings just strewn throughout the room, as well as plastic bags full of clothing, stacked four high against three of the walls. It was as if a hoarder had lived there and had left everything in situ before moving out. The potential for it to have been a massive fire was obvious to the eye, but oddly enough, the only thing that had been on fire was the body lying in the middle of the floor. We looked closer at the body, who looked like a young male, and observed what can only be described as a ligature, partially burnt, wrapped around his neck. This, without doubt in our minds, must be a murder scene, so we took great care to ensure nothing was disturbed and carefully left the room to stand and wait for the first Constable to arrive.

When the Police arrived, we entered the room again and Gashy pointed out the ligature to the Constable, but to our surprise he didn't seem that interested, commenting that although the ligature around the neck might look suspicious, "it was a well-known fact that some kids tighten things around their necks in order to enhance the sensation when glue sniffing". He then pointed out a canister, lying close to the body, that had contained lighter fluid, which the kids apparently sniffed regularly. Only this particular canister looked 50 years old, and had probably been lying in that room since the house was last lived in. I wasn't convinced and neither was Gashy; in fact, the whole crew found it unbelievable, but we had no choice but to leave the scene to the Police and go back to station to complete our paperwork, including our witness reports.

We felt frustration that it appeared Sunderland Police were palming this death off as another glue sniffing incident gone wrong, with a Senior Police Officer summing the incident up to the press as 'solvent abuse and experimentation with fire', which certainly didn't reflect on what we had found at the scene.

The body was identified as 15-year-old David Hanson, who lived locally with his parents and attended the local high school, Monkwearmouth School, as it was called then (now called Monkwearmouth Academy School). Again, the local press took their lead from the Police and reported the death as being linked to glue sniffing, but after what we had witnessed, we found this hard to take. At this point we had no real reason to link Thomas Kelly's death to David Hanson, apart from the glue sniffing angle, which we didn't believe to be true. However, within the space of just over five weeks, we had two young persons found dead in a fire situation. These weren't normal times.

BACK TO THE ALLOTMENT

Three weeks later, on Friday, 25th February, we were coming to the end of a busy day shift, when we got a call to smoke that could be seen coming from the allotments just off Newcastle Road, Fulwell. We cheered as the bells went down, as we thought this shout might get us an hour in overtime payment. We drove out of the station with a sense of joy, but returned with our hearts filled with despondency and anger.

I was riding M01, and we skirted around the outside of the allotment to try and get a better location to the fire. We could see a small amount of smoke floating in the air and just assumed it was a garden fire that had been left smouldering. Nevertheless, we were there to put it out, so looked to gain access to the allotment involved. After assessing the situation, we decided that the nearest road for us to use would be Wearmouth Drive, where the back gardens backed onto the allotments. We pulled up into Wearmouth Drive and Gashy knocked on the nearest house, where he asked the owner if it was okay for us to go through his back garden to sort the fire out. The gentleman agreed, so we pulled the hose-reel up his garden path and through into the rear of his premise.

When we got to the back garden, we could see that the smoke was coming from a greenhouse just the other side of a couple of

6-foot fences. I scrambled over the fences and jumped down between a shed and the greenhouse. I asked the lads to feed the hose-reel over the fence, and as they were doing that, I cracked open the greenhouse door to ascertain how developed the fire was. To my shock, I found myself looking at the body of a male that was still smouldering from the fire.

I quickly closed the door and shouted more hastily for the hose-reel, whilst spluttering to Gashy, who was just the other side of the fence, that we had another one. I don't think it registered with Gashy immediately, as he asked me what I meant. I replied, "Another young lad, and that's all that's on fire." It didn't take much water to put out the fire, and by then Gashy had jumped over the fence to see what I was dealing with. It was obviously a young lad, as I recognised the boots he was wearing as Caterpillar boots which were in fashion at the time, especially amongst young teens. We stood there in a semi-state of shock, neither of us having much to say to each other, as we looked at the young body whilst contemplating what on earth was going on in our area.

As we awaited the arrival of the Police, we again looked over the fire scene and found it unbelievable that all that was on fire was the lad himself. Even plastic potting plants close by had mainly remained intact, but the body had severe burns, making us think that an accelerant had been poured over the lad's clothing but nowhere else. To add to our suspicions, around his neck there was again a ligature.

The initial Police attendance turned up, and by then I was starting to get a bit angry with them. I said to the Constable, "When are you going to take these deaths seriously?" "What other deaths?" he replied. He really had no idea that there had been other 'recent' deaths in the area. I pointed out the burned-out allotment shed a mere 50 feet away, stating, "The young lad who died there two months ago, and the poor lad down on the seafront three weeks ago." He looked gobsmacked; it appeared the different shifts at the cop shop didn't really liaise with each other, so he really was unaware. I mentioned the ligature around the neck of David Hanson and that the deceased in the greenhouse also had a ligature. At last, his interest seemed to rise, and he got straight on to CID to attend.

We finished up and returned to home station, leaving the scene for SOCO to do their work. I felt confident that at last the wheels were going to be set in motion and the deaths were going to be taken seriously. We felt there was a serial killer out there that seriously needed to be caught before any other youngster suffered like these boys had. I prayed for the souls of those who had been killed in such a wicked way, and hoped for the families that the person responsible would be brought to justice.

Within a very short period of time, the Police released the name of the lad in the greenhouse. He was called David Grieff – another 15-year-old, who also went to Monkwearmouth School. Yet again, he was a local lad who had been brought up in a very respectable family. He was also a very close friend of David Hanson.

UTTER FRUSTRATION

The following day, police officers turned up at the station to take witness statements from all of those that had been at the job. One by one we sat with a Constable and relayed everything we had seen and done. During this time, all the lads tried to get a feeling of what the thoughts of the Police were, and whether they had any idea who might be committing these atrocities. The statements were signed off and the officers left, but the general thoughts of the lads on Watch were that either the Police weren't giving much away, or they simply didn't have a clue who the perpetrator was.

What happened next not only shocked us, but angered us to the core. It appeared, according to the local press, that the Police were yet again putting the last death down to substance abuse that had gone badly wrong. Did they have other evidence to support this? Had they received information from a reliable source? Were we totally wrong in what we thought? The questions with no answers bounced around the room as we struggled to fathom the logic behind the Police decisions. We were all as frustrated as hell, but felt powerless to judge the findings of the Police, as they must have surely made their decisions on solid evidence.

The problem we had was that in the 1990s Sunderland Police had a poor reputation when it came to solving murders, so we had little faith in their ability when it came to these deaths. A number of murders in Sunderland had been left unsolved, and two involving young kids – Simon Martin in 1990, and Nikki Allan, a seven-year-old, in 1992, in particular – had left the public feeling that the Police had let them down. This was made worse by the facts that the Police had arrested and charged a young lad for the murder of Simon, only for it to be quashed under circumstances surrounding forensic evidence. Also, a 24-year-old neighbour of Nikki, George Heron, had been charged with her murder, only for him to be cleared at court after the judge accused the Police of heavy-handed tactics whilst obtaining an inadmissible taped confession.

The topic of these boys' deaths was all we talked about over tea-breaks, and no-one was more frustrated than Gashy, who was born and bred in Sunderland and very proud of his city. He was not happy that the Police appeared to be trying to sweep all the deaths under the carpet just to save their reputations, and wondered if the parents knew all the true facts about the jobs. However, knowing that the Brigade, as well as the Police, would take a dim view of a Station Officer releasing any information from the incidents, had put him in a difficult situation, which only fuelled his frustration. So, feeling that his hands were tied, we had to hope that the parents wouldn't just accept the deaths and would fight for the truth to come out.

Thankfully, the parents did refuse to accept the Police findings and, bonded together by their pain and suffering, began a campaign, with the help of the local press, to get the Police to review their conclusions. The pressure the families were putting on the Police was not going to go away, and we all felt it would just be a matter of time before the Police attitudes towards the case had to change.

SUNDERLAND STRANGLER

Within days of David Grieff's death, rumours had started to circulate around the local area, naming a person who was suspected of committing the murders. The name, Steven John

Grieveson, was rife throughout Monkwearmouth School, and a number of lads on the Watch recognised his name, stating that he had a history of being a nasty character. In fact, one of the lads swore he had seen Grieveson standing at the bottom of the lane when we were at the David Hanson job. All this was reported to the Police, but nothing seemed to change.

Eventually, all the pressure from families for a review began to pay dividends. The local press, having now come around to believing there was more to these fatalities, added their weight for all the circumstances of the deaths to be re-examined.

Without warning, Sunderland Police were taken off the case and a team of detectives from Gateshead Police took over the reins. This team was headed up by a dogged Detective Superintendent called Dave Wilson, who immediately recognised that the deaths had been suspicious. He called in a pathologist expert to re-examine the autopsy reports, and sent his team to re-interview us all down at the station, to go over every inch of our witness statements. This time we felt the job was getting done right.

Within a short period of Dave Wilson taking up the case, Grieveson was arrested and charged with three counts of murder. The press named him 'The Sunderland Strangler', and after a six-week trial he was found guilty of the murders and sentenced to a minimum of 35 years. The motive behind the murders was that he was a closet homosexual who had sexually abused the boys, but didn't want the secret of his sexuality to get out.

The brutality of what he had done to those boys sickened me to the pit of my stomach. It is a case that will forever be in my memory, and I just hope that Grieveson is never again allowed to walk the streets as a free man.

Fast forward to 2012, and I had left Tyne and Wear to live in the Isle of Man, where I was serving as a firefighter in the Isle of Man Fire and Rescue Service. Out of the blue, I received a telephone call from a detective in Northumbria Police. She confirmed that I was the right person, and stated that Grieveson was about to be charged with the murder of Simon Martin. She also asked that I leave certain dates in 2013 free, as I, along with all others who had attended the murder scene, might be called to give evidence at court in regard to the case. "No problem," I replied, as she also stated that she would be in touch in the near future with further information.

Months later, she called again, to say that Grieveson was holding his hands up to the murder and that my attendance at court wouldn't be required. I felt a sense of calm come over me, as I reflected on the day that Simon's body had been found, thinking to myself that justice would finally be served for that poor innocent child who had died so many years ago.

Grieveson pleaded guilty at Newcastle Crown Court, and on the 14th October, 2013, he received a further life sentence with a tariff of 35 years. This meant that Grieveson will not be eligible to apply for parole until he reaches the age of 78, in the year 2048. It had been over 20 years since the murder of Simon, but at least now his family could have some peace, knowing his assailant had been found and incarcerated.

CHAPTER SEVENTEEN

THE FULL MONTY

At times on Green Watch, we felt as if we were jinxed at getting all the big jobs that the station turned out to. I am sure it was not the case, and that the other three Watches were getting their fair share, but we were certainly averaging a sad number of jobs that occurred with fatalities. Apart from the ones I have mentioned, we also had a bad spate of road traffic collisions resulting in fatalities. We also attended a number of incidents to assist the ambulance service in body retrievals, and even had an elderly gentleman collapse and die right in front of the station, where we were unable to revive him. The list seemed endless, and each one deserves a mention to say they were not just a statistic, but a person with a family who cared.

But it was not all doom and gloom, and we had loads of good times, with many incidents that we attended ending successfully and other jobs that creased us with laughter. We had become a really good Watch, and a lot of us socialised together, becoming more like family than just work colleagues.

One day, Gashy came in and announced that his wife Jane was coming up to her 40th birthday, and that he had decided to throw a party for her in the social club that was affixed to the station. We were all, of course, invited with our partners. He then said that he wanted to make it a night that she wouldn't forget, adding that he had an idea and wanted to see what we all thought about it. He said that he and Jane had been watching *The Full Monty* – the movie about a group of unemployed men who decided to raise some extra cash by doing a striptease show dressed as security men. The film is really funny, and as they were watching it, Gashy had commented to Jane that he could do that, causing her to laugh out loud at the mere thought of it.

We laughed about it over a cup of tea, but Gashy had cleverly planted the seed, knowing that we wouldn't let him down. "Yes," we said, "it would be funny for you to do it, but surely it would be more effective if we all did it as a group, just like the film?" Before long, all those on Watch who weren't embarrassed with their bodies and knew how to have a laugh, volunteered to be part of the show.

We had a few weeks before the big event and were determined to put on a good show, so each lunchtime, as well as any stand down periods, we sloped off to the social club and practised our moves on the dance floor. The laughs we had during these times were insane; not only were we poor dancers, but our synchronisations were all over the place. We had more fun doing this than at any other time we had had on the Watch. As a team building exercise, everyone should attempt this, no matter what profession they are in.

Garry 'Teasa' Teasdale and Neil Harrison decided that they needed to look their best for all the ladies in the room, so had regular visits to a solarium to obtain that bronzed, macho look. The rest of us decided to save our money for beer on the night. We practised and practised and the night was getting closer, but something was missing. We knew we couldn't go completely naked, as the social club's committee would go nuts, so we had to cover our bits up with something at the last minute. We were all sent out to get thongs, or similar items that might do the job. Again, at rehearsals we laughed out loud at some of the items that the lads wanted to wear. A lot were voting for boxer shorts, but my slinky, black, shiny thong stole the show. It covered enough and left your ass free to the air, which Teasa thought would drive the women wild. I was immediately dispatched to buy the same thongs for everyone. The shop assistant looked puzzled as to why I wanted so many of the same one, and tried to sell me a kinky little red one. However, my heart was set on the black ones, although I almost relented and was very tempted to buy Teasa a special thong of his own, with an elephant's trunk attached!

The party date had just about arrived when Gashy announced that all the invitations had been sent out, stating there were going to be over 120 people in the room on the night. A lot of Jane's relations were coming, so we wondered how our sense of humour would go down with these non-Fire Service people. A few of the lads were getting jittery about the whole event and starting to have second thoughts, but they knew they couldn't let anyone down, not least their own boss.

Over a cup of tea, we discussed other ideas that could add to the entertainment on the night, when someone suggested doing a take on 'Through the Keyhole'. This had been a popular television show, where guests tried to work out whose house was being videoed, by being shown various clues on camera. Gashy thought this was a great idea, foolishly trusting us with his house keys to go and do some film work, while he conveniently took Jane out. What he didn't know was that we were going to fill his house with props that were not there when we started.

The night arrived, and we all waited in anticipation of the main event. The room was packed, and a few of the lads were downing a few shorts to build up Dutch courage. Before that, though, we had to sit through the episode of 'Through the Keyhole'. The compere for the evening, Station Officer Tommy Taylor, introduced the video by asking the audience if anyone out there could recognise this house. He then had the crowd in hysterics as the film went from room to room, with Tommy making the appropriate comments. Jane, from the first clip up the garden path, knew it was her house, and her face went bright red with embarrassment.

Entering the house, we had stockpiled every pair of shoes we could find into the entrance area, making it look as if Jane had a serious shoe fetish. We moved through the lounge, which we had turned into a right tip, as if Jane just didn't bother with housework. She was mortified. Into the kitchen, every pot, pan, and plate was heaped into the kitchen sink, whilst an amount of cereal was poured over the worktops. Jane just wanted to crawl into a hole. Up the stairs and into the main bedroom, one of the lads – wearing a bondage mask – was tied to the bed, surrounded by an array of sex toys which had been strategically placed around the room. To add to Jane's increasing discomfort, her knicker drawer was then raided, with the contents being held up high for all to see. We finished off by showing one of the lads, again with mask on, having a shower in the bathroom. By now the room was in hysterics, and not just at Tommy's comments, but at Jane's total embarrassment. I looked across and could see the ribbing that she was receiving from her family, but could also see that Jane could appreciate the humour.

She thought that would be the end of the show, so settled down to chat to her guests, not realising that we were leaving the room one by one. As the party continued, we quickly changed into our fire kit, complete with thongs! However, Teasa and Neil Harrison, being a bit vain with their false tans, must also have been a bit self-conscious with their manhood, as they both swiftly rolled-up a pair of socks and packed them tightly into their thongs, which caused a huge amount of amusement amongst the rest of us, along with a fair bit of light-hearted ribbing.

Eventually, it was showtime, and Gashy entered the club in fire kit, with Jane wondering what the hell he was doing. Gashy took the mic and placed a chair in the centre of the dance floor, where he asked Jane to join him, and sat her down. He explained to the room that he and Jane had watched *The Full Monty* and how he had said that he could do that, to which Jane had just laughed. The cheering and shouting from the crowd became deafening, with the sound reverberating through the doors as we waited for our cue to enter from the hallway. Standing waiting there, in those few minutes, became unnerving, allowing stage fright to creep in amongst a few of the boys. It honestly became that bad that a few of the lads were absolutely bricking it, causing them to seriously reconsider doing our practised routine.

Jane, by this time, realised what was about to happen and held her face in her hands. However, she was not expecting us as well! The lights came down, with the Hot Chocolate music from the film being cued, and on the first beat, the hallway door opened, and we proudly paraded in. The place fell about, and I can honestly say it was the loudest crowd that has ever attended that social club.

Jane was giggling away with embarrassment as we circled her menacingly, then we got straight into the routine. Bit by bit, the kit came off, just as we had practised, although some of the funnier moments were made better by the fire boots, which seemed to stick to some of our feet and needed an extra hard tug to get them off. Tunics were unfastened and bare chests were exposed to the screams of the women in attendance. Tunics were then taken off and swung around our heads to be flung at Jane. Leggings came next, to reveal boxer shorts which had Jane's 40th written on them. Not yet fully satisfied, the crowd bayed for more, with the ladies in the room screaming for full nudity. So, we ultimately lined up in front of Jane, and on the final note, whipped off our boxer shorts. These had been strategically pre-ripped and lightly stitched back together, so tore off easily to reveal our shiny thongs and bare arses. Feeling more than a bit exposed, we then quickly made a run for the door, leaving the hysterical crowd chanting for more!

It was one of the best social events we had as a Watch, but more importantly, Gashy had given Jane a birthday to remember.

CHAPTER EIGHTEEN

CHARACTERS AND A SERIES OF HUMOROUS EVENTS

The Fire Service seems to attract a right mixture of people to its ranks. There are definitely some weird and wonderful personalities, including oddballs and eccentrics, but ultimately most have joined for the right reasons and basically just want to help and serve the public in the best way that they can. Throughout my Fire Service career, I have served with some really special characters – some were intentionally funny, while others were just naturally funny, and there was a whole bunch who were not funny at all. We did, however, have to get along to ensure the job was done right, as living in each other's pockets while we were on duty tended to bond Watches together. Of course, there were, without a doubt, individuals that I served with that left a lasting impression on me, and I have no doubt they would say the same thing about me.

My theory about work is that if you're enjoying what you are doing, and try to have the occasional laugh along the way, the days and nights just seem to fly by. I am sure my sense of humour wasn't always appreciated, and sometimes it meant that I was the only one that was smiling, but one thing that was always undisputable with me was that when those bells went down, I always got serious to get the job done.

From my first day in service until the last, I met and worked with some incredible people, some I have already mentioned and a few below who have a story attached.

ON MANOEUVRES

Derek '999' Smith was ex-Army who served with me on my first Watch at Victor. It wasn't the fact that his Brigade number was

999, which I thought was pretty cool, that I remember him. It was the fact that every so often on a nightshift, while everyone was fast asleep in the sleeping quarters, Derek would sleep crawl. What I mean by this is that when Derek would be fast asleep, and obviously dreaming of his past life, he would go on midnight manoeuvres, crawling military-style around the dormitory, then eventually back to his bed. The first time I witnessed it, it scared the life out of me, but the lads told me not to wake him as it was better that he just made his own way back to bed. Weird, but true!

SWEET TOOTH

Kenny Sharpe, my first Sub Officer at Station Mike. His claim to fame was that he had an unmatched fondness for midget gems, the fruit-flavoured, hard jelly sweet. He would spend the day popping these sweets into his mouth from a packet he always kept in his pocket, chewing away to his heart's content. This was pretty normal, but what wasn't normal was that you would be in a BA job and all of a sudden you would hear 'PSSSST', then a few minutes later 'PSSST'. You would turn around and there would be Kenny, breaking the seal of his mask, whilst popping a midget gem into his mouth. It always made me smile.

MYSTICAL BOB

Bob Carr was a firefighter based on my station, but worked on the Red Watch. Bob is special because he has a gift, and his gift is that he is a faith healer. All I can say to those non-believers is "don't knock it till you've tried it". Playing sport throughout my life has often meant that I have picked up the occasional sprain or muscle damage. When I first heard that Bob often treated some of the lads on the station for minor injuries, I was sceptical. However, one day I turned into work carrying a shoulder injury from playing basketball. I was sore, but was determined that I wasn't going to go sick. It was a dayshift for me, but I knew Bob would be coming on duty later in the day for a Red Watch nightshift, so I decided that I would try and see him then. Bob arrived on station and I approached him with my issue, where he immediately agreed to try and help, ushering me up to the lecture room for a more private consultation.

I sat there while Bob focused himself and then, without touching me, he moved his hands over my shoulder and neck area. What happened next is inexplicable; my neck and shoulder area went freezing cold, and then within minutes the area went really hot. This happened a few times, and by the end of 20 minutes I found that I could raise my arms above my head, which was something I couldn't do before Bob arrived. He explained what I had injured, and said I needed a couple of more sessions with him and everything should be okay. Those 20 minutes turned me into a believer rather than the sceptic, and I have been treated by Bob for numerous injuries throughout the years.

Bob also helped my wife Lorna when she suffered a whiplash injury following a car accident. She was a definite non-believer until her first session, but after receiving the treatment, the movement and pain in her neck definitely improved to the extent that even I could see the physical difference. There are, of course, plenty of injuries that Bob cannot help with, but even then, in the majority of cases, he was still able to explain what the injury was and how it should be treated.

As a strange twist, Bob's brother is a Catholic priest and a definite non-believer in Bob's healing powers. Apparently, they have had numerous discussions about it at family get-togethers, with his brother becoming a bit heated at times, even though Bob never laid a hand on him!

BLESS YOU

Ray Richardson was a firefighter with me during my time at Mike. Ray was also a Methodist Minister in his own right, and regularly gave religious services in a church in South Shields. One day we turned up to a guy threatening to throw himself off the cliffs on Roker seafront. Ray approached the guy to try and talk to him, but he insisted that he just wanted to talk to a priest. Ray ran back to the truck, whipped his fire tunic off and placed his dog collar around his neck. He then returned to speak to the guy again, but he thought Ray was taking the piss and almost threw himself off the cliff there and then. The Reverend Ray convinced him otherwise, and everything ended nicely.

EXPLODING BEDS

Gary Lowes, as mentioned previously, was a fellow firefighter on Green Watch, and had served in the Parachute regiment before joining the Brigade. At 5'6" Gary is a pocket rocket of a man, who knows no fear and is as strong as an ox. On arriving on station, he was told by the Station Officer that as long as he stayed away from me and Billy, he should do alright. Alas, with his sense of humour, it didn't take him long to become the third Dangerous Brother, and we have remained friends all these years.

Now, one thing that used to annoy Gary was that the firefighter who had the bed next to him in the dormitory, snored like a trooper. Eddie Moore was his name, and he was one of the old sweats on the Watch, but he was a lovely fella and worked as hard as anyone else on the crew. During one tour of duty, Gary was feeling tired, so was desperate for a good night's sleep. The dormitory had just been fitted with new fold-down beds that were fantastic, and being fold-down meant the room could be used as a lecture/training area during the daytime hours. It was our first nightshift, and Eddy must have really enjoyed his new bed, because as soon as his head hit the pillow, he started snoring really loud, much to the disgruntlement of Gary. Anyway, we turned out a few times that night, so nobody got any real sleep.

Before going off duty the next morning, Gary told me that he was going to fix Eddie's snoring once and for all. I asked what his plan was, and he stated that when he left the Paras, he had accidentally brought some flashbangs home, so he was going to put one under Eddie's bed if he started snoring. (Flashbangs are used by the military and police as a distraction device. When set off, it explodes, temporarily creating a blinding flash, as well as a deafening sound). I told Gary that it would be best to put the device in a pan or another container so that it wouldn't damage the new bed.

We came on duty for our second nightshift, and Gary told me he had brought the device in. The night ticked on, and around midnight I turned in to see that Eddie was already in bed, but not snoring. Gary turned in, and I thought that would be that, but less than an hour later Eddie began his regular snore pattern. I looked across at Gary who was twittering away to himself, when suddenly he got up and went out. He came back with a pan from the kitchen and proceeded to pull the pin from his flashbang, placed it in the pan, put the lid on, and then slid it under Eddie's bed. 'BANG!' The noise was deafening, and Eddie's bed jumped two foot into the air before slamming back down to the floor. Everyone shot up, apart from me, as I was chuckling away under my sleeping bag. The smoke started to fill the room and the fire alarm went off. Gary scarpered to silence the alarm before Gashy or the Junior Officers came across to investigate, while the boys opened windows to disperse the smoke. Gary told Eddie he had more flashbangs, and surprisingly enough, Eddie didn't snore again that night.

Morning came and we started to make up our beds, unfortunately when Eddie raised his to fold it away, there was a circular hole measuring 12 inches in diameter, carved into the wood panel. The flashbang had exploded with such force, that it had blew the lid off the pan straight into the underside of the bed. The shock on Eddies face was a picture to see and I could hardly stand as tears of laughter rolled down my cheeks. Gary stood chuckling like a naughty schoolboy, as the older member of the Watch stood in a state of panic, as if they were the ones who had created the damage.

Just at that moment we could hear Gashy coming up the stairs on his way to the mess room. As he passed the dormitory, I mischievously called to him that he should come and look at the new beds. Gashy, being too wise to get involved in one of my japes, simply replied, "If it has anything to do with the fire alarm going off last night, I don't want to know! JUST FIX IT!" At least now we all knew what needed to be done.

The other reason Gary was smiling was that in an hour's time he was to start his annual leave, and he and his wife Julie were going off to the United States for a few weeks. That meant me and Billy would have to cover for him and get the bed sorted. The first port of call was to the company who fitted the beds less than two weeks before. We explained our predicament and the company said they could repair the bed, but it would cost just over £1000 for a replacement. We said we would get back to them if required. Not!

Eddie, despite being blown up – bless him – suggested we got some veneered plywood sheets to match the rest of the beds and just adhesive it to the existing base. Figuring that this was the cheapest option, we took the measurement of the base of the bed and, with the pan lid-sized sample, we headed off to Homeworthy, who specialised in veneer furniture. We arrived and asked to speak to the manager, who listened with a grin on his face as we described what we needed to do. Having been to Homeworthy for a dust silo fire quite recently, the manager was more than happy to help. We showed him the sample and he came back with an almost match, which we figured would save us £1000. To top it off, the manager refused to take any payment, as he said the story of how it happened was enough for him. We headed back to station, and with Eddie's help we stuck the veneer to the base. We stood back to admire our handiwork and to look around at the rosewood beds all folded up neat and tidy, and the one teak bed that stuck out like a sore thumb!

SOCK RAT

As I have already stated, Billy was hyperactive and just couldn't settle if we were having a quiet night. To combat this, he used to think up some incredible japes to play on the other members of the Watch. But it was one of the simplest japes that we always went back to, especially if we were working nightshift on a Friday, Saturday, or Sunday, when we could have a little fun with the general public.

Within an area of 100 metres from the station, we had two pubs, a working men's club, and a chip shop. This meant that on a weekend the footfall across the front of the station could be quite high. It also meant that come kicking out time at the pubs, we would see some right sights as a procession of drunken people headed home. Some staggered and weaved, taking two steps forward then one step back. Others munched on their supper from the chippy, with more food hitting the ground than their mouths. Some held each other up as they sang their way past, while others took a deep breath whilst marching in what they thought was a straight line. It was hilarious to observe, especially when you were sober, and it was one of the highlights of working weekend nights.

We would wait until the main bulk of people had passed and then we would bring out Roland, our sock rat. It's amazing how a sock stuffed with padding, and with mouth, ears, and whiskers felt tip penned on, could look like a real rodent after eight or so pints. We would attach Roland to fishing line and, when it was clear, one of the lads would cross the road, dumping Roland just outside of the shops which stood opposite the station.

The lights in the appliance room would be turned off and the appliance door raised two inches. Then we would wait for our first victim. As the victim approached where the rat was, we would start to reel in the fishing line, which couldn't be seen in the dim street lighting. It was comical watching people's reaction. Women screamed, chips were dropped, and a number of times some individuals even tried to stamp on him, but we were too quick and reeled Roland into safety. One night, we giggled away behind closed doors as one guy tried stamping on it a dozen times, only for us to move it just in time. He followed Roland across the road while still stamping, and looked bemused as it slid under the door. Not one for letting go of the chase, the guy rang the front doorbell to tell us we had a rat on the station. We asked him what he meant, and he said that he had chased the rat right under the door. "Ah," we said, "that must have been Roland. He's the station's mascot and always comes in at this time for food." The guy looked dumbfounded and apologised for trying to kill Roland, muttering away to himself as he quickly turned around to continue on his merry way, closely observed by all the guys who stood chuckling to themselves as they hid behind the appliance room doors with Roland.

SCUD MISSILE

One of the shops opposite the station was a carpet shop, and one day Billy popped across to see if they had any of the cardboard tubes that the carpets are rolled onto. Back he came, carrying a few, with members of the Watch wondering what ridiculous plan Billy had now.

It was at the time of the Gulf War, codenamed Operation Desert Storm, and the press was full of what was happening in the Middle East. It was then that Billy told me we were going to build our defences against an Iraqi attack, starting with some scud missiles on the top of the drill tower (I told you he was hyperactive). I helped him get the tubes up the tower, and after a while he was finished. To be fair, when you looked up from ground level, you would swear that it was a missile launcher. Soon the local kids were inquisitive, asking what the guns were on the tower, so we told them straight 'Scud Missiles'. Before long, the local press had got wind of a big story of defence guns being set up, with them even sending a photographer down to take a picture. They had also phoned Brigade Headquarters for the story, and soon the station's Divisional Officer was on the phone, demanding to know what was going on. The scuds came down a lot quicker than they went up!

PSYCHO

Sometimes a decent jape took a while to set up. One of these involved the Leading Firefighter on the Watch called Noel Thompson. Billy had suggested setting Noel up for a decent shock, and explained his plan to me. The first thing we had to do was to put doubt in Noel's mind that something was amiss on the station, and that there was a possibility of the building being haunted. Sounds ridiculous, I agree, but Noel tended to be a bit gullible.

The Junior Officers' dormitory and showers were on the other side of the station from the rest of the lads, and directly below the social club attached to the station. For security reasons, you could access the club from the top floor of the main station, with the club also having a pole-shaft that went down to the appliance room.

We would wait for the club to close and for Noel to go to bed, then we would go through to the club and rattle pans directly above the Junior Officers' dormitory. One of us would keep watch, and as we heard Noel coming up the stairs to investigate, we would swiftly slide down the pole to the appliance room, before disappearing into our dormitory to quickly get into bed. Noel would always pop his head into our dormitory on his way back down the stairs to see if anyone was up, and we would all pretend to be asleep. Next morning, Noel would ask if anyone else had heard banging last night, and we would all look at him as if he was hearing things. We continued this for a few weeks, and Noel was twittering on that he thought people were getting in the club after it closed. We relayed a story to him of a man's death that had occurred on the stairs of the club (not true) and that it might be his spirit rattling around.

Eventually we got to the stage where Noel was pretty nervous of going anywhere near the club, and we could tell that he was really unsettled whenever he was the only Junior Officer sleeping at that side of the station. So, we figured the next time he was sleeping alone on that side of the station, that would be the time to strike!

That nightshift came around, and Billy and I prepared for the conclusion of the jape. We had just got back from a job in the middle of the night and had started getting cleaned up. Noel was pretty dirty, so we knew he would be taking a shower. For those of you who know the *Psycho* film, starring Norman Bates and the famous shower scene, you can guess what comes next.

We had a cassette recording of the music that accompanied the scene of the attack in the shower, with a ghetto blaster ready to blast it out. I held a squeezy bottle full of red water-based paint whilst Billy had a toy-rubber knife. We could hear Noel in the shower and just gave him enough time to start shampooing his hair when we pounced. The lights went off and the music was switched on, loudly belting out the shrieks. Instantly, Billy started striking at the shower curtain with the rubber knife while I sprayed the red paint over the top of the curtain. It was a quick strike and must have frightened the life out of poor Noel, who was screaming for help while trying to fathom out what was happening. We retreated and switched the lights on, as there were more screams from Noel, who suddenly saw all the red and assumed he was bleeding heavily. It was only when Billy and I burst out laughing that he realised he had been had. Disappointingly, Noel had the last laugh, as the red paint stained all the grout in the shower, which took us ages to clean using a load of bleach as well as a load of our personal time.

CAT PRINTS

One day we received a call to a cat stuck in a car engine, and half expected the cat to be dead on arrival. But when we got to the scene, the cat was very much alive and had just gotten itself stuck. The owner of the car didn't recognise the moggy and was unsure how long it had been there. We took no time at all in retrieving the animal, then contacted the RSPCA to see if they could take it off our hands. They agreed and said they would come to the station later that afternoon to pick it up. We got back to the station and gave the cat some food and water, then placed it in the downstairs toilet to await the arrival of the RSPCA.

Unknown to most of the crew, the RSPCA actually turned up within 30 minutes of us arriving back onto the station and Billy had safely handed over the cat. But instead of just leaving it as a job well done, he decided to try and pull the wool over the eyes of the Watch. He took a potato from the kitchen, cut it in half, and shaped a paw print into it. When he was happy with his fake paw, he retrieved the left-over red paint that was in his locker from Noel's shower jape, and led a trail of prints from the downstairs toilet to the basement. Now, although the basement was relatively small, it also housed the large boilers that heated the station. Lighting wasn't great in the basement, and it was pretty tight to move around the room due to the boilers and associated pipework, so it was quite feasible that a cat could hide there.

The lads came down from tea-break to be told the cat had escaped from the toilet and must be carrying an injury to its paw.

For the next hour or so, the lads searched not only the basement, but also the rest of the station, yet not one of them mentioned that the RSPCA hadn't turned up. But it didn't stop there. The next Watch came on, and they looked around the station, but the conclusion was that the cat must have escaped to the outside. Next day, towards the end of the shift, Billy printed more footprints, leading from the basement and fading out after a couple of steps up the stairs. One of the other lads noticed them and the search began again, including the oncoming nightshift joining the hunt. Billy eventually came clean, much to my amusement, but also to the disgust of the nightshift. Some Watches just don't appreciate humour!

UNCLE FESTER

Between Billy and I, we could probably write a book on tricks and japes that we have been involved in throughout our careers. The list is endless, with the likes of the story of hiding a caravan – belonging to a lad on the Watch – in the middle of the night. He was due to go on holiday direct from work, and when he came back from a shout and saw the caravan was gone from the yard, he nearly crashed the appliance he was driving. He pulled up and rushed off the truck into the station office, to quickly call the Police to report it stolen. He then had to call the Police back and explain it was a mistake when he realised it was just us messing him about. Or the time we hauled a 125cc motorbike, that belonged to one of our colleagues, to the 4th floor of the tower, with just the handle bars out the window. I still don't know how he retrieved it or how long it took him to get it down, as we went home and left him to it!

It may appear that we were the ones doing all the joking about, but the Watch did get regular paybacks, including a time when they stitched a fresh fish into the lining of my fire tunic. It stunk for weeks, no matter how many times I washed it, until they came clean and told me the source. I tried to remove what was left, but by then it was decided I needed a new tunic anyway, so it just got replaced.

Occasionally, we also had to laugh at ourselves for things that happened on shouts, including one incident that I attended in Sunderland city centre. It happened in late November 1991, and I was acting Leading Firefighter, riding as the OIC of the aerial appliance M03, when a call came in to attend a reported fire in the city centre. I responded, knowing that station November would be in attendance within minutes, as the call was just around the corner from them.

First message came through to confirm it was a kitchen fire in a pub below the Odeon Cinema. We pulled up, and I went straight to the OIC of the incident to see what he required from us. He confirmed that he had two BA teams in, but there was a lot of smoke, so we would need to evacuate the cinema as a precautionary measure. I told him to leave that with me, and proceeded to head towards the main doors of the cinema with a crew member from November in tow.

I entered the premises and asked to speak to the manager. I explained the situation and stated that the cinema needed to be evacuated. The manager seemed a bit flustered, so I suggested that I would make the announcement from the front of the stage. As the movie had already started, I told him I would wait until he had stopped the film and switched on the auditorium lights.

The lights came on as the movie stopped, so I took my fire helmet off and stepped out from the wings onto the front of the stage. I announced in my loudest voice, which seemed to echo round the hall, that there was no need to panic, but due to a small fire in the pub below we were going to have to evacuate the cinema. Just then some smart arse in the upper level shouted out, "It's Uncle Fester!" and started singing the Addams Family tune. The place fell about laughing, and within seconds the majority of the people in there started clicking their fingers and singing along with him. It hit me straight away that the movie that had been showing was *The Addams Family* – a movie-length version of the popular American TV show. The character the lad was referring to was a bald headed, not-so-good-looking guy, who walked around wearing a long dark coat done up to the neck. I looked

112

down at my navy fire tunic, done up to the neck, and thought *fair play*, as I turned and abruptly took my bald head off the stage.

The problem was that I probably would have got away with my slightly embarrassing moment had I been alone, but the lad from November had been standing in the wings and he was practically wetting himself with laughter as I silently sloped off the stage. *No way would I be able to keep the incident a secret*, I thought, and I prepared myself to receive plenty of ribbing from the station November crew. Right enough, from that afternoon on, they took every opportunity that came their way to remind me of it. Whenever I came in contact with them at a job, or was detached to their station for a duty, they would, in unison, start clicking their fingers and attempt to sing that dreadful theme tune.

CHAPTER NINETEEN

THE DEVIL WITHIN

Sometimes in life, something inside you makes you do things or react to things that afterwards you think, *Why the hell did I do that?* Some people call it 'devilment', but not everything you do is for devilment purposes. A lot of these moments that happened with me were purely for self-humour or for the humour of others. And because a lot of humour is in the spur of the moment, there were a few instances where afterwards I thought, *Bloody hell, that could have gone wrong!*

SPOOK A BOBBY

One house fire I attended in the middle of the night was a bit suspicious, so the Police were required to attend. As the electrics had been involved in the fire, the main circuit board was isolated, so the only lighting we had in the house were our torches and a couple of portable lights powered by a generator. The fire had been started in an upstairs bedroom, which caused severe damage to that room and heavy smoke logging to the rest of the house. A light was set up in the bedroom, but it was still dark with casting shadows. We seemed to wait ages for the Police to attend, and we were getting restless, so we started larking around. Suddenly I had this thought that the lads should cover me up on the bed that was in the room, and I would then jump out at the copper whenever he arrived. The lads thought it would be a hoot, so played along with me.

The Station Officer was outside waiting for the Police, so knew nothing about the jape. As the copper turned up, I got covered up just as he was escorted in to view the bedroom. I waited patiently, lying as still as I could, until he came alongside the bed. Then as quick as a flash, I stuck my arm out and grabbed his leg. He screamed, the Station Officer yelled, and the lads outside the room burst out laughing. Bravado kicked in with the copper, who sort of saw the funny side, but the Gaffer went nuts, as he knew it was a potential crime scene. *Ah well*, I thought, *you can't please everyone.*

IT'S JUST NOT CRICKET

That wasn't the only time I had the Police jumping, but this time it wasn't my fault – just the nature of the game. We had received a call to smoke issuing from the local cricket club, and when we arrived on scene we could see it was going to be a working job, as all the windows on the clubhouse were heavily blackened. The front of the club had huge windows, with 8ft x 10ft panes of glass facing out to the cricket pitch to allow members to watch the game from inside, with a gin and tonic in hand!

The BA wearers started getting themselves ready to go in, whilst a covering line of hose and two hose-reels were placed ready to be used. As this was happening, a panda car had pulled up and two coppers got out and made their way to watch the action. Unfortunately for them, they were standing far too close for their own good. I kept low and opened the door to the premises when, within seconds, the Beast inside decided to feed on the intake of air. Boom went a window, when the gases inside ignited as the backdraught occurred. The noise was immense, and the flames shot out from the shattered window. I looked behind me to see the coppers running across the wicket, their figures illuminated in the glow of the fire. I restrained myself from shouting 'HOWZAT' and got on with the job of putting the Beast back in the box.

SLIP OR PUSH

One of the jobs that M03 tended to turn out to on a regular basis, was to the report of persons on top of either the Wearmouth Bridge or the Queen Alexandra Bridge. Both bridges crossed from

Mike's area (north of the River Wear) to Station November's area (south side of the River Wear). Sometimes it would be kids just messing or running from police, other times it would be a cry for help, and sadly sometimes we were too late to stop people jumping/falling. For those who had mental health difficulties and required help, my heart goes out to them; those who climbed up there for a joke, or just to be a nuisance, I had no time for.

One man in his early twenties would climb up the Wearmouth Bridge practically every weekend. It was always around the same time, between midnight and 01.00hrs, and after he had had a skinful in one of the local pubs/clubs. We would turn up with the ALP, go up, talk to him, give him a cigarette, put a harness on and bring him down. He would then be handed over to the Police, with us having the knowledge that the whole saga would start again the following week. It wasn't just our Watch that got him; the other Watches on station did as well, and we were, quite frankly, getting really sick of him and his antics.

One particular Saturday night when we were on duty, the bells went down, and before the print out was even read out, we guessed where we would be going. With blue lights rolling, we arrived at the Wearmouth Bridge within a few minutes, only to find that our assumptions were correct and yet again our regular had climbed to the top of the bridge. The Leading Firefighter was just about to put his harness on when I asked if I could go up for the experience. I put my harness on and got launched by the ALP operator, who was working the turret controls, to an area near to where the lad had last been seen. I then took over the controls from within the cage for the delicate work of manoeuvring between the bridge structure. Once through a gap, the lad came close to me to chat, and looked as happy as a pig in muck.

First thing he said to me was, "Have you got a fag?" to which I replied that I didn't smoke. He told me all the other lads have cigarettes and that he wanted me to get him some. I told him all the smokers on the Watch were off on leave, but if he came down, I was sure the coppers would give him one. He ranted how all coppers were bastards and wouldn't trust any of them.

I then politely asked him to put a harness on, but he defiantly said, "No, I am thinking of jumping." I could tell by his mannerisms that he had no intention of jumping, and that he was just enjoying being a nuisance. So, I asked him again to put the harness on, even if it was only for a short time while he considered what he was going to do. "After all," I added, "I would hate to see you slip." He agreed, so I helped him to get into the harness, which also happened to be securely attached to a fixing point on the cage. I had just checked to make sure it was nice and snug when, would you believe it, he **slipped**.

What happened next not only scared the life out of him, but also shocked me. Down he went like a bag of cement. The fall arrest on the harness took some of the strain, but the boom on the Alp decided it was time to give me a ride. Boy, did it bounce like a bungee as I gripped the cage rail as tight as was humanly possible. The bouncing only lasted a few seconds, but a few seconds – I can confirm – can feel like a lifetime. The turret operator took control and lowered the lad down, where he was screaming blue murder, stating that he wanted me locked up because I had pushed him off the bridge. "He slipped!" I exclaimed. "He fxxxing pushed me!" he yelled. Either way, we never did see him up on that bridge again!

CHAPTER TWENTY

SPORTS AND SOCIAL

Sport has always played a big part in my life, from participating in every sport that was offered at school to playing semi-professional basketball for 15 years. I have a competitive nature and hate to lose, but more importantly I love being part of a team, with all the banter that goes along with being part of a group.

The Fire Service lends itself to this team aspect in a lot of ways, and when you join a Watch, you feel part of a team. From your first cup of tea with the rest of the Watch, to everything you do on the drill ground, the emphasis is placed on team building. All this bonding, with time spent together, allows the Watch to perform at their best when it's required at incidents, with everyone having full confidence in all their colleagues working alongside them.

Therefore, it was no surprise that the job really suited my personality, and I flourished in this team building atmosphere which, as a side effect, also happened to improve my team ethos when playing my personal sports. This being the case, I took every sports opportunity that came my way in the Fire Service, and there were plenty of opportunities to be taken. Sport in the Fire Service is huge; each Brigade normally has a sports and social club which organises events in-house, nationally, and even internationally. I took part in a range of different sports and loved every minute. It provided me with some great memories and experiences that I still fondly look back on, ranging from a game of volleyball in the station yard to an international football tournament in Rotterdam.

When I first joined the Service, it was part of Watch life to play volleyball, which was deemed a sport that even those less sporty could join in and still be part of the team. At least a couple of times a week, we would put the net up, pick sides, and play until we were told to stop, or the older hands got too tired. It was great fun and a good way to keep your fitness levels up, as you really built up a good sweat. Every point mattered, and the banter between us was infectious, with even the older, more sensible members of the Watch taking the opportunity to mock anyone that made a mistake. For me, being tall was a great advantage whilst playing volleyball, and when I got detached to other stations it usually meant that I was one of the first to be picked for a game, as they expected me to be a great shot blocker; I hope I didn't disappoint. Playing volleyball was also a great way to get to know the personalities on the station that you were detached to, and once you had played, you tended to blend into their way of thinking, which made working at any incidents with them so much easier, as you already had a feel of what your work colleagues expected of you. Unfortunately, as with any sport, injuries occur, so a lot of Fire Services across the country have banned volleyball on health and safety grounds. It is a shame, as the camaraderie that was formed playing against each other is different from any you can get lifting weights on a machine, or sitting peddling an exercise bike to keep your fitness levels up.

Another popular sport on station was a game called plates, which is basically table tennis with a difference. A plate (preferably metal) is placed at each end of the table, one bat's length from the baseline. The game is normally played as first to 21 points, and the points are scored by hitting a plate, then the point becomes live. If the ball is returned and hits another plate, that would be two points, and so on until the ball is dead. The thing is, when the ball hits the plate, it pings off in all directions, making the shots unpredictable and helping to even the game out for those not so good at proper table tennis. Some people just hate to lose, and I was not the only one! So when the ball had gone in a different direction to what you expected, players would dive full length to try and return it, making the game so funny to watch. The reason metal plates are preferred is solely for the noise that is made when the ball hits it. It gives a proper ping compared to an ordinary plate. We used to play this for hours on any stand down periods, and it wasn't uncommon for a few players to end up with slightly pulled muscles after they had overstretched trying to return a point.

But as I have already stated, it wasn't just sports held on stations that you could get involved in. Tyne and Wear Fire Brigade Sports and Social Club organised a lot of different events on a yearly basis, from inter-station football and golf competitions, to hiking and mountain climbing. They even organised popular holidays abroad, which were exclusive to Fire Service personnel. So, if you really wanted to, you could almost fill your social life purely around Fire Service events, although I tended to stick to the sporting events.

INTERNATIONAL FOOTBALL

Football in the North East is a passion for a lot of people, and it is no different for those who serve in the Fire Service. TWMFB has always prided itself on having a decent football team, which is made up purely from serving members of the Brigade, and they regularly compete against other services, such as police, army, navy, or indeed other Fire Services from throughout the country. Players who played for the team were extremely proud of being part of a select group, and some even classed it as it as a badge of honour.

One year the Brigade decided to enter a football competition in Rotterdam, The Netherlands. It was a big tournament, which attracted teams from all over Europe, all bidding to be the proud winners of such a prestigious competition. As it happened, the Assistant Chief Fire Officer of Tyne and Wear Metropolitan Fire Brigade, Jim Bremner, was a very keen supporter of the football team, so he decided that he wanted our Brigade team to enter the tournament, adding that he would also be attending to support them in their bid for glory.

However, there was an issue with the team. The regular Brigade goalkeeper was injured, and nobody else on the team fancied playing in goal at such a big tournament as this, especially as the ACO would be attending in person. So, being left with little choice, the selectors of the team had decided to try and recruit a goalkeeper from the inter-station football tournament that was to be held a few weeks prior to the Rotterdam trip.

The inter-station tournament arrived, and I was asked to play in goal for Station Mike. I agreed to play, even though rugby was always my choice of field sport, thinking that I could just chalk it down as a one-off experience. Nonetheless, I performed reasonably well at the tournament, and felt that I hadn't let the station or the team down with my performance, even though we were knocked out at the semi-final stage. However, I wasn't the only one who thought I had done okay, as no sooner had I got myself showered than I was approached by the Brigade football team selector. He stated that I had played a really good tournament, and asked if I fancied playing for the Brigade team in Rotterdam. He also emphasised that I would be letting the Brigade down if I said "no", so I felt immediately obliged to say "yes". Besides, I knew that a couple of lads from Mike – and a couple of others I knew – were going on the trip, so I thought it would be a good social event.

We arrived in Rotterdam, and before the first game ACO Bremner had a quick chat with some of the regular players that he knew. He then came to me, wearing the goalkeeper's jersey, and asked how long I had been playing. I told him that apart from school and the inter-station tournament, I hadn't played football at all. He wished me the best of luck, but I could tell that he didn't hold out much hope for the team. The games started, and to be fair I was doing okay, saving the occasional shot, whilst trying to appear that I was an experienced goalkeeper who had played in goal for years. Luckily for me, I was also fortunate in having a great defensive back four, who protected me extremely well so that my goalkeeping skills would be kept to a minimum. To top it off, our striker played superbly in that tournament and just kept scoring goals at the other end of the pitch. To my surprise, we kept winning all our games, and before we knew it, we had reached the final against Rotterdam Fire, the home team. ACO Bremner was quite excited at our progression and came across to give us a quick pep talk before the final began. Although, as he talked, he gave the impression that he was still very nervous about my lack of goalkeeping experience.

The final started and we immediately came under a little bit of pressure from the Dutch, but to my credit, every ball they played into the box I claimed with a new-found confidence. Having played basketball for so long, my eye-to-ball co-ordination was, as expected, excellent, which allowed me to calmly pluck any crosses that came my way, and well before their strikers could get anywhere near the ball. Plus, for a big fella, I was also reasonably agile, so when a couple of their players broke through with only me to beat, I managed to dive quickly at their feet to claim the ball, which undoubtably prevented a couple of guaranteed goals.

It was a tight game, but we came through it to win the match and the tournament. The ACO was absolutely delighted and came bounding excitedly onto the pitch to congratulate us all, and kindly offering to buy us all drinks in the bar to celebrate. He even took a moment to praise me for what he called 'some outstanding saves, that without doubt had secured the trophy'.

The celebrations continued in the clubhouse and the drinks flowed freely. The atmosphere was electric, leaving me feeling unbelievably happy that I had said "yes" to going on the trip. I had played the whole tournament without picking up any injuries, so felt pleased in that respect, but little did I know that the night would end with me picking up the most unusual football injury.

The clubhouse had a large table football game, and everyone was playing whilst enjoying the post-tournament event that had been laid on by the hosts. The table had been placed in the room, with a ceiling fan directly above it to keep the players cool in the sticky summer heat. Halfway through the night, I was invited by a fellow goalkeeper from another team to play in a doubles match with him, and for the sake of international relations I accepted his kind offer.

The game began, and it was a close matchup against a couple of French lads, with the scoreboard swinging one way, then the other. It came to a point where the next goal would win the game. So, showing great finesse, I took control of the ball and, with a quick flick of the wrist, the ball flew into the French goal to win the match. I was ecstatic, and punched the air in celebration, totally forgetting about the ceiling fan rotating around my head.

Surprisingly, the consumed alcohol must have dumbed my senses as I felt no pain, but when I looked at my hand, I could see that the fan had sliced a two-inch cut into my finger. We all laughed as I left the room to get the cut seen to, and once washed it was obvious that it was nothing that some pressure and a Band Aid couldn't deal with.

Once the cut was treated, I continued enjoying the rest of the evening, celebrating what had been a very memorable trip. However, the saga was not over yet. I shortly found out that when my injury had occurred, some 'plum' had been on the phone to someone back in Tyne and Wear, and in his drunken/excited state, he had reported that I had lost three fingers in the accident and would, without a doubt, be out of the job. The rumour mill spread rapidly, and when I got home the next day, I discovered that a collection had already been started for me, with a couple of hundred pounds having already been raised. The truth of the injury came out and all monies collected were handed over to charity, much to my amusement and the plum's embarrassment.

THREE PEAKS CHALLENGE

Another event I entered was the 'Three Peaks Challenge', which was a test of your ability to climb the three tallest peaks in Britain within a 24-hour deadline. I have always enjoyed hiking, especially hill walking, and every summer I would join a group of friends from Station Kilo (South Shields) to head off to the Lake District for several days. Once there, we would do long walks and hill climbing before retiring to a bar for a few beers and a lot of laughter. Due to these happy experiences, I thought the Three Peaks Challenge would be an easy event for me to do, so I decided to compete along with a group from our station, including Gary Lowes the ex-Para.

We arrived up in Scotland the day before the start, and I must admit we maybe had a whisky or two too many in the hotel bar before heading off to bed far too late. I awoke the next morning with a heavy head, and had to force some breakfast down in preparation of the challenge that lay ahead.

Putting my heavy head and churning stomach to the back of my mind, I jumped in the minibus with the rest of our team and headed down to the start line to sign the register. Once booked in, we immediately began climbing the mountain that lay ahead of us, and we strode out at a reasonable rate, with Gary egging everyone on that we were going to do a fast time.

Now Ben Nevis on a nice day is fantastic, and this was a nice, warm, sunny day and the views were something else. I didn't see much of it, though, as my eyes were on the path in front of me, trying to keep up with Gary who was yomping quickly up the track. Before too long we had reached the top, where we got our forms signed to say we had made it. I sat down to enjoy the scenery, and pulled out a banana to eat as I poured a hot cup of coffee. But before I could take a sip, Gary was up on his feet and putting his rucksack back on. "Let's go, boys, it's time to get down," he stated. I was not amused, but felt obliged to hurry or be left behind, so I stuffed the banana down my throat and took a mouthful of coffee. I stood to put on my rucksack, but before I had it over one shoulder, Gary was off like a greyhound out of a box.

I am not kidding when I say we ran down the mountain, passing all sorts of groups who looked at us as if we were mad. We got down to the bottom and piled into the minibus before heading straight off down the road, towards Scarfell, which stood waiting for us in the Lake District. I was complaining big style to Gary that I was not built to go up or down mountains that quick, and that he was an arse for not spending a few minutes at the top to enjoy the view. He just laughed and told me not to be a wimp, and to be ready for the next one! So, we sat in the bus, stuffing homemade tuna pasta into our bodies, to hopefully help replenish the carbs lost, in preparation of what lay ahead.

Now I had climbed Scarfell Pike a few times with my South Shields buddies, but never as quickly as we did this time. It became obvious to everyone that Gary was on a mission to have a fast time, and a few of the lads were happy to go along with it. I felt that I had no option but to keep plodding on as fast as I could, if only to just to keep them in view. By the time we had got back down, I felt as if I had physically run up and down Scarfell, so I complained again, telling him that it was supposed to be an enjoyable hike not a sprint, to which Gary yet again just laughed.

We got back to the minibus and quickly loaded up to begin our trip to Wales. It was essential to refuel my aching body, so I started to force more pasta inside me, whilst continuing to let Gary know that he was being an arse for forcing me up the mountain at that pace. He just chuckled away to himself, and I could tell that he was taking great pleasure in seeing my discomfort. I knew that my whingeing was going straight over his head, but sometimes it's just nice to get it off your chest.

However, being totally exhausted, the smell of the tuna and sweat in the bus, mixed with the effects of overindulgence from the night before, was having a negative effect on me. I was starting to feel a bit green, so I gave up complaining and put my head down to try and sleep away my sick feeling. I must have been out for the count, because before I knew it, I was awoken by the lads to say that we had arrived at the bottom of Snowdon.

On arrival, Gary was again full of beans, trying to get everyone to make one last push. But by then I had stiffened up, and insisted on a gentle start before turning up the pace. A few others were feeling tired and agreed with me for a change, so we set off at a reasonable pace. By now my old knee injury was starting to act up, so I knew it would be tough going, but I was determined to make it to the top, where the challenge from hell would finish. On arrival, we booked in and recorded our time, which was respectable enough, but nowhere near the top ten percent, which was Gary's aim. How these other teams were making their times was a puzzle to us, but we had done our best, and I made a mental promise to myself that I would never do it again. Gary, being the mad Para he is, wanted us to hike back down to the minibus, but as there is a tram that goes from the top of Snowdon to the bottom, you can guess what my reply to him was!

WORLD POLICE AND FIRE GAMES

The World Police and Fire Games is a sporting event held every two years for anyone working in Law Enforcement, Firefighting,

Border Protection, Customs, Immigration, and the Prison Service. It regularly has over 10,000 athletes competing, making it second in size only to the Summer Olympic Games. Athletes from over 70 countries compete in a variety of sports, including basketball, athletics, swimming, bowling, golf, boxing, cycling, shooting events, darts, martial arts, lacrosse, paintball, dodgeball, rowing, sailing... the list is endless, and even includes police service dogs, and of course 'The Ultimate Firefighter'. It is an event that has been held in a number of countries, including Australia, China, U.S.A., Canada, and Northern Ireland.

It was always an ambition of mine to compete at the event, and that ambition was realised in 2011 when I took a team from the Isle of Man Fire and Rescue Service (IOMFRS) to New York to compete in the 3v3 basketball competition. It was a fantastic event, with the basketball being held in the Javits Centre in Downtown Manhattan. This was great news for us, as it allowed us to book into a hotel just off Times Square and still be within walking distance of the arena. We had a fantastic time and competed really well, beating two American teams – a team from the US Customs, and one from Border Control. They were not a happy bunch at being beaten by a team from across the Atlantic, especially as basketball is seen as their national game. However, we ended up losing to the eventual winners of the tournament – a mixed team of police and fire from Iceland, who were all huge. But we had done ourselves proud, having finished the tournament placed a lot higher than we ourselves had predicted.

On the way back to the hotel after our final game, I told the team how proud I was of them for stepping up to the mark and getting a few wins that would stay in my memory. I told them that at the first pub we came across, I would do the honourable thing, as a proud Coach, and buy them all a few drinks. The chosen team drink during our time in America was a bourbon called Knob Creek, which we all enjoyed in moderation, so I looked forward to toasting the team's success with the first shot of the day. We entered the first pub we came across, which happened to be reasonably busy, and I proceeded straight to the bar to order the first round.

The bartender came up and asked what he could get me, to which I replied, "Could I have six Knobs, please?" He smiled and suddenly announced to the room, "This guy wants six Knobs, can anyone assist?" The place fell about laughing, and it was at that point that I saw the rainbow flags hanging behind the bar, making me realise that we were in an LGBT bar, and a lot of the clientele were most likely gay. So asking for six Knobs was maybe not the right drink to request in this establishment. The barman laughed and said, "I presume it's the bourbon you're after." I smiled meekly and paid for the drinks. Of course, the rest of the team thought it was hilarious, and ribbed me about it for the rest of the trip. But to be fair, the locals made us feel very welcome, and we had a laugh with a few of the guys in there who were genuinely interested in the WPFG tournament. We left after a few drinks and moved on to continue our celebrations at a Brazilian restaurant near to the hotel, which again proved to be a winner. The whole trip was an incredible experience, and I would recommend anybody from any of the Services to at least attend one tournament in their career.

I personally had enjoyed the New York trip so much that I decided to attend another WPFG in 2015. These games were held in Fairfax, Virginia, and this time I travelled with two guys from Laxey Station on the Isle of Man, Neil Parsons and John Boyde. Neil is a former Commonwealth Games participant, whose passion is in any shooting events, especially Olympic Skeet. John is a Retired Station Officer who has supported Neil at all types of events over the years, going on these trips with the intention of meeting new people and to have a great social experience.

The three of us had such an enjoyable time in Fairfax that we decided to stay on an extra couple of days after the tournament had finished, and travelled to Washington DC to visit the sights. At the Games, Neil had cleaned up at most of the events he entered, coming back to the Isle of Man with a clutch of medals. He had teamed up with a great set of firefighters from Canada and the USA who were also pretty good shooters, helping him to a fantastic medal hoard that would take some beating. Neil and his team have remained close friends ever since, and a couple of them even took the time to go to his wedding in the Isle of Man. This just shows you the friendships that can be built at these events, where you can be guaranteed of meeting like-minded people who share the same passions. The beauty of the World Police and Fire Games is that you're never too old to compete in something, as most of the 60+ sports available to enter often have a veteran or masters class, which even caters to retired personnel. Therefore a lot of the participants use it as an excuse to link up with old friends from around the world, who you have once seriously competed against but have ultimately bonded with.

CHAPTER TWENTY-ONE

SECONDARY EMPLOYMENT

The nature of the shift system – two dayshifts, followed by two nightshifts, followed by four days off (although technically this is only three days off, as you have already worked from midnight till 0900hrs on the first day) – allows some firefighters to pick up other employment to subsidise their salary. Some Brigades are totally against this, but my view is that as long as the secondary employment doesn't interfere with their main employment, why shouldn't personnel have the opportunity to earn a few extra pounds for their families? The Fire Service is full of all types of people, often with a number that have been trained in trades such as plumbing or joinery, with quite a few electricians and bricklayers thrown into the mix. The skills that these people have are often called upon when we attend incidents, so what is the harm of allowing them to practise their trade on their days off?

Personally, I wish that I had got myself a trade before I joined the job, as you will never see an electrician or plumber out of work. However, that didn't stop me from trying to enhance my own salary in order to attain better things for my wife and kids. My first secondary employment came about from my old pal Jim McCabe, who obviously never forgot who pulled him through training school. Jim had got some work as a stagehand at music events, and put my name forward when they needed more personnel. The job entailed helping the riggers to build the stage for the event, and once that was complete, we could also earn extra by acting as security in the pits (front of stage). Once the show was finished, we would assist on the derig, as well as loading the trucks for the show to move on to the next venue. They were long tiring days, but effectively easy money, with the added bonus that you got to see some great acts for free.

I was fortunate enough to work in the pits for Queen when they played at St James Park, where I stood in awe at the fabulous performance of Freddie Mercury live on stage. I also enjoyed other big shows, including Michael Jackson, Tina Turner, Kylie Minogue, Rod Stewart, Simply Red, Eurythmics, Status Quo, Elton John, Erasure, along with numerous other smaller bands thrown into the mix. Added to this list were other types of acts, such as comedians like Billy Connolly and Jim Davison, along with one-off sporting occasions that needed staging. Considering the shows that I have seen over the years, I must have saved a fortune in ticket prices.

At no time did I think that working these events affected my job as a firefighter, but the extra cash certainly came in handy with a young family to support. Another job that Jim got me into was an annual event of putting up Christmas decorations in shopping malls and big open areas. This took us up and down the country, where we would enter the shopping mall after it had closed, and work through the night until an hour before the mall re-opened. The company who employed us enjoyed having firefighters onboard, as they felt that we were happy working nights, could work comfortably at height, and could usually operate machinery such as cherry pickers without requiring too much supervision. It was always satisfying to finish working at a mall, and to look up to see everything in place and working. The difference we made to some places was incredible, and we regularly turned some drab-looking shopping spaces into a winter wonderland. The malls inside were always nice and warm and comfortable to work in, but occasionally we had to brave the winter's cold and do the outside decorations, which was always tough going. One year we did the Albert Dock area of Liverpool, which has several small shops and restaurants leading directly onto the dockside. The wind from the Irish Sea was blowing a hooley the whole time we were there, which left me hating every minute of the installation. I felt frozen from arriving until we packed up and loaded the vans to leave, but better things were to come.

We left Liverpool and travelled down to France, where we had the job of doing Christmas decorations for Euro Disney. It was great fun, as we worked hard during the night and were allowed a few free rides in the park during the day. It's surprising how many firefighters are kids at heart, and we screamed and hollered on the big rides before eating candy floss and ice cream. But having been to Florida a number of times, I know which Disney I prefer and the Florida sunshine gets my vote every time. The cold air of France in the middle of October meant you had to wrap up tight before you went out to enjoy yourself, so my favourite holiday Hawaiian shirt had to remain packed away. Nevertheless, I found the France trip a fantastic experience, and even though I had used up a fair bit of leave to go there, it was still worthwhile, especially since the pay helped massively towards the cost of Christmas back home.

The company we worked for was the best in the U.K. and had a good reputation, not only in Britain but also in Europe. They paid fairly, and always used the best hotels to ensure we were well rested in-between shifts. The quality of the decorations used were of the highest standard, and completely transformed every centre we visited. Each gang of men had at least one qualified electrician and a member of the company's design team, who would explain what would be required for the job, before allowing the rest of the team to get to work.

Everything usually went smoothly, and I can't recall any real incidents, except for one night in a shopping mall in Southampton. We had just erected a 9-metre pencil tree (a skinny, artificial Christmas tree), putting thousands of Christmas lights onto it, ready for the electrician to wire them all together on a circuit board. The electrician did his job and the tree lit up beautifully. Luckily for us, we were still on site when the tree suddenly burst into flames, and we quickly extinguished the flames and convinced the mall's Security Officers that there was no need to call the Fire Brigade, as we were all firefighters. The thought of the embarrassment that would have occurred if the Hampshire Fire Service had come to the mall only to find some of Tyne and Wear's best trying to burn down their shopping mall, caused a giggle or two amongst the crew. Luckily, the tree had been put out before any real damage was done, and we returned the following night to finish off the installation, complete with new tree.

CHAPTER TWENTY-TWO

THE BIG MOVE

Woefully, my time with Tyne and Wear Metropolitan Fire Brigade was coming to an end. I had enjoyed every second that I had served, but due to family commitments it was time to move on. My wife Lorna had been brought up on the Isle of Man, and we often discussed how the island was a great place to bring up kids, with its lush green hills, numerous beaches, and secluded glens. I had visited the Island in 1983 and 1985, to do some basketball coaching, and had loved the place ever since. As fate would have it, I met Lorna years later, stepping off a Metro in the North East, so it seemed my destiny would be to eventually move and live on the island.

Once my son was born in 1996, we started to look at how we could make the life-changing move, and checked out the feasibility of transferring to the Isle of Man Fire and Rescue Service. We realised that Lorna, having been brought up on the island, put me in a favourable position where I wouldn't require a work permit to comply with the island's employment laws, so we just kept checking to see when the IOMFRS would be recruiting.

In 1997, a job recruitment advert was released by the IOMFRS, and I immediately applied for the role, sending off my curriculum vitae. When I was invited to attend Fire Headquarters for an interview, I immediately booked leave and planned our trip to the island. As this was my first job interview in over 10-years, I was understandably a bit anxious, but also really excited at the prospect of moving to the island whilst hopefully remaining in a job that I so dearly loved.

The interview panel consisted of Chief Fire Officer Alan Christian, Deputy Chief Fire Officer Brian Draper, and Divisional Officer John Cliffe. They seemed very interested in my Fire Service history, and I answered every question with ease. The interview had gone as well as it could have, leaving me hopeful of a positive outcome... but alas, it was not to be. Having returned to the North East, I received a letter through the post stating that I had been unsuccessful in my application to join the IOMFRS, whilst also wishing me good luck for the future. It was a big blow, as jobs in the IOMFRS were few and far between, and I didn't expect to see any further recruitment in the foreseeable future.

Just as a follow-up and to find out where I had gone wrong, I decided to telephone Divisional Officer Cliffe to receive some feedback, and to be fair to him, he gave me the truth. He stated that my experience was immense and that I had had the best interview out of all the applicants. He also added that any other Brigade in the UK would snap me up if I were to apply to any of them. On hearing this, I queried why I hadn't got the job, to which he said that he shouldn't really say, but off the record, the job was given to the Chief Fire Officer's son. It was blatant nepotism, but I wasn't annoyed in the least and just felt that it was just the island's way.

As it happens, Mark Christian, the Chief's son who got the job, has a passion for what he is doing, along with a great desire to progress in the Service. This passion will eventually push him to the top job, where he will be a fantastic Chief Fire Officer, to which I wholeheartedly wish him the best of luck in climbing to that position. And, although I disagree with nepotism in the Fire Service, in some ways I can clearly understand the benefits of giving jobs to sons and daughters of serving personnel. On an island that runs a Wholetime and a Retained Service, these kids have been brought up listening to their parents tell stories of incidents that they have attended, as well as witnessing their fire alerters going off, to see their mum or dad turn out to their stations at any time of day and night. This has to leave an impression on them, which would put them in good stead for living the life of a firefighter on the island. Nonetheless, in order to ensure a fairness and equality, whenever recruitment is taking place, Human Resource Departments are now being asked to play a bigger role in the processes, ensuring nepotism is a thing of a bygone era.

In early 2000, the IOMFRS once again posted that they had job vacancies so, now having a baby girl as well as a son, I decided to reapply. However, I had also noticed that the Isle of Man Constabulary were recruiting at the same time, so I decided it would be best if I applied to them as well. I thought this could be an ideal back-up, if for whatever reason I failed again to get accepted into the IOMFRS. I notified the Fire Service of my intention of applying for both Services, and to be fair to them, on hearing this they went out of their way to arrange for me to have my fire interview around the same time as the Police were doing their recruitment process. This meant I only needed to travel across to the island once, although it put a little pressure on me to prepare for both jobs.

I arrived at Fire Headquarters, and again the interview seemed to be going well, and I appeared to be getting a good vibe from the panel which sat in front of me. But despite this, Chief Fire Officer Christian said two things that put doubt in my mind. First, he stated that because I was used to working on a busy station, he felt I would quickly get bored at the number of incidents that I would attend on the island. He then also added that he couldn't give me an answer straight away as to whether I had the job or not, because he was going on holiday, and on his return, he would be interviewing some Retained personnel who had also applied for the Wholetime position. I left the building slightly disillusioned, wondering how many sons, daughters, nieces or nephews the Chief had. I then questioned whether I was deluding myself that he would give me a job over anyone that was already living on the island. It was at this point that I decided to put all my efforts into becoming a Police Constable on the island, even if it meant giving up on my dream job.

The next day I attended Police Headquarters, where I completed the fitness stage of the Police recruitment process, including a bleep test, which I managed with ease. I travelled back to Wearside, feeling confident that the Constabulary route was going to be my only option if I wanted the dream move to the island to come to become a reality.

A couple of days later I received official notification from the Constabulary that I had passed the fitness stage, and was invited to the next phase of the process. This would include a two-day stay at an outside adventure centre, where we would complete scenario-based assessments covering the six core values of the Constabulary, which are Caring, Professionalism, Challenge, Service, Respect, and Responsibility.

This stage was tough going, and the instructors ran you ragged for the whole period you were there, ensuring that everyone was worked as hard as they could, whilst allowing very little sleep to recover. This was done with the intention of testing you to see how well you coped under pressure, especially when tiredness started to kick in and mistakes are being made. The instructors observed everyone closely and seemed to take a sharper interest the more tired you appeared; they wanted to see how you endeavoured in this state of mind in remaining part of the team around you.

My experiences in the Fire Service, and the fact that I had done a 15-week recruits' course, held me in good stead for these two days, and I came through the weekend with flying colours. Having completed the hard part, I only had the medical and interview to get through and the big move would be on. I passed both with ease, and began putting things in place to relocate to the island in preparation to start my police training and to begin the next chapter of my life.

CHAPTER TWENTY-THREE

THE POLICING YEARS

BRUCHE

I moved to the island at the beginning of September 2000, leaving Lorna to follow on a couple of months later with Kai and his little sister Gemma. After a week of induction on the island at the Constabulary, I left to go to Bruche Police Training Centre, which is located just outside Warrington. It was to be a 15-week residential course, with only weekends free. This allowed the Isle of Man Constables to fly back to the island on the Friday evening and then return to Bruche on the Sunday evening, ready to start the new week on the Monday. The Centre trained officers from all over the country, with each course hosting a variety of different Constabularies, all mixed in together. For example, on the course that I attended, there were a number of officers from Merseyside, Greater Manchester, North Wales, West Yorkshire, Lancashire, Cumbria, North Yorkshire, and Wiltshire, and of course the Isle of Man. The centre was headed up by a Kommandant called Inspector Christmas and, believe it or not, he was married to a lady called Mary, which I found slightly amusing. The training consisted of a lot of role play scenarios, as well as classroom work that covered all aspects of the law. We also had weekly sessions based on officer safety tactics, which included self-defence classes which taught you how to use your baton to disarm individuals.

I would like to say that I enjoyed the course, but having done a 15-week fire recruits' course, I found a lot of aspects of Bruche very disappointing. I found the discipline amongst the Probationary Constables very poor, with the instructors allowing the students to get away with an awful amount of pettiness and misconduct that wouldn't have been acceptable on a fire recruits' course.

I asked myself if times had changed that much to the extent that even the standard of your uniform didn't seem to matter anymore, or was it more the fact that the Police Forces have such a turnover of staff that they can't be overly fussy on the standard of recruits that they take on. Anyhow, it was my job now, and I had to knuckle down to make the best of it. I focused on getting through the 15 weeks and returning to the Isle of Man to do some proper police work, whilst hopefully maintaining my own high standards that I set myself.

Note: My thoughts on the lack of discipline amongst Probationary Officers at Bruche was proven to be true when a BBC *Panorama* programme called 'The Secret Policeman' was broadcast. An undercover investigative journalist managed to get himself onto a course at Bruche, where he filmed a lot of racist behaviour and language. The centre took a battering from the press and never really recovered, finally closing its doors for good in May 2006.

TUTOR CONSTABLE

Having passed out from Bruche, I returned to the island to spend a couple of weeks in the classroom 'Manxiefying' the laws that we had been taught. The Isle of Man is a self-governing British Crown dependency, with its Head of State, Queen Elizabeth, holding the title of Lord of Mann. It has its own Parliament, called Tynwald, and abides by its own laws, although it predominantly follows the UK's laws with various amendments and changes that are more suited to life on the island.

Once we finished our classroom work, we were allocated a tutor Constable, whom we would shadow and learn from until it was felt that we were competent enough to patrol alone. My tutor Constable was an officer called Wayne Milne, who stood at 6' 2"and had a belly to match his love of pies. Wayne had a good sense of humour, so we naturally got on well, although one gripe I did have about him was that he would never let me drive the panda car, even though I considered myself to be a more competent driver than him. We were predominantly based out of Kirk

Michael, a small village on the west coast of the island, but would spend a lot of our time in Ramsey, a larger town in the north, as well as patrolling the surrounding country areas.

Policing on an island is totally different from policing in a major city in the UK. The island has a population of around 80,000 people, with the crime rate being at a reasonably low level. Nevertheless, it still has its issues, along with its fair share of drug and domestic violence cases, which the law take very seriously, serving out punishments that are much higher than those dealt in the UK. However, the overall mentality on the island is definitely more relaxed than in the UK, and where I was used to turning out to stolen cars that had been torched (set on fire), on the island, in a rare instance when there is a stolen car, it just seems to get parked up somewhere undamaged.

Policing the north and west of the island with Wayne was like a game of cat and mouse. Because of the size of the area we were policing, you tended to know who the villains were, and they of course knew who you were. If something happened, you knew exactly who to call on, and if they saw you coming, they tended to hold their hands up and come quietly. But every now and again, you would get something just a little bit out of the ordinary, and these were the jobs I cherished.

ENFORCER

One day, Wayne and I got word that the Drug Squad was coming up to Ramsey from Douglas to execute a search warrant, and that they needed us to give them back-up. The main post office in Douglas had intercepted a parcel that appeared to contain drugs, so they had notified the Drug Squad, who decided the best tactic would be to let the postman deliver the parcel before pouncing on the address.

We gathered at Ramsey Police Station for a briefing, where the excitement amongst everyone in the building could immediately be felt. The Drug Squad arrived, and the officer leading them took one look at my physical size and asked if I had ever used an enforcer tool. Commonly known as the big red key, every fire engine carries one to smash open locked doors to gain entry to a premise. I happily told him that the enforcer was like an old friend, and that I would love to show him how it worked. The briefing started, and I was told that my role would be to break open the front door of the property, once the postman had posted the parcel. I was then to step back and allow the Drug Squad to storm the place. Message received and understood. So we all loaded into our vehicles and positioned ourselves where we could see the target house.

The postman arrived on scene, and he must have had notification of what was about to happen, as he seemed to deliberately take his time, stopping to chat to people and delivering to every other house in the street. He even walked past the target house to deliver two doors up, before eventually turning around and walking up the path of the correct house. As soon as the parcel went through the letterbox, we screeched up to the address and jumped out of the vans. I was out first, and with one swing of the enforcer, the door was smashed open. I stepped back, and six officers piled into the house. Within seconds, there was a shout from two officers, who had gone directly up the stairs, to say that they had come across a locked door. I reacted immediately and bounded up the stairs with enforcer in hand. Now, an internal door is nowhere near as strong as a front or back door, but nevertheless I still swung the enforcer with as much force as I could muster. The door came off its hinges and crashed into the room, and immediately one of the officers, standing beside me, jumped on the door to scan the room for persons. "It's clear, nobody in here!" he called. To which a voice under the door called back, "I am under here, you bastards." The skinny little drug peddler had been about to open the door and had his hand on the lock when suddenly, with one big bang, it had come crashing down on top him. We all laughed as we lifted the door off the lad, helping him to his feet, where he was then promptly arrested for the importation of drugs to the island. We returned to the station where a Drug Squad officer decided I needed a nickname, and as quick as a flash he decided to call me 'Bluto', after the muscle-bound character that appears in 'Popeye the Sailor'.

MIDNIGHT RUN

One late shift, Wayne and I were sitting having a cup of tea at Ramsey Station when, just after midnight, a call came in to respond to a domestic incident at an address on the Pondy Estate in Ramsey. Although the estate has now been refurbished and updated, back then it was like a concrete maze, with a mixture of two- and three-bedroom, ground and first floor flats, built in a 1970s style, with a few maisonette-type houses thrown into the mix.

Street lighting wasn't great on the estate, but Wayne knew his way round reasonably well since he had, in the past, made quite a few arrests at various addresses on the Pondy. The address we were going to just happened to house someone that Wayne had come across before, and he warned me that the lad probably wouldn't come quietly. We pulled up as close as possible to the property in question and got out of the car to investigate what was going on. As we approached the front door, we could hear a lot of shouting and a woman screaming. Just then, the door flew open, and the lad who Wayne had previously arrested came out, spotted us, and took to his heels before either of us could grab him.

Wayne told me to chase him, whilst he would get in the car to try and cut him off, so I took off as fast as I could. Now, running with running shoes on is one thing, but running with work boots on, whilst wearing a stab vest fully loaded with all relevant equipment, is another. The lad understandably started to pull away from me, but I figured if I could just keep him in sight, he might tire, giving Wayne a chance to intercept him with the car. For some reason, all I could think of whilst running was that the chase was like the 'Tortoise and the Hare' story and I just happened to be a rather large tortoise who would eventually win the race.

He kept turning corners and I would almost lose sight, then just get a glimpse as he turned another corner. This went on for a few minutes, and I was trying to relay messages to Wayne as to my whereabouts, but unless I saw a street name, I didn't have a clue where I was. Eventually, the lad jumped a fence onto the school fields, where I could make out his outline running towards the main road. I could tell he was tiring, and he kept looking back to see if I was closing on him. He got to the main road and jumped over a wall, with me on his tail just a couple of metres behind him. But more importantly, I could relay exactly where we were to Wayne. I vaulted over the wall and landed a metre behind, and within seconds I rugby-tackled him to the ground. He was exhausted, so didn't put up a fight as I placed the cuffs on him, before sitting him up into a more comfortable position. Within seconds, Wayne came shooting up the road with blue lights flashing, and in a 'better late than never' display came screeching to a halt right beside us. However, as Wayne got out of the car, the lad recognised him from a previous arrest and stated that it was a shame that it wasn't 'that fat bastard' who was chasing him, as he would have easily got away. I chuckled to myself, but Wayne took huge offence and roughly placed the lad in the car to commence his trip to the cells.

JUMPING KANGEROO

One Sunday evening, Wayne and I were catching up on some paperwork at Ramsey Police Station when an Irish gentleman came in and appeared to be a little flustered. I asked if I could help him and he said, "I know you won't believe me, but there is a kangaroo jumping all over the road near Sulby." I laughed and asked if he had been drinking, to which he replied he had not had a drop, and that he knew I wouldn't believe him.

I calmed him down and assured him that we would attend the scene to make sure it had hopped to safety. I laughed as he left muttering to himself, but when I relayed his story to Wayne, he said that it wouldn't be a kangaroo but a wallaby. I thought Wayne was pulling my leg until he said that we should go out and make sure the road was clear.

On the way, Wayne explained that a couple of wallabies had escaped from the Wildlife Park back in 1965, and were living in the hills around the Sulby area. He also stated that apparently the numbers had bred over the years and there were now approximately 160 wallabies running wild.

Dusk was settling in as we turned onto the main road heading to Sulby. I looked ahead and, right enough, sat there right in the middle of the road was a large wallaby! Wayne told me to get out of the car and he would drive past the wallaby, turn around, and then drive towards it, to hopefully steer him towards me. "What do I do then?" I asked. "Try and shepherd him off the road," he replied.

I got out of the vehicle and withdrew my baton, although I had no idea what I was supposed to do with it, while Wayne slowly manoeuvred the car past the wallaby and did a U-turn. He then put the blue lights on and started weaving back towards me. Just then, a double decker bus came along and followed behind Wayne. I could see the passengers straining to see what was happening, and I thought, *That's great, now I have an audience watching me make a fool of myself.*

The wallaby looked at the car approaching and stood tall. *Wow*, I thought, *he must be over 1.5 metres tall.* Not to be outdone by the wallaby, I stood as tall as I could, with my arms spread out to the side. Wayne later joked that I must have looked like the 'Angel of the North' to the passengers on the bus, who were intently watching the action.

The wallaby started to move towards me and then gathered a bit of speed. My immediate thought was that I would rather have faced a mass brawl than be face-to-face with this thing, as it bounded closer and closer. It was only metres away from me and didn't seem to show any fear, while I stood there cringing that it was going to bowl me over. But just before it reached me, it deviated direction and jumped straight over my outstretched baton, just as if it was a circus act. I turned, a little bit shocked, just in time to see it take one further bound as it leapt into the trees and disappeared into the dusk. The bus driver gave me the thumbs up, as I noticed him and his passengers having a good laugh at what they had seen. I quickly jumped in the car whilst trying to be calm and collected, but Wayne had obviously enjoyed the whole encounter and just burst out laughing at the look of shock that showed on my face.

THE FAT CONTROLLER

One afternoon, Wayne and I responded to a call that a man was threatening his wife with a knife. The man in question had been a Scenes of Crime Officer (SOCO) in the Greater Manchester Police, and on his retirement had relocated to the island. Wayne had dealt with him before, and told me just before we arrived that the gentleman often had issues with his mental health and could be very unpredictable.

We pulled up at the address and approached the front door just as a middle-aged lady opened it. It was evident that she was extremely upset and had been crying. She stated that her husband had a knife in his hands and was threatening to harm himself, as well as her. She also stated that his mental health hadn't been too good in a while, and that he was due to go to the UK to stay in a specialist unit for a few weeks to hopefully receive some treatment. She added that all she wanted was to get the knife off him, so that he would calm down enough to take his medication. At that point, Wayne let me know that he thought it best that I enter the house to do the talking, as the last time he had dealt with the gentleman he had taken an instant dislike to Wayne.

I entered the house with the man's wife standing directly behind me, and saw a man in his early 60s sitting in an armchair. He was hiding something down by his side, which I presumed would be the knife, so I kept a close eye on that arm as I tried to calm the situation. He obviously knew a lot of the Ramsey Police, as the first thing he said to me was that he didn't recognise me, and asked if I was new to the Force. I replied that I was, and on hearing my Geordie accent, he started reminiscing about a Geordie that he had worked with in Manchester.

He then pulled the knife into view, and when I asked him to put the knife down, he simply stated that he had pulled the knife from the body of a girl that had been murdered in Manchester. Although it didn't ring true, as all items from such a scene would have been bagged and recorded as evidence, I played along with him and listened to some of his horrific stories of when he had worked as a SOCO.

143

I was just starting to get a rapport with him, and the situation seemed to be getting calmer, when suddenly he spotted Wayne standing behind me in the doorway. "Ah," he said, "it's the Fat Controller." Wayne entered the room and the man said, "I don't like you, and this knife is going to be embedded into that big fat stomach of yours."

Both Wayne and I shouted simultaneously at the man to put the knife down, whilst at the same time withdrawing our CS gas (a non-lethal incapacitant spray) from their holders. The man started to get up from the chair and half lunged at Wayne, when we immediately deployed the CS straight into his face. He fell back into the chair and I grabbed his arm, managing to free the knife from his grip, and quickly slipped the handcuffs on him. Restraining the man, I wondered to myself why Wayne wasn't helping, until I looked behind me and saw that as well as the man, both Wayne and the gentleman's wife were struggling badly with the effects of the CS in the confined space of the room. There were tears and snot everywhere, and I ushered the three of them out of the house into the fresh air. My sinuses, however, had spent years in smoke-filled atmospheres, so I found that I was not really affected by the gas. I got some water from the kitchen and proceeded to try and wash the irritant from their eyes before we would begin transporting the prisoner to Douglas.

Wayne was still suffering and could hardly see out of his eyes, but unbelievably he still wouldn't let me drive the van across the mountain road to the cells in Douglas. Instead, we drove with all the windows open, stopping a couple of times for Wayne to clear the tears from his face. I was a bit annoyed that he didn't trust me to drive, so I started ribbing him about being called the Fat Controller, which I said was a great description of him. (The Fat Controller is a fictional character from 'Thomas the Tank Engine and Friends', a set of books designed for children. He has a large stomach and a jolly-looking, round face).

We arrived at the cell block and took our prisoner inside, where the remnants of the CS gas left on our clothing started to affect the Custody Sergeant, so much so that his eyes started streaming as well. The prisoner was quickly booked in and the Sergeant chased us to get a change of clothing.

As routine, I put together a file on the case and presented it to my Inspector. He could see that the gentleman needed help, not a criminal record, so after the man had been bailed to his home address, the Inspector visited him. He explained that if he committed to going to the UK for specialised help, all charges would be dropped. In my eyes, this was the right decision, as I believed the gentleman would benefit immensely from getting the right treatment.

DANCE TO THY DADDY

My work with Wayne was done, as I was deemed competent to police without a tutor, and I got transferred from Kirk Michael to Ramsey Station, where I was to partner up with an officer called Will Moffatt. Will was a couple of years younger than me, but shared similar interests such as sport, and especially rugby, so naturally we hit it off straight away. Although being partners, sometimes we would patrol individually, but more often than not we would double up, especially on a nightshift where there would only be the two of us to patrol the north of the island once all the pubs and clubs were closed for the night.

One such night, we received a telephone call stating that lights could be seen in a property on the mountain road, and that the property was supposed to be empty. In his laid-back way, Will decided that we should have a drive up, if only to check out what was going on. The property was just down from Waterworks, which is close to the start of the mountain road running between Ramsey and Douglas. It was an old, isolated, detached building, difficult to see from the road due to it being surrounded by trees, so anyone in there would have felt comfortable putting the lights on, thinking they wouldn't be seen.

We parked up in the nearby car park and made our way down to the house, using only our flashlights to guide the way. On arrival, we could see light shining through the cracks in the boarded-up windows, and there was also smoke coming from the chimney pot. Several voices could be heard, so Will decided that we should call for back-up before proceeding. This would mean support coming from Douglas or Peel, which would be a minimum of a twenty-minute wait. As we waited, we listened carefully to try and figure out the number of people inside the building. Within a short period of time, we agreed that there were at least six different voices, and that they all sounded reasonably young.

The back-up arrived, so we approached the front door. I banged my fist against the wood, calling out, "Police, open the door!" The voices went silent, and the light went out. I banged again and bellowed, "If the door isn't opened in the next ten seconds, we are sending the dogs in!" We didn't actually have any dogs on scene, so I just made barking sounds which seemed to do the trick, as the door opened and a voice inside said, "Keep your dogs back, I have opened the door."

We entered the building and switched a light on to find six teenagers sitting in a lounge area, with the strong smell of marijuana hanging heavy in the air. It was pretty obvious what had been going on, but the boys weren't giving anything up and just sat there not saying a word.

I told the boys that the other officers were going to search all the rooms of the house, while we played a little game of hot and cold. I could tell by their body language that they were unsure of me, as I stood there towering over them with my strange Geordie accent. So, I decided to try to unsettle them. I said that I was going to search this room, and if I was getting close to where the drugs were hidden, they were to say *hotter*, and if I was moving away from the drugs, they were to say *colder*. I started singing an old North East folk song called 'When the boat comes in' and really emphasised the chorus 'Dance to thy Daddy, sing to thy Mammy', where I would pick up cushions or open cupboards and stare at them until I got an answer to hot or cold. Before long, they were desperate to help me find the hoard, calling out hotter and colder, until I finally came across a large bag of drugs. We transported them across to Douglas, but for some inexplicable reason none of them wanted to get in my vehicle. They truly thought I was nuts and would likely do them in on the way to Douglas. The effects of marijuana on a young person's brain is a strange thing indeed.

POLICE LIKE A FIREMAN

As I have already mentioned, policing on an island is totally different from policing in a large city. For instance, you just don't have the resources to arrest everyone that you feel should be locked up, and you certainly don't have as much back-up as you would like when you are dealing with violent situations. Therefore, you must adjust your method of policing by using your head to speak to people in a manner in which they appreciate, hopefully defusing whatever the situation is before it can escalate into something more serious.

I felt that my life experience in the Fire Service had equipped me to handle members of the public well, and believed that my communication skills were a key to me becoming a good copper, able to diffuse situations just by talking to people. This was highlighted to me when some of the other officers on the island were having a nightmare time with some of the local youth. I can honestly say that none of them ever gave me any grief, and that was because I took the time to speak to them, listening to their issues in a manner that they respected. Some would say that at times I was too soft with them, but in my book, I saw it as building trust and rapport.

Also, knowing that back-up is twenty minutes away, you tend to try and defuse situations rapidly by using good communication skills, which can often result in you changing what you thought your initial course of action was going to be. This happened on more than one occasion when I would be dealing with drunken people. Rather than lock them up for being Drunk and Incapable, I would take them home, knock on their front door, and if a parent or partner were willing to take them in, I would leave them to sort themselves out. This would also mean that I remained available in the area to police more crucial incidents, instead of having to drive the drunk across the mountain to spend the night in the cells. (Note that I only took non-violent, happy drunks home; anyone that was violent had a trip straight to the cells.) Often, in the following days of such a job, a parent, or even the drunk themselves, would stop me in the street and thank me for the way I had handled the situation. After all, just because they have slipped up and had a few drinks too many, that doesn't make them a bad person.

Policing can be a lonely occupation, as you tend to do a lot of work on your own either patrolling or doing administration. This isn't helped by the way that many of the public perceive the role of a Police Officer. In fact, most do not want anything to do with them until, of course, they require Police attendance in their hour of need. There is an old saying that everyone loves a fireman, but no-one likes a copper. And having worked both roles, I can honestly say there is some truth in that statement. However, I felt that being a Police Officer hadn't changed my personality, and as it was my personality that had left a lasting impression on all my fire colleagues, why couldn't I police like a fireman? My wife disagreed and stated that once I became a Police Officer, my personality definitely changed. She said that I became more cynical than usual and became suspicious of everyone I met. I must admit that I had noticed that on nights out, I would be more comfortable with my back to the wall, where I could scan everyone in the room just to see if I recognised their faces. This is particularly so on the island, where you know all the bad guys and they know you. But I maintain that during this period of my career, I still had a mischievous streak and a sense of humour. I always tried to bring a smile to most people I came across, whilst endeavouring to be fair to everyone I dealt with. Besides, I got the impression that most people appreciated how I was policing, so I must have been doing something right.

CHAPTER TWENTY-FOUR

DOUGLAS SECTION

As part of my development to become a more rounded Constable, I was moved from Ramsey to work as part of a Section in Douglas, the capital of the Isle of Man. Working in Douglas is totally different from working in the other towns and villages on the island. The population is around 30,000, and with a fair number of hotels and B&Bs, it gets a higher number of visitors staying in the town than anywhere else on the island. This meant that, unlike working in Ramsey where you knew all the local villains, in Douglas you always had someone new on the block to be aware of.

Being the newbie on the Section, I was kept busy, and found myself continuously deep in paperwork. Not only did I have a heavy case load, with statement-taking and case file preparation, but I also had my Personal Development Programme (PDP) that needed to be kept up-to-date. This heavy workload made me appreciate why, to the general public, there appear to be fewer and fewer officers on the beat. To this day, I still carry a load of sympathy towards those officers sitting behind a desk doing administration work, as I know most of them would readily swap the form-filling and relevant paperwork to be on the streets dealing with people. Nevertheless, the amount of paperwork required for each case investigated is ridiculous, so unless something drastic is to change in the law, officers will still have to be in the office, sitting for long periods of their shift, ensuring all essential administration is completed.

But to me, being on the beat was the best part of the job. Going out and talking to people, while trying to resolve any issues they had, gave me a good sense of purpose. I would therefore try and get through my paperwork as quickly and efficiently as possible, just to get out on the beat. I soon learned that doing this usually meant that Control would send you to any incidents that were called in, rather than disturbing officers that were doing paperwork. This suited me, and helped fulfil my need for an adrenalin rush, although to be honest I never found any aspect of police work to be as thrilling as the adrenalin rush I used to get whenever I attended incidents with the Fire Service. Nevertheless, I still enjoyed getting my blood pumping, and thankfully I managed to be available at the right times to attend a fair number of incidents during my time in Douglas, with a few of them being somewhat memorable.

KUNG FU EXPERT

Being 6'6" tall and reasonably well built (once being described by Lenny Henry, the comedian, as being built like a shithouse door), it came as no surprise that if a prisoner was kicking off whilst on his way to the cells, Control would radio up for me to be part of the reception committee, ready to take the prisoner from the van into the custody block. This happened on a number of occasions, and usually when the van door opened, I – with others – would fill the door opening space, leaving the prisoner with no option but to come quietly, knowing that he had no chance if he attempted to get the better of us.

On the other hand, there is always an exception where somebody wants to fight the world, which can be amplified if they are under the influence of something. This is exactly what happened when an Asian guy, visiting the island, had an episode which resulted in him being locked up.

It was a beautiful sunny day, and I had managed to get out of the station early to start walking the beat through the streets of Douglas. All of a sudden, the radio became alive with an incident that had occurred in Laxey, which is a small village on the coast between Douglas and Ramsey. The report was that an Asian-looking male was in the village, and was trying to open a number of front doors in an attempt to gain entry to the properties. Officers were dispatched, but on arrival they could find no sign of the man. The next sighting of the man was when another report came in that a semi-naked male was acting strangely, after crashing his moped into a road sign. This occurred at the far side of Laxey, and by the time the officers arrived on scene, the male had once again disappeared. It seemed that the male was destined to get away with whatever he was up to, as the radio fell quiet for a lengthy period of time.

But approximately 40 minutes later, a radio message was passed for Ramsey officers to attend a property just around the corner from the Police Station. The report had come from two young girls who were inside the house, stating that a male was trying to break in, even though he had seen them at the window.

Police Constable Eric Sloane was first in attendance, and his first radio message was an immediate call for assistance. Eric had turned up to witness the man halfway through the window, so grabbed him by the waist and dragged him back out. It was then that the male took up a Kung-Fu posture and started throwing kicks and punches at Eric. Eric withdrew his CS gas and baton, and fended off the attacker whilst he waited for back-up to arrive. Help came, but still the male wouldn't come quietly, and he appeared to be under the influence of drugs, making him extremely violent. Eventually, it took six officers to hold him down, placing him in handcuffs and securing his legs, before placing him in the van for the trip to the cell block in Douglas.

That's when I got the call to attend the custody block, along with another big strong copper called Tony Lawler. We sat waiting, conversing that it always seemed to be us that got the short end of the straw to be the reception committee, while we also discussed how on earth one man could cause so much trouble to warrant the number of officers that it took to lock him up. The van arrived and, along with two others, we carried the prisoner into the cell block to face the Custody Sergeant. He was writhing and spitting, so the Sergeant told us to place him straight in a cell and that he would get the doctor to come in for a mental health evaluation of the prisoner.

The doctor arrived and was escorted by Tony and me to the cell holding the man. At this point in time, the male was still wearing the handcuffs, and his legs remained bound. The first thing the doctor said was that there was no surprise that the man was kicking off, being trussed up like a turkey. He said, "Take those cuffs off straight away." I asked if he was sure and he said, "Definitely, that's why he's so angry." I released the handcuffs, and immediately the man kicked off again, throwing punches at the doctor, as he struggled to stand with his legs still strapped together. The doctor hastily ran out of the cell, leaving me and Tony to pin the lad down and place him back in cuffs.

We returned to the Sergeant, who explained that the doctor had left with the recommendation that we take the detainee to A&E to see if they could assess him. So, once again we went into the cell and carried the man directly into the back of a van. On the way to the hospital, the man was continuously talking to himself and acting in the strangest way, so much so that I was starting to believe that it was more than just drug abuse, but more like some kind of mental breakdown. I hoped that a doctor at the hospital would at least assess him correctly, so that the man could receive the help he so obviously needed.

We carried him into A&E and were placed in a side room, where a nurse tried to talk to the prisoner, but just ended up getting spat at. The nurse told us to wait, and a doctor would be along shortly. *Fair enough*, I thought, but it was difficult to control the prisoner, as the whole time we were there, Tony had to pin him to the bed whilst I held his legs down. Whilst pinned down, the lad continued to talk to an imaginary friend called George, and after a while we worked out that George was his pet rabbit. Working this out made me recall the tale of another rabbit, so I – without thought to any consequences – started to tell Tony the story of 'Gashy and his famous Curried Rabbit'. The lad was obviously listening intently, because as soon as I got to the part of Gashy chopping the rabbit up, he went crazy. It felt that he had the strength of ten men, and it took all of our joint strength just to pin him down. The doctor came in at this point and decided that there was no way he could assess/treat the man, and told us to take him back to the Police Station.

We arrived back at the cell block and lifted him into the cell, where we took off his cuffs and leg bounds, then made a hasty retreat from the cell. By then it was the end of my shift, so I headed off home, hoping that the lad would settle down and get sorted once the effects of any drugs had worn off.

The next morning, I arrived at work to see the riot squad getting dressed into all their protective gear. I asked if they had a drugs raid on, and they replied that they were dressed like that to take a prisoner out of their cell. I enquired if it was the same Asian lad that was a Kung-Fu expert, and they replied that it was. They explained that he was naked, and that he had smeared his own faeces all over his body, as well as covering the cell walls. I was glad I wasn't being called to go back in, and stood and watched as eight of the team entered the cell, dragging the lad out to be placed back in the van, where he was then to be taken to the mental health hospital.

No charges were ever brought against the lad, as I believe he was quickly moved off the island to a specialised mental health centre in the UK. Hopefully, he received the correct care at the centre and made a full recovery.

MASS BRAWL

One bright Sunday afternoon, I was patrolling in a van, alongside a colleague from my section who had slightly less time in the job than me. He was a nice lad, but we must have looked an odd couple, as he was only 5'6" tall compared to my 6'6", so it was probably best that we patrolled from a vehicle rather than on foot.

All of a sudden, a call came in for a number of units to attend Castle Street in Douglas, to reports of a mass fight outside the Irish bar, O'Donnell's. We were already driving along Douglas promenade, going in the right direction, so I knew we would likely be the first ones on scene. This made proceeding to the incident all the more exciting for me, but I could tell that my partner wasn't feeling it the same way; he continually asked me to slow down, while I sped to the incident with blue lights flashing and two tones wailing. Within minutes, I pulled around the corner into Castle Street, and slammed on my brakes to observe a mass fight happening directly outside the pub. I could see that a number of the pub's door security men were involved in the fighting, so figured something must have happened inside, or that they were trying to prevent a group from entering. I relayed a message back to Control and started to get out of the van, when I glanced across at my partner, who was just sitting staring at the scene before him. I told him he had to get out of the van, but he replied, "I can't do this." I didn't know what to make of the situation with him, but I knew further back-up would be arriving shortly, so I continued out of the van.

There appeared to be six or seven separate fights going on, and I approached the nearest one, where a man was viciously kicking another man who was on the ground. I pulled out my baton and struck the man who was doing the kicking, on the side of the leg, bundling him over onto the ground. I was just getting him into a position where I could get the cuffs on him, when I could see someone about to strike me. I lowered my head, expecting to feel a strike, but none came. My partner had got out of the van and was wrestling with a woman who was waving her shoe around, trying to hit me. More reinforcements arrived, and before long a number of arrests were made. It came to light that the people fighting were all from the same family, who were notoriously well known to the Police. They had taken objection to not being allowed into the pub, due to one of them already being barred, so had then started fighting with the door staff.

As for my partner, he decided that the job wasn't his cup of tea and immediately handed in his notice on return to station. He is now perfectly happy working as a postman.

KNOCK ON THE DOOR

I had plenty of empathy with the lad who had left the Police to become a postman. I could see where he was coming from; being a Police Officer isn't always a nice job, and it certainly isn't one that suits everybody. At times, it can seem that no matter how well you do your job, certain members of society go out of their way to criticise and ridicule everything you do, making you feel totally under-appreciated by those you are ultimately there to help.

Despite this, I still recognised that it was a good solid career, so with a young family to support, I resigned myself to being a Police Officer for the rest of my working life. Besides, I was at the stage where I was becoming confident in all aspects of my policing role. Every incident I attended just added to my levels of experience, which in turn allowed me to understand more fully what was expected of me. As this happened, I became more relaxed at dealing with different situations, and this helped to reduce any stress levels, making the job a lot easier and more fun to do.

But I still missed the buzz of going to fires, even though I was still managing to get an adrenalin rush when attending police jobs. Before I joined the Police, I had accepted that I would miss the Fire Service when I first made the career change, but I had also reckoned that within a short period of time I would develop new friends with fresh tales to tell, that would ultimately help build new memories. Being a sociable type of person, I soon made friends amongst my Police colleagues. But with a bank full of Fire Service memories firmly embedded into the back of my mind, I guessed it was going to take me a lot longer to settle into my new role than I first envisaged. What didn't help was the fact that I would fondly reminisce about my time in Tyne and Wear with any Police colleague that I was partnered up with. These stories always made me smile, but also made me feel as if I was a firefighter doing a Police job. I acknowledged that the job wasn't a secondment from the Fire Service, so figured that I would have to change my mentality towards it, or the future years were going to be one big, unyielding slog.

Just when I had my future figured out in my mind and was determined to do the best that I could in the Constabulary, I received a surprise knock on the door of my house. I opened the door to find an officer from Isle of Man Fire and Rescue Service stood in front of me, in full undress uniform. I instantly recognised him from my previous visits to the IOMFRS, as being the officer in charge of their Training Department. He explained that word had got back to his Senior Management Team that I was living on the island and they wondered whether I would be interested in joining

155

the Fire Service again. He added that a number of vacancies were about to be advertised, but they had wanted him to speak to me in person. I initially thought it was some kind of joke being played on me, making me sceptical of what he was saying and wondering to myself what his real motives could possibly be. He told me to have a think about it, and left it at that.

I decided to make some subtle enquiries, and quickly established that he had been telling the truth. A reliable source that I knew confirmed that there were three vacancies available, and that one was definitely being earmarked for me. All I had to do was show them I still had an interest in joining the Fire Service, and they would set the wheels in motion. From that moment, I suddenly felt as if the weight of the world had been lifted off my shoulders, which only reinforced my initial thoughts that it would be a no brainer to switch back to the job I was so obviously missing. I sat envisaging the move back, and my excited mind raced at the notion that I would once again be dancing with the Angels!

After further discussion, I accepted the IOMFRS offer and tendered my resignation. I immediately got summonsed to the Chief Constable's office, where he did his best to persuade me to remain a Police Officer. He said that my career had been noted and that he expected me to become a Sergeant within two years. But I felt that due to my physical size the Sergeant's job would be one on the beat and not in areas such as CID or Traffic, which might have tempted me to stay. I stuck to my decision, and a date was set for me to join the Fire Service, but only after the busy TT fortnight had been completed. (The Isle of Man TT, or Tourist Trophy races, are an annual motorcycle sport event run on the island and draw visitors from all over the world. During a fortnight period in May/June, around 46000 visitors arrive, making it an extremely busy time for all the emergency services.)

LAST JOB

About a week before I was due to leave the Police and join the Fire Service, I was on foot patrol along the promenade on a busy

Saturday night. The pubs were busy, and drink was getting the better of some people, who were finding themselves locked up for the night for being drunk and disorderly. The cells seemed to be filling fast, but so far I hadn't had to arrest anyone, and instead used my charm and wit to diffuse certain situations.

I was standing outside a popular bar on the promenade when a gentleman approached me with blood dripping from his nose. He was loud and brash, and was insisting that I go into the pub and lock up the lad who had punched him on the nose. Now, in situations like this, there are always two sides to the story, so I was in no rush to lock anyone up before I gathered all the facts. I asked if there were any witnesses to the assault, and he pointed out a couple who were just leaving the pub. I spoke to them and they told me that the gentleman with the bloody nose had been making a nuisance of himself, shouting and arguing with everybody, and had aggressively pushed the lad a few times, who had then responded by punching him just the once. I took down their details before letting them go, and went back to the man who was still trying to stop his nose from bleeding. I explained to him what the witnesses had told me and stated that if he still wanted to proceed with the accusation of assault, I had no doubt in my mind that both of them would be charged with disorderly conduct on licensed premises, where they would both end up being barred from all the pubs.

At that time there was a great push to ban anyone from licensed premises who caused any type of disorderly behaviour, especially those that had been fighting. I figured that by laying out the potential outcome, the aggrieved man might want to think about how he wanted to proceed. I gave him my collar number and stated that I thought he should go away and sleep on it, and if he still felt aggrieved in the morning, to contact me at Douglas Police Station and we would take it from there. I asked him if he knew the person who had punched him, and he stated that his name was Hinds and that he was a firefighter. He also added that they had previous history with each other, and had not liked each other for years. *That's all I need*, I thought, *arresting a firefighter a week before I joined the Fire Service.*

I entered the pub and spoke to Hinds, who relayed the same version of events as the witnesses I had spoken to outside. Having listened to him justifying his actions, I then took the opportunity to give Hinds a bit of a dressing down, even though I did have some sympathy towards him, as it appeared that he wasn't the one who had started the commotion. I explained that just because he thought the lad deserved a smack on the nose, it was not for him to take the law into his own hands, adding that he had been stupid in allowing the incident to develop to that stage and that he should have just simply walked away. I informed him that the aggrieved was going to sleep on how he wanted to proceed, and if he did decide to press charges, I would most likely be knocking on his door the following day. Before I left, I made a note of his details, as well as the details of a few other bystanders who had witnessed the incident – all of whom verified that the gentleman with the bloody nose was the one who had instigated the disagreement, leaving me in no doubt who had done what.

The next day I came back on duty, where I immediately telephoned the aggrieved to see how his bloodied nose was, and to ask how he wanted me to handle the incident. Having slept off the effects of one too many beers, the gentleman decided that he didn't want to take it any further, and hoped that would be the end of the matter. He had made the right decision, as he knew that it would not have ended happily for either of them. I gave him some strong advice on how he should behave whilst on licensed premises, stating that I would also be giving Hinds the same advice.

I would like to say that I enjoyed my time in the Constabulary, but in reality, compared to my time in the Fire Brigade, I found it fairly stressful. Every job you went to seemed to involve hassle, and even when you attended events such as school fetes, etc, there was always someone ready to give you grief. Don't get me wrong, I did have some good times in the Police and met some wonderful people who appreciated what we were doing, but overall, the bad parts of the job totally outweighed the good points.

As in any organisation, there are good people and there are some not so good. Unfortunately, in the Police it only takes one or two bad apples to create an image representing the whole force. However, having worked amongst them, I can honestly say that there are a lot of really good people in the Isle of Man Constabulary, who are there for the right reasons. Their goal is to protect and serve the good people of the Isle of Man, and I wish them all the best throughout their endeavours.

CHAPTER TWENTY-FIVE

GOOD TO BE BACK

In July 2002, having spent almost two years in the wilderness, I turned up at Douglas Fire Station ready to start the next chapter of my life. It felt good to be back, and I looked forward to getting settled onto a Watch and meeting my new colleagues.

Due to my experience gained in Tyne and Wear, along with the fact that I hadn't been out of the Fire Service too long, the Senior Management Team felt that refresher training on station would be sufficient to get me up to scratch. So, while two other new starters went off to do a full recruit course in England, I spent the next two weeks drilling with the four different Watches.

IOMFRS SET-UP

The Isle of Man Fire and Rescue Service has a different set-up to what I was used to in Tyne and Wear. The shift pattern was similar, but it also included Retained responsibilities as well.

The island has one Wholetime station in Douglas, and six Retained stations located in Laxey, Ramsey, Kirk Michael, Peel, Port Erin, and Castletown. The Wholetime personnel, based at Douglas Station, work a two dayshift and two nightshift system similar to the UK, but they also carry an alerter which, when activated, enables them to respond to the station on their days/nights off. Douglas Station also has a number of Retained personnel who supplement the numbers on each Watch. These Retained personnel, as well as all the others on the other six stations, drill once a week and respond to their respective stations whenever they are alerted by Control.

At the time I joined Douglas Station, the Watch strength was nine persons, with a minimum of seven being on duty at any one time. The station carried a vast amount of equipment and had a fleet of appliances second to none. The appliance room held three pumping appliances, a Heavy Rescue Unit, a Foam Tender, a Turntable Ladder, and a Hydraulic Platform. As well as the appliances, a number of trailers were stored at the rear of the premises ready for various incidents, including Line Rescue, Water Rescue, and Chemical Decontamination. These trailers would be towed either by the station's pick-up truck, or by a number of Pinzgauer off-road vehicles, which were parked up and ready to mobilise. Having come from TWMFB, where all the specialist resources are spread across different stations, it was an eye-opener to see all the specialist equipment in one place. But with only one full-time station on the island, it made sense that all the specialist equipment would be located where the Wholetime firefighters could use and test everything. Having it on the Douglas Station also helped to ensure that the Wholetime firefighters were able to maintain their competencies in its usage.

For someone who was captivated with anything to do with the Fire Service, it was a dream come true to have all these appliances, along with a load of specialised equipment, just sitting there waiting to be used. I was also thrilled by the fact that when the bells went down for an incident, the on-duty Watch would take the necessary appliance for their initial attendance, and other personnel – responding to the station on their alerters – would bring on any subsequent vehicles or equipment that would be required. The notion of sliding down the pole with the knowledge that you may be riding a different appliance to the one you started the shift on certainly intrigued me, and I often described the concept as being not too dissimilar to the television programme, 'Thunderbirds', which I regularly watched as a child. Depending on the type of incident they were being mobilised to, the Thunderbirds' characters (albeit puppets on a string) would choose to mobilise in an array of different vehicles, each with a distinctive look and Thunderbird call sign. Every episode was different, but with the awesome amount of technical equipment and specialised vehicles they had at their disposal, it came as no surprise that every incident attended by the Thunderbirds always ended with a positive outcome. It was, of course, a totally different system to what I had been used to in Tyne and Wear, and I knew that we were not puppets on a TV show, but I appreciated all the equipment the IOMFRS carried, and was confident that I would soon adjust to my new surroundings and embrace the different working practices from those I was used to.

PIE-EATING WATCH

Having finished my refresher training, I was notified that I was to join Red Watch. They were a good set of lads, but seemed to have a passion for pies and pasties, purchased from the local pie shop. If it was your birthday, you bought the pies; if you were going on leave, you bought the pies; if you came back from leave, you bought the pies. It seemed like someone every shift had to buy the pies, and it was starting to show on some of the Watch.

I settled in well, but was a bit concerned that my sense of humour wasn't really appreciated by the Watch, as they took every opportunity to remind me that I wasn't Manx and that there was a boat leaving the island every day. In fact, once they even went as far as to get me a one-way ticket, which I took as a sign of affection, so I stayed just to annoy the hell out of them.

I was loving being back in the job, and just wanted to play with as much equipment as I could and as often as I was allowed. This usually meant the other lads would be made to join me. This was generally appreciated by the younger members of the Watch, who enjoyed the extra training, but not by the more senior members of the Watch, as it obviously ate into their pie-eating time, so they just tended to huff and puff until we were finished playing.

DRIVE PAST

I adjusted well to the shift pattern, including the Retained side of the job, and excitedly awaited getting turned out from home on my alerter. I lived just under two miles from the station, and would get such an adrenalin rush as I dashed down to the station whenever my alerter activated. You were supposed to adhere to the rules of the road, including the speed limits, but when you turned out in the middle of the night and the roads were quiet, it was hard not to break the speed limit. You knew that if it was a working job, the on-duty Watch would be eagerly awaiting your back-up.

One night, just after one o'clock in the morning, my alerter activated, waking me from a deep sleep. My heart rate raced as I jumped out of bed and got dressed as swiftly as I could, before piling into the car to head to the station.

The quickest way for me to get there was via a road called Johnny Watterson's Lane. However, as I turned onto the road, I was suddenly confronted with a huge amount of smoke billowing from a house on my left. I braked, realising that this must be what we were turning out to. Hesitating for a second, I considered stopping, but was aware that if I didn't get to the station, there might not be enough personnel to mobilise the second pump. *Besides, what could I do without a BA set to wear?* I reasoned to myself.

My mind was made up and I decided to carry on towards the station, where almost immediately I could see the Duty Watch coming up the road at speed towards me. I continued driving as swiftly as I could and got to the station in rapid time, then hurriedly grabbed my fire kit and jumped on the second pump to make my way back to the incident.

The job turned out to be a living room fire, and sadly a middle-aged lady was found lying on the settee by the first BA team in. She had suffered severe burns, and it was obvious to those involved that nothing could be done to save her. It played on my mind that maybe I could have made a difference if only I had stopped, but the paramedics on scene stated that she had been deceased for some time, and certainly well before the arrival of the Fire Service. This helped put my mind at ease, knowing that even if I had stopped, I would have been too late to save her.

I found the whole incident a strange experience, as it was the first time that I had ever driven past a fire to come back to it. With this being the case, I obviously wanted to stay until the job was fully wrapped up and join in the full debrief. However, it was made clear to me that it was a Blue Watch job and that we were just the back-up, which meant that the full debrief of the incident was only going to be given to Blue Watch once they had fully finished at the incident. My Watch and the other Retained personnel that attended were stood down once our work was done, so missed out on getting a full understanding of what had occurred; we merely returned back to station, cleaned up, and went home to bed. It took a while for me to get used to this way of working, but we got turned out from home on such a regular basis that it soon became second nature.

FLYING BUDGIE

There are certain things that pass you in life that will remind you of an incident you have attended, or an event that you have been part of. One such reminder for me is when I see a budgerigar in a house or pet shop.

I turned out with Red Watch to a report of a kitchen fire in a house on the Willaston Estate in Douglas. On arrival, I donned my BA set and entered the property with my BA buddy and found a well-established fire in the kitchen, which we quickly extinguished. The owner of the house was outside the property when we arrived and was saying that her budgie was still inside, so after knocking down the fire, we searched the smoke-logged house for it. We found the cage in the lounge and I took the budgie, which was not showing any signs of life, to the outside, to see if we could give it some oxygen therapy. I had been to jobs before where, after giving oxygen, pets such as cats and dogs have come around after suffering the effects of smoke. So I thought it was worth a go.

I handed the budgie over to firefighter Gary Kirby, who was holding the oxygen cylinder, and told him to try to resuscitate the bird with some oxygen. I watched closely as he placed the budgie on the palm of his hand and turned the cylinder on, with the mask sitting close to the budgie's beak. As soon as the oxygen was turned on, the budgie flew out of Gary's hand, hit a fence, and went crashing to the ground. I struggled to contain my laughter, as the owner became excited at the thought that the budgie was still alive and flying, until Gary pointed out that it was as dead as a dodo, and that its last flight was purely down to the pressure being delivered by the cylinder. To be fair to Gary, he felt so bad about what had happened that he took the time to find a small box, and buried the budgie for the owner in the back garden. But, boy, did I rib him about it once we were safely out of earshot of the owner and back on the appliance, heading to home station.

FIGHT NIGHT

The budgie was not the only thing that Gary Kirby was famous for on Douglas Station; he was also renowned for his boxing. Anyone on the island that was involved in boxing had heard the story of how Gary had turned up to a venue in England to box, only to find that the person he was due to fight had not turned up. Another fighter on the card to fight that night had also suffered a no-show, so Gary was asked if he fancied going against him instead. Gary, having spent money and time travelling from the island, thought he had nothing to lose, so agreed to the fight and got himself prepared to go into the ring.

After getting battered for three rounds, Gary finished the fight, having come in second place. He asked who it was he had just boxed, as he thought that the lad was pretty good. "Ricky Hatton," came the reply, and Gary recognised the name of the man who was to go on to hold multiple World Championships at Light-welterweight and one at Welterweight.

Having heard this story on a number of occasions, I suggested to Gary that on a nightshift we put a bit of a show on for the rest of the lads on Red Watch. Always up for a bit of a box, he agreed instantly, and preparations for the fight between 'Ricky's Whipping Boy' and 'The Geordie Bomber' were set in place. All the beds in the dormitory were manoeuvred around to form a boxing ring, with some of the mattresses being placed in strategic places to stop us from hurting ourselves. Soon, everything was in place, and the Watch gathered to see the welterweight Kirby give the heavyweight Kirkham a good beating.

We got changed into shorts and gloves, and as we waited for the entrance music, I said to Gary that we should go in and dance around the ring, just throwing a few gentle jabs here and there to add to the show. I said that it was just a bit of fun, and for him not to take it too seriously. He agreed just as the music to the *Rocky* film blasted out from a stereo unit, which was our cue to enter the ring, as the rest of the lads roared their encouragement for the big fight to begin.

Looking like Muhammed Ali, I danced around on my toes, as was the plan, but the music must have got to Gary and he abruptly came wading in, throwing jabs and right hooks as if his life depended on it. *You little sod*, I thought. So, being twice the size of him, I literally picked him up and threw him onto a mattress, where I jumped on top and battered him with the oversized training gloves we were wearing. The place was in hysterics – so much so, in fact, that we missed the station alarm going off, and it wasn't until the firefighter manning the control room came running through that we realised that we had a fire call.

Fortunately, it was only a small waste bin on fire, and we all had a good laugh about the fight as we travelled down to it, with the lads begging for a rematch on our return to station. However, I convinced them that the weight difference was just too much, and that it would be much more enjoyable to watch Gary fight someone his own height/weight. The seed was sown, and it didn't take too long to convince another firefighter, Justin McMullin, that he should challenge Gary, as we all had faith that he could beat him. Now, Justin is no athlete, and has a body the shape of a space hopper, but he is always game for a laugh, so boldly agreed to his first ever fight. The problem with Justin was that once he was committed to the fight, we just couldn't shut him up. He kept going on and on about how he would box Gary's ears off, and that he was going in there for the big K.O.

We returned to station and told Gary of all Justin's audacious tittle-tattle, leaving Gary feeling a bit insulted, and as a result, he accepted the challenge with a look of fury in his eyes. The stage was set for fight two of fight night. Gary 'Killer' Kirby was ready to go to war with Justin 'Butterbean' McMullin, in a boxing match that will be forever remembered by those who were there.

From the off, Gary pummelled Justin, who covered up nicely. But we didn't want Justin just to stand there and be a punchbag; we wanted him to engage fully into the fight and at least throw one punch. So, we loudly encouraged him to do so, which certainly seemed to help his confidence, as he relaxed his covering up stance and attempted to throw a swift left-hand jab. Unfortunately for him, as an experienced boxer, Gary easily saw this coming and delivered a whopping great right hand of his own, which landed squarely on Justin's jaw, knocking him straight onto his backside with a look on his face that told you he was seeing stars. The place fell about in hysterics and tears rolled down my face, with the laughter increasing as we watched Justin attempt to get back to his feet. But his legs had turned to jelly, so once again he wobbled back down to the floor. Gary stood triumphantly looking down at his battered opponent, raising his arms in a victory salute. At last, Gary had won a big fight, although this time not against a world boxing champion, but a world doughnut-eating champion.

Tyne and Wear Metropolitan Fire Brigade Recruit Class September 1987. I am sitting front row far left and I appear to be the only one happy to be there (TWFRS)

Fulwell Fire Station, Sunderland. The TWMFB South Division Social Club was located above the appliance room bays.
A fine place to learn my trade (TWFRS)

Climbing back up Bradda Head (Isle of Man), to continue damping
down the gorse fire which took days to fully extinguish.
The surrounding landscape allowed you to enjoy some fantastic
views as you battled to contain the blaze (J. McMullin)

Members of the IOMFRS Colour Party in full regalia used for
ceremonial purposes including funerals.
From L-R Paul 'Rothy' Rothwell, Andrew 'Duggy' Dugdale, Keith
'Jugs' Moore and Justin 'Butterbean' McMullin (J.McMullin)

Delamere Hotel Fire, Douglas, Isle of Man, shortly after the roof and internal floors suffered a total collapse (P.Killey)

Turntable ladder tackling the fire spread from the Delamere Hotel to the opposite hotel roofs on Empire Terrace. (P.Killey)

The full scale of the fire damage to the Delamere Hotel can be seen from this aerial photograph taken from the Turntable Ladder as the crews continue to dampen down the remains (P. Killey)

All dressed and ready to enter the hotels on Empire Terrace to help prevent the fire spread from the loft space into the rest of the building, I am the tall good looking one on the left (P.Killey)

The IOMFR's two Aerial Ladder Platforms (ALP's) posing for the camera outside Douglas Fire Station (J. McMullin)

Using the ALP (Aerial Ladder Platform) to damp down the fire at the
Mount Murray Hotel and Country Club (J.McMullin)

The extent of the 17 million pounds worth of damage, caused by the fire
at the Mount Murray Hotel and Country Club, could be viewed from
this angle on the front lawns (P.Killey)

CHAPTER TWENTY-SIX

ALP TIME

After about a year on station, I was approached by the Deputy Chief Fire Officer Brian Draper (who was to become Chief Fire Officer in 2004), to ask if I would be interested in assisting the Head of Transport, Station Officer Alan Gawne, in putting together a business case for a new aerial appliance to replace the aging Turntable Ladder that was part of the fleet. He stated that they were particularly interested in getting an Aerial Ladder Platform (ALP), and knew that I had worked on an ALP station in my years in Tyne and Wear. The secondment would mean coming off Watch for a few months, and working a dayshift duty pattern. I agreed without a second thought, as life on Red Watch was not as fast paced as I was used to, having been really busy in Tyne and Wear and then snowed under with my work in the Police. Besides, all those pies were starting to have an effect on my waistline, so I figured the change would be a good thing.

The dayshift duty pattern was explained to me, and straight away I realised that I probably wouldn't miss as many fire calls as I initially thought I would. This was due to the fact that I would be on station Monday to Friday, and had the potential to pick up jobs with all the Watches that came on duty to do their dayshifts. Plus, being Day Staff, you had to cover two Watches on your alerter, which meant I was still getting my fair share of incidents during the evenings after I had finished work for the day, responding not only to Red Watch but also to White Watch alerters.

I started the secondment and moved into Alan's office, where I was basically told that I had *carte blanche* to put together a package of what I thought the island needed in an ALP. I was then to put together a training package and lead the team in getting the ALP ready to go on the run. It all sounded simple enough, although it seemed like a huge workload for someone who hadn't done anything like this before. But as always, I was up for the challenge.

I sat and planned my strategy of how I was going to complete this mission, figuring that the first thing I needed to do was to find out what was already out there in the ALP world. In order to achieve this, I put together a business case, to be presented to DCFO Draper, hoping that it would encourage him to grant the necessary permissions for me to go across to the UK. This trip, I explained, would basically be a road trip, visiting various Brigades that already had ALPs in their fleet. Whilst there, I would be able to evaluate what sort of ALP would be best suited to the needs of the IOMFRS.

Eventually the trip was approved, and I travelled across to the UK to head to Strathclyde in Scotland, Tyne and Wear, North Yorkshire, Merseyside, and North Wales, collecting as much information that I could about the different types of ALP in use. I also collected an array of training notes and policies and procedures from the different Brigades, with the intention of taking them back to the island to later plagiarise them into documents that would be suitable to use with the ALP that the IOMFRS planned on purchasing.

Having now established what we wanted, Alan and I, along with DCFO Draper, visited Angloco – a company in Dewsbury, West Yorkshire. Angloco build all sorts of fire appliances and had a fantastic reputation as a company who specialised in building ALPs, so a meeting was arranged to go through what we required for the island's ALP. It was exciting to be there and all very new to me, but Alan had been the Brigade's Transport Officer for a number of years, putting in place a continuous replacement programme for all the appliances on the island, so he was used to being in this sort of environment. I was also finding the whole thing extremely enthralling, aware that I sat there at the start of the build with the knowledge that I would be seeing the project right through to the end.

The meeting got underway, with Angloco suggesting a few amendments to the initial specifications that we had previously sent over to them. These amendments obviously came with a cost attached, so the DCFO would then discuss the proposed changes with Alan and me, to see if we were in agreement. Some items we accepted, and others we declined, but before long the final specification was agreed. Everything went well and we were well hosted by Angloco, who even invited us to the main ALP factory in Finland, to get a better insight into how ALPs are produced. All costs were to be covered by them, so it seemed an ideal opportunity to see the inside workings of an ALP, as they are usually built in Finland before being shipped to Angloco, who finish off the body work and add the extras required by the different Brigades.

We flew out to Finland just before Christmas 2003, arriving at the ALP factory, which seemed to be in the middle of nowhere. On arrival, we had the full tour, and I was flabbergasted at the size of some of the vehicles being built. One vehicle had wheels that were taller than me, with a 100m aerial platform on top. To put it into perspective, our ALP was only going to have a 30m extension. I learned a lot about ALPs that day, which made the whole trip worthwhile. After the tour, we went out for dinner, where I ate the local delicacy of reindeer, which was very nice, but it didn't go down too well with my kids when I phoned home and told them that I had just eaten Rudolph, so Father Christmas was going to be one reindeer short that year.

Finally, the build was complete, and the ALP was delivered to the island in 2004. My design of a safety rail all around the deck area of the ALP had been well liked by Angloco, who went on to sell quite a few more appliances that were identical to ours, to other Brigades across the UK. However, buying the ALP was the easy part. Now we had to produce the training notes, along with policies and procedures, as well as train up all the Watches before the ALP could go on the run.

Fortunately, during my initial road trip to the UK, I had met an ALP instructor from North Wales who had gone through a similar experience. I asked the DCFO if it was possible for him to speak to his counterpart in North Wales Fire and Rescue Service, to see if we could borrow their ALP instructor for a week or two, in order for him to oversee the start of the initial training. A few phone calls were made, and the deal was struck. The instructor happily came across to the island, where he helped train up six of our own instructors, who would then go on to train the rest of the lads on the Watches.

I had really enjoyed the experience of being involved on a different side of the Fire Service, and found dealing with private sector companies, especially those outside the Isle of Man, very rewarding. This being the case, I hoped that I had made a good enough impression on the DCFO that I might be offered any future secondments of a similar nature. To see a project through to its conclusion had been absorbing, and I felt that I had taken on so much knowledge in such a short space of time, that I hoped I would get to use these new found skills again. I really appreciated being given so much responsibility to secure the new ALP, but also knew that the DCFO was keen for the IOMFRS to have the best equipment across the board, so I presumed that there might be more work of this type to come, and I desperately wanted to be a part of it.

What had surprised me was how much work was required behind the scenes to plan, source, and secure the new ALP, and I had learned that even the smallest piece of equipment involved more than just going online to purchase. A lot of other aspects need to be looked at, including budgets, risk assessments, evaluations, training packages, storage space, etc, before any equipment is allowed to be used by the front-line firefighters. But it was rewarding work, knowing that the end result would help the firefighters to do their jobs more effectively. As it happened, the ALP was well received by the Service across the board, and I was commended by the Chief for the work I had put into it. More importantly for me was the fact that the lads on all the Watches were enjoying using it.

A second ALP was purchased a couple of years later, to replace the Hydraulic Platform that was starting to show its age. Because all the work had already been done for the first ALP, the process was straightforward. However, the funding for it had to be raised on the back of it being used for another means.

I knew from my policing days that any fatal road accident on the island was investigated by the Constabulary's Road Policing

Unit, who photograph and evidence the scene for use in a Coroner's Court. I took the new ALP up to a car park adjacent to the Police Headquarters and invited the head of the Unit, John Kinrade, to take a ride up in the cage of the ALP. I explained how good the photographs would be for the Coroner from that angle, as you could see round bends, as well as picking up any skid marks from vehicles. Being that high up, you could also see damp patches, or micro-climates on the road that would not necessarily be seen at ground level, and that could give a fuller picture to what had occurred. John was impressed, and he informed his officers to call up the ALP to any serious or fatal Road Traffic Collision (RTC). This intention of use by the Police certainly helped in the business case, and allowed us to receive the funding for the second ALP.

My foresight into how good an asset the ALP could be to the Police was to be proven from its first usage at a fatal RTC. A deadly collision had occurred up on the mountain road, involving a car and a motorbike. With it being the ALP's first use at one of these incidents, the Fire Service Duty Officer suggested that I should take it up to the scene, in case there were any issues, and to operate the cage with the SOCO onboard.

The ALP operated without a hitch and the SOCO took a decent number of photographs, asking me to position the cage at different heights and positions to get a thorough picture of the incident. When the case got to court, the Coroner was amazed at the clarity of the photographs, and stated that they allowed him to see exactly what had happened and he recommended that the same standard of photography, especially the aerial shots, be part of any future investigations. Praise indeed for the ALP.

CHAPTER TWENTY-SEVEN

DELAMERE HOTEL FIRE

Whilst seconded to the day shift role, I still attended a fair number of fires, and one of the more destructive ones was a blaze at the Delamere Hotel. The Delamere was a large hotel, sitting on Mona Drive in Douglas, and at the time of the fire it was in the process of a renovation project. White Watch was on duty that night, and were turned out in the early hours of the morning to reports of smoke issuing from the building. On arrival, a BA team – led by a firefighter called Keith Moore – entered the premises and proceeded up the stairs of the property. The place was full of black smoke, and they were having difficulty locating the source of the fire.

Keith was a very experienced firefighter, and something about this job just didn't feel right to him. The temperature seemed to be rapidly rising and the smoke was making it difficult to proceed, so he made the decision to withdraw his team to see if there was a better access to where the fire was situated. No sooner had the BA crew stepped outside into the street, when all hell let loose. The whole structure turned into a massive fireball, as a flashover engulfed the whole building. Windows exploded out, showering those below with shards of broken glass and leaving flames free to rise from within the building into the early morning sky. If Keith hadn't had the instinct that things were not right and withdrawn his team, I have no doubt that there would have been firefighter casualties that night.

Prompted by what had just happened, the OIC radioed for extra pumps and the island's two aerial appliances to be dispatched. All alerters were set off, and every resource available was sent to help fight the blaze. The Turntable Ladder (T.L.) that was due to be replaced, turned up to fight one of its last fires on the island, with a crew onboard that were determined to be at the front of the action.

The driver, David Craine, arrived on scene and assessed where best to position the T.L. for it to have its best impact. But rows of parked cars, as well as the steep sloping road of Mona Drive, made it difficult to find a suitable position to the front of the Delamare. So, David pulled the appliance around the corner, into Empire Terrace, to set up and fight the inferno from that side of the building. Quickly setting up, Leading Firefighter Ken Carney jumped into the cage to operate the monitor, while David – operating the turret – launched him swiftly up into the air, to position him high above the Delamere. But as soon as Ken reached his operational height, the wind direction changed, blowing in directly from the sea, and pushing the flames directly at the cage in which Ken stood.

Ken screamed into the appliance intercom system, telling David to get him down quickly, as flames licked all around him. Fortunately, a firefighter manning a hose line on the ground could see Ken's predicament, and he immediately started spraying up into the air, in the direction of the T.L. cage, in an effort to offer Ken some protection, and allowing David the time to take control and rapidly bring the cage back down to the ground. This action probably saved Ken from receiving some nasty burns, but not before the side of the appliance and the cage were noticeably scorched by the heat of the fire. They hastily repositioned the appliance to attack the fire again, but knew that a load of paperwork was facing them once the job was sorted.

The increasing strength of the wind blowing in from the sea, started to cause another issue. Embers from the Delamere were being blown onto the roofs of a number of hotels in Empire Terrace. The problem was that the roof tiles on these hotels were made of compressed cedar wood, which were starting to ignite. The turntable ladder had to suspend its fight against the Delamere blaze to do a 180-degree turn in order to put water on the affected hotels, whilst BA teams were deployed to fight the fire from within the relevant loft spaces. In total, I had four separate BA wears at the Delamere fire, and although thoroughly exhausted by the end of the job, I enjoyed every minute of it. Nobody was injured, and the hotels opposite were more or less saved, although the top floor of two of them had suffered a fair bit of damage. The Delamere suffered a total collapse before the fire was finally extinguished, and today a new set of flats stands in its place.

FIRE IN THE HILLS

Another fire that took a lot of resources to bring to a conclusion was a gorse fire on the hills at Bradda Head, a headland on the south of the island. Early afternoon on Friday, 17th October, 2003, embers from a small rubbish fire ignited the gorse and heathland behind a house on Bradda East Road. The fire spread rapidly, pushed along by strong winds, and four fire appliances were dispatched to tackle the blaze. The dry conditions didn't help matters, and soon the blaze was raging out of control, and further resources were hastily requested. The six-foot high gorse bushes were making fighting the fire difficult, as the blaze spread up the hill towards the coastline and Fleshwick Bay, before turning inland and heading towards the plantation at Fleshwick.

It took three full days to finally get the fire surrounded, and at one point 70 personnel and 11 vehicles were on site, helping in the struggle against this fierce conflagration. On the 19th October, things were finally under control, allowing operations to be scaled back, although a Fire Service attendance remained in place, damping down, until the 25th October.

Though not on the same scale of what is seen during wildfires in California and Australia, the fire had stretched the IOMFRS resources to its limits, so it is only right that a special mention should be made of those Retained personnel that attended the incident. Their contribution in putting an end to this fire proved to be invaluable.

Apart from the environmental aspect that the fire had on the land, the only other damage done was to some farm hedging and fencing, which resulted in the owner of the farm taking out a grievance against the Fire Service. However, as I said, no buildings or lives were lost, and no farm animals injured. So I think overall, for a fire of this scale, it was a job well done when you consider all the factors that the Fire Service were facing, including ensuring crew safety when working close to cliff edges against such an unpredictable fire.

The only other damage was to a Pinzguaer off-road vehicle which also dented the pride of one firefighter. A Retained Firefighter had driven the off-road vehicle onto the side of the hill to commence firefighting operations by using a hose-reel. He jumped out of the vehicle and grabbed the hose-reel, engaged the pump, and started to squirt water towards the fire. He heard the hose-reel unwinding itself from the drum, and turned around to see the appliance rolling down the hill towards the cliffs. He had forgotten to put the hand brake on, and gravity was taking its toll. Now, anyone in their right mind would let go of the hose-reel, but he thought he could pull the Pinny back up the hill. Alas, as soon as the last of the reel came off the drum, the firefighter started flying down the hill, just as if he was water skiing.

Witnesses said that they had never seen anything like it in their lives, and they were left really disappointed that they hadn't got their phones out to film the calamity. Apparently, the appliance took to the air and leapt over one wall, which is when the hapless Retained Firefighter thought it best to let fate take its course, and he sensibly let go of the hose-reel. Only one wall stood between the Pinny and the cliff, but as luck would have it, instead of going over the second wall, the vehicle rolled and slammed to a stop into it, saving the Pinny from a watery grave in the sea below. Damage to the vehicle was immense, but at least it was repairable. As for the Firefighter – he suffered a few bruises and a lot of ribbing from his colleagues for the rest of his service.

As a side note, there is a road bridge on the island called the Fairy Bridge, and local folklore states that when crossing the bridge, you should wish the little people Good Morning "Moghrey mie" or Good Afternoon "Fastyr mie". If you fail to do this, the folklore states that you will be cursed with bad luck. I must admit I had a wry smile on my face as I travelled down to Bradda Head in the Fire Service minibus. As we passed the Fairy Bridge, all these hairy-arsed Firefighters were saying "Fastyr mie" quietly under their breath and giving a little wave out of the window. But although I was smiling, to make sure I didn't receive any bad luck at the job, I thought it best to give a little wave as well – just to be on the safe side.

CHAPTER TWENTY-EIGHT

BACK TO RED

Soon enough, I was back on Red Watch. Although I will never be Manx, my wife and I welcomed a new baby daughter called Zoe, who was born on the island, and as a result, the Watch kind of figured I was here to stay, so stopped trying to get me on the boat every day. Besides, I think I had proved myself to them on the fireground, and was more than they could handle in the sense of humour stakes, so they finally just accepted me as someone else to pay for the pies.

SHADOW

As a Watch, we were getting our fair share of fires, especially since a known arsonist had been released from prison and appeared to be getting up to his old tricks. The lads on the station had given him the nickname of 'Shadow', and he thrived on being given such a name by people he thought of as his heroes. As it happened, he was more of a danger to himself than others, and most of his fires were small rubbish fires that only caused a trivial amount of disruption. But as we know, fire is not a force to be played with, so every now and then Shadow needed to be caught and sent to prison.

We would often see him on our way back from an incident, and we would speculate that he had somehow had something to do with the fire that we had just put out. Of course, we couldn't prove that he was involved, so the driver would just beep his horn and the lads in the back would light their cigarette lighters for Shadow to see, just to let him know we were onto him. He would smile and wave, and we just knew we would be turning out to somewhere else within the hour, which would of course be at a place near to where he was last seen. Like I say, the majority of his fires were just rubbish bins, but every now and then he would do something really silly and set fire to a building, stay inside, and wait patiently to be rescued.

One such incident happened at a large, terraced house in Royal Avenue, Onchan, about a three-mile run from Douglas Fire Station. Shadow had set his fire in a bedroom, phoned the Fire Service to report the fire, and sat in the wardrobe to await rescue. We turned up to the house that was heavily smoke-logged, but didn't take long to locate the small fire in the bedroom. We had been told that everyone was out of the building, until someone mentioned that Shadow lived there, so a more thorough search was made. There he was, in the wardrobe, suffering the effects of smoke inhalation, but as happy as a pig in muck to be carried out of the premises. However, once he was checked over by the attending ambulance, guess where he was heading? Straight back to jail!

CHIEF ON A CRANE

In 2004, Brian Draper took on the role of Chief Fire Officer of the Isle of Man Fire and Rescue Service. His appointment was well received by all within the service, and with him being fairly young in age, it was presumed he would serve for many years in that role. I had spoken to CFO Draper prior to his appointment, and had mentioned that my old CFO in Tyne and Wear was in his early forties when he took the top job, and that he been like a breath of fresh air to the Brigade. I somehow knew that Brian would make a cracking Chief, and the fact that he still turned up to stations to get some hands-on experience with the tools, kept him close to what was happening within the Service. By doing this, he gained a lot of respect from everyone he dealt with at station level. To top it off, having taken the job, Brian still wanted to remain part of the fully trained Line Rescue Team, and would turn out on his alerter whenever the team was required.

One such incident occurred when my Watch were on duty on a weekend night shift. We were turned out to a man that had climbed up a crane on Douglas Promenade and was threatening to throw himself off. As we arrived on scene to access the situation, the OIC immediately requested the attendance of the Line Rescue Team, so we settled down to wait for their attendance whilst monitoring the safety of the man on the crane. However, after a short period of time, the only member of the team to show up was the Chief. Apparently, the rest of the team had been booked off by mistake, and were all attending a retirement party. The only other members of the team that were available were two members of Red Watch, who were riding alongside me as members of the on-duty Watch, so they didn't have any of their line rescue gear with them.

CFO Draper would address the lack of attendance at another time, but right there and then he had a job to do. Respect to him; he donned his harness and climbed the crane to successfully rescue the gentleman, who by now was extremely cold from the strong wind that had been blowing in from the sea, so was just really happy to have his feet back on *terra firma*. As this was taking place, I reminisced about the fire that I had attended at the mill in Sunderland, when I had witnessed ACFO Bremner getting stuck into the job and even climbing a ladder to fight the fire. I thought then that it would be the last time I saw any Senior Officer getting his hands dirty, but how wrong I was, and I stood admiring CFO Draper do his rescue, proving to all that he was a true firefighter at heart and that being part of the Line Rescue Team wasn't just for show.

GRUELLING RESCUE

One nightshift, just after midnight, the bells went down to a report of a house fire in Demesne Road, Douglas. I knew the road, due to the fact that I had been sent to a domestic incident there when I was in the Constabulary. At the time I'd had to question where I was going, because Demesne is pronounced 'Demain', so I was asking where 'The Main Road' was in Douglas, as I hadn't heard of it. Control corrected me on that occasion, but it had delayed my arrival at the job. The other officers attending thought it was amusing, as due to my delay I had missed locking someone up, so I therefore had never forgotten the street. I also remembered that the houses on the street were tall, terraced buildings, with most of them converted into flats or bedsits, where tenants had their own room but shared bathroom and kitchen facilities. So I thought that this could have the makings of a decent fire job.

I was a designated BA wearer that night, partnering up with firefighter Bobby Moore. We arrived on scene and could see straight away that smoke was coming from a first-floor window of a property at the end of the street. Bobby and I quickly started to don our sets, whilst the OIC, Sub Officer Martyn Rundle, forced open the front door of the property. He could see smoke rolling down the stairs, but the ground floor was clear, so he entered to bang on a flat door that was directly ahead of him. A young couple came to the door, and as they were evacuated out of the building, Martyn asked if there was anyone in the rooms upstairs. They stated that there was a baby who was asleep in a cot in the first bedsit and that she was alone, as the mother had gone out nightclubbing. They said the mother had asked them to only check on the baby if they heard her crying.

Martyn relayed to us what the couple had said, and the adrenalin flooded our veins with the news that it was now a 'persons reported' job. Bobby and I urgently dragged a hose-reel up the stairs to fight the fire as fast as we could, as we were aware that time was critical in our bid to save the baby. With all my senses being fully activated, I kicked into gear one, but my heart was in my mouth with the dread that we wouldn't be quick enough to successfully retrieve the baby before she succumbed to the deadly effects of the smoke. The knowledge that the baby's life depended on just the two of us weighed heavy on our shoulders, as we knew that the second BA team would be at least 10-12 minutes away. The alerters would have been set off as we left the station, but taking into account travel time, we knew how long we would have to wait for back-up to arrive. We also knew that the baby wouldn't last that long in the thick smoke, which seemed to be getting worse, so we just had to crack on and do our best.

We reached the first floor, and visibility was close to zero, but we could just make out a glow coming from a room to our right-hand side where the fire was obviously developing. Bobby started to attack the fire, whilst I started a left-hand search, quickly finding a door to a room which I hoped would be the one containing the baby. I lay flat on the floor where the smoke was less dense, and shone my BA Wolf lamp across the room. My eyes keenly tried to pierce through the smoke as I scanned for anything that may help me. Almost immediately, just to the left of me, I could make out the shape of the legs of a cot, so I swiftly jumped to my feet and reached into the darkness, and instantly I could feel the baby wrapped tightly in the sheets. Grabbing the baby to my chest and covering her face with the blanket, I rushed out of the room and dashed straight down the stairs with this precious bundle held tight. Martyn was lying flat at the bottom of the stairs trying to assess where we were up to, when I suddenly appeared out of the smoke, bounding briskly down the stairs towards him. I quickly handed him the baby and watched as Martyn darted to the outside, where he delivered the baby to a waiting ambulance crew.

I proceeded back up to the first floor, feeling relieved that we had found the baby alive, and continued searching, as Bobby was still firefighting in what we now knew to be a kitchen area. I entered another room, and again the smoke was unbelievably thick; even though I tried to get low, I couldn't see a thing. Commencing a search pattern, I came across what I believed to be a sofa, and to my disbelief, as I swiped along what should have been the front of the sofa, my hand hit what I thought was an arm. I reached onto the sofa and found that I had located a second casualty, and immediately started to drag him out. As I got to the entrance to the room, I urgently shouted to Bobby that I had a casualty and needed help. He immediately dropped the hose-reel and grabbed the legs of the unconscious male, and we carried him down the stairs to safety.

The second pump still hadn't arrived by this time, so Bobby and I went back up to the first floor to continue searching, as he was sure that he had extinguished the fire. Within a few minutes I was confident that the first floor was clear of any further casualties, so we moved on to search the rest of the premises, trying to complete as much as we could before we would be relieved by another BA team, once they arrived on scene.

Continuing on, we located a set of stairs next to the kitchen, which appeared to be heading up to the second floor. We started to proceed up the stairs, but after the second step, we struggled to advance any further, due to the fact that the stairs were packed with bags, boxes, and a ton of other items that were blocking our way. Feeling frustrated, we hurriedly snatched at the items until we had cleared a path through to the top of the stairs, only to find a door that was locked. It was difficult to get any purchase on the door to force it open, because we were standing on a small area of stair, but Bobby was determined to get through it. He managed to use all his weight to burst the lock from the frame, enabling us to enter to begin a search of the second floor.

We quickly decided that it would be best if we took a risk and split up from each other. Bobby started a left-hand search, while I began a right-hand search pattern. I quickly came across a room that I worked out to be a kitchen, and was just going to advance further into the room when I heard Bobby calling me in an urgent manner that he had found a casualty. I made my way back and met him just as he was dragging an unconscious male out of a bedroom. I grabbed the casualty by his legs and we carefully negotiated him down the partially blocked flight of stairs. We had made it halfway down the stairs when we came across another BA team that was coming up. The second pump had arrived! Boy, I was so pleased to see them. I was starting to gasp for air at the exertion of what we had done up to that stage, so we quite happily handed the casualty over to the second team, for them to awkwardly manhandle him down the rest of the stairs. By now, both Bobby and I were getting low on air, but we returned up the stairs to complete a rapid search of the rest of the second floor. We finally made our way back outside just as both of our whistles, warning of low air, activated.

A BA servicing area had been set up on the pavement, so we took our sets off and sat on the pavement to try and recover, drinking water as if it had gone out of fashion. I was absolutely knackered at what had been an incredibly exhausting job, and just sat quietly reflecting on what we had been through, letting my body settle down before servicing my BA set for the next job.

About 15 minutes later, the baby girl's mother turned up, and I looked at her while trying to figure out how a mother could leave a baby by themselves whilst she went clubbing. But I am not a judge and jury, and was just happy that we had saved the baby. My thoughts went to my own three kids, who were at home, where their mother was taking care of them, probably fast asleep and totally unaware of what their dad had just encountered.

Both Bobby and I had thought we had done an exceptional job saving three lives, then word got around that it didn't look as if the last casualty was going to make it, which really put a damper on our spirits. Sadly, the male from the second floor had passed away. We returned to station to complete our reports, and thought nothing more of the job until we were summonsed to the Coroner's Court to give evidence.

The fire was discovered to be caused by a faulty toaster; the first adult we rescued gave evidence stating that he had been out for a few drinks and had got home feeling a bit hungry. He put some bread in the toaster then lay on the sofa, where he must have fallen asleep. The bread had got stuck and continued cooking until it burst into flames, igniting other items on the worktop. The fire continued to develop, but the flats were not fitted with any detection system, so everybody in the premises was left unaware. A man passing by the building had noticed the smoke and called the Fire Service.

The Coroner was pretty harsh on the lad, and emphasised the dangers of cooking whilst under the influence of alcohol. He also told him that if it hadn't been for the swift actions of the Fire Service, he would be looking at three deaths not just the one. Bobby and I gave our evidence and were thanked by the Coroner for our efforts.

On leaving the Court, an Advocate for the deceased approached us and asked if the family could have a word. They came across and thanked us for our efforts in trying to save their family member, and it was such a heart-rending moment. All we could say was that we were sorry for their loss, and that we were so sad that we had not been able to reach him in time. The lad that was saved also spoke to us, bursting into tears as he thanked us for saving his life. I choked up as well, as you could see that he blamed himself for the fire, leaving me with the impression that the guilt was going to live with him for a very long time. It was so sad that a simple act of making some toast had led to such a tragic event, leaving one family bereaved and another young man having to live with the consequences of that night.

CHAPTER TWENTY-NINE

PROMOTION AND NEW RESPONSIBILITIES

In January 2006, a position became vacant in the Corporate Services Department for a Leading Firefighter (Crew Manager). The job was to involve sourcing, evaluating, and procuring of fire equipment. Following the good experience that I had had during the ALP build, I decided to apply for it. I interviewed well and got the offered job, leaving Red Watch once more, to have Alan Gawne as my line manager yet again.

As before, I still carried an alerter and was attached to two Watches, but this time I had the rank of Leading Firefighter, so I was expected to take charge of appliances whenever the need arose. Having enjoyed acting up to the same rank during my years in Tyne and Wear, I knew what was expected of me and I looked forward to the challenge ahead.

I soon settled into my dayshift role and started to really enjoy the task of sourcing the best equipment that our budget would allow. Every year there appeared to be something new coming onto the fire market, offering opportunities to progress the Service into a safer place to work. This being the case, I decided to make it my philosophy that the majority of my budget would be spent on equipment that increased safety for the firefighter, which in turn would increase efficiency for the Service when dealing with incidents.

But rather than it being just me saying that this piece of equipment would be good for the Service, or that this equipment was far superior to what we currently used, I decided I needed to attend procurement meetings that were being held jointly by all the North West of England Brigades. This consortium of Brigades made it their policy to actively evaluate all equipment, including fire kit, with the intention of going to tender as a group and ensuring they received the best equipment at the lowest prices from all their suppliers. Knowing that all the equipment that they purchased had been fully evaluated, it would give any equipment I bought in conjunction with them the added credibility that I was looking for.

As I sought permission to attend the meetings, I learned that the last person who had been in my role had himself attended some of these meetings, but had not really enjoyed them and so simply stopped going. Consequently, our Service hadn't been represented for some time, but I truly felt that attending would not only be good for my development, but also benefit all who served on the Isle of Man. With this in mind, I approached the Senior Management Team with a business case, explaining the reasons behind me wanting to join the consortium. I emphasised the fact that as well as the equipment side of the meetings, a variety of other subjects were also discussed, including Health and Safety issues, which would of course be very beneficial for our Service.

Eventually, the required permissions were granted, leaving me to book my flight to attend my first meeting, which was programmed to be held at the headquarters of Merseyside Fire and Rescue Service. I travelled to the meeting in a suit and was so glad I had, as the first thing I noticed was that, apart from a couple of civilian representatives, the rest of the group were all high-ranking officers. The room was full of Divisional Officers, with a few Station Officers thrown into the mix. I figured that having to deal with so many high-ranking officers was probably the reason why my predecessor had not enjoyed the meetings. But being dressed in a suit meant that they had no idea of my rank, and I didn't feel obliged to tell them.

As expected, I found the meetings to be a really valuable source of information, as the different Brigades would discuss any issues that they were finding with any equipment or fire kit, passing on that knowledge to each other to improve standards across the board. It was therefore an ideal group for the IOMFRS to be involved with, and we benefited immensely from the association, especially as I now had colleagues I could turn to if I had any doubts about the suitability of any pieces of equipment.

Being such a small Fire Service, we could never commit the number of personnel required to proficiently test any new equipment coming onto the market. So being part of a group that ensured all equipment was evaluated and tested, allowed me to purchase equipment with added confidence. Added to this was the fact that being part of the group meant that the suppliers had to treat the IOMFRS the same as the larger Brigades, or face being dropped by the group, and this ensured that we received the same pricing as the others. The consortium worked well, and they went out to contract for a whole range of items, from work shirts to fire kit, or lifesaving equipment to hand-held radios. This meant that the savings I made by being involved with the consortium, allowed me to get the most from my annual budget, enabling me to buy extra equipment to the benefit of the IOMFRS.

At every meeting I attended, I learned something new to take back to the island. As most of the people at the meetings had spent most of their careers in procurement, they had become experts in their own fields, so I only needed to ask a question to be fully informed on any issue regarding any equipment or fire kit. I was like a sponge soaking up all the information, and knew that if I continued to attend these meetings, I could improve on the equipment that the IOMFRS already had.

LUNCH WITH BIG H

Just when I was getting used to my new role, I thought I was going to lose my newly acquired rank of Leading Firefighter, and possibly even more. Being day staff, I tended to eat lunch with the Duty Watch, rather than go home to eat. On this particular day, Green Watch were on duty, and as I was out and about in the station van, I decide to buy fish and chips with a carton of curry sauce to take back to the station for my meal. I arrived back and went up to the dining area, where I observed that Green Watch had almost finished eating. I proceeded to the kitchen where I plated up my food and poured the curry sauce over the top. On carrying it to the table, I placed it down at a free space, and returned to the kitchen to get a drink. On returning to the table, my food was nowhere to be seen, and a firefighter called Paul Hunt was sitting in the seat that I was going to use. Paul was a larger-than-life character, who goes by the name of 'Big H', although he is only 6'3". I always assumed the big part was either for his attitude or the big pock marks on his face. I asked him where my lunch was, and he said that it was in the bin. When I asked him why, he replied that he was sitting in that chair and that the food on the table had been in his space.

I could feel my blood starting to boil, but thought it best just to check that he was telling the truth before I took it any further. Walking calmly over to the bin, I opened the lid, and there sitting on the top of the rubbish was my plate, laid down without a chip out of place. To say I wasn't amused is an understatement. I have always followed the ethos that you should never mess with anyone's food, especially on station, where food was often left standing due to turning out to shouts.

I turned around and noticed that the whole room had gone incredibly quiet, while the other firefighters watched closely to see what might happen. Now, I have never been one to take a step back from a challenge, and I could feel the fury starting to flood my body as I looked again at the plate of food that I was never going to eat after being in the trash can. I contemplated my next move as I slowly picked the plate out of the bin, knowing that my reputation stood on the line in front of the whole of Green Watch. I knew then that I couldn't let Big H get away with embarrassing me in this way, without some sort of retribution. So I just marched across to where he was sitting, and in one quick swoosh, I smashed the plate of food straight into his face. Before he could react, I stepped back and angrily ripped my jacket off, raising my fists in order to get ready to rumble. He jumped to his feet, and as we faced each other, the rest of the Watch suddenly responded and jumped in between us before the fight could escalate any further.

I was still fuming, but knew that this would not end up well for either of us, so I turned around and walked out of the room, heading straight to the Station Commander's office, where I threw my rank markings down on his table, stating, "You might as well have these now." He obviously didn't have a clue what had just happened, and just sat there speechless as I left the room to go down to the washroom to clean up.

Big H was already down in the washroom when I arrived, trying to wash the curry sauce out of his eyes. When he saw me, he just burst out laughing, which started me off laughing as well at the stupidity of the whole incident. I think he admired me for not bowing down to his bullying ways, and years later, we still go out for lunch once a week. Thinking about it, though, he never seems to order fish and chips with curry sauce. The curry sauce, however, did wonders for his pock marked skin, and gave him a glowing complexion for weeks afterwards. As for my rank, I returned to my office after the lunch break and explained to Alan what had happened. He disappeared to smooth things over with the Station Commander, and nothing more was said of the incident, although Green Watch loved to remind me of it over the following years.

BUILDING KNOWLEDGE

Apart from the North West Procurement meetings, I also got myself invited to the Scottish Fire Services Consortium meetings. The IOMFRS had sent all of its full-time firefighters on an Urban Search and Rescue Course that was being run by Strathclyde Fire and Rescue Service. While I was there, I used the opportunity to get to know who their Procurement Officers were, and had the full tour of all their appliances, along with all the associated equipment. I had mentioned the North West Consortium meetings that I was attending, and before I knew it, they kindly asked if the IOMFRS would be interested in joining their consortium, too.

The Scottish Brigades were going through a big change to become Fire Scotland – one big organisation, rather than separate Brigades – and were in the process of standardising fire kit and equipment right across Scotland. The meetings were chaired by the Chief Fire Officer of Strathclyde, and he told me that having me attending their meetings was a great benefit to Fire

Scotland, as my knowledge of what the North West Brigades had achieved was assisting them in determining which direction they should go in. For me, it was just another avenue for learning what other Brigades were doing in their quest to provide better personal protective equipment (PPE) for firefighters on the frontline, but I also saw the opportunity as being a great benefit to the IOMFRS in building good relationships with Brigades right across the UK.

As an added incentive, being part of two large organisations that trialled and tested a huge amount of kit meant that I was assured that any kit I bought had already been thoroughly tested by a number of different Brigades. Additionally, although we were linked to the North West and Scotland Consortiums, and were included in a lot of their contracts for fire kit and equipment, the IOMFRS still maintained an independence which allowed me to pick and choose what I thought would be best for the island.

This was the case when the North West put out an expression of interest for suppliers to provide fire helmets. Suppliers wishing to be part of the tender process put forward their most recent helmets, which then went on to be tested by a number of Brigades. This process can take months, with everything taken into account, such as comfort, durability, strength tests, costs, after service, etc. The trials included the helmets being tried in different situations with and without BA being worn, and the results were graded using a scoring scale. Eventually, all the facts were brought together at a final meeting to decide which supplier had won the tender. Ultimately, the Brigades agreed that the Rosenbauer Hero's Helmet had scored the most highly in the wearer trials, but the Gallet, which was second best in wearer trials, was the most cost effective. The North West signed the contract for the Gallet, but I opted the IOMFRS out and went for the Rosenbauer instead, which had been rated higher by firefighters across the board. As it happened, the North West changed to the Rosenbauer a few years later when the contract went out again, so I felt justified in the decision I had made years earlier.

FIRE EXHIBITIONS

As well as the consortium meetings, I also attended the annual Fire Exhibition Show, which was based just outside of Birmingham. The exhibition was huge, and with all the big fire suppliers in attendance, it offered me an ideal opportunity to meet up with all my business contacts face-to-face, which I always found to be a lot more personal and more productive, than dealing with them over the telephone.

Having all the suppliers together in one place also meant some good financial savings for the IOMFRS, as it isn't cost effective to fly from the island across to the UK just to sign equipment contracts, or to attend any demonstrations of new equipment to the fire market that any suppliers were offering. Therefore, when scheduling in my attendance at the Exhibition, I would always look at the list of suppliers who were presenting at the show, and arrange face-to-face meetings with any I needed to deal with. These meetings gave me ample opportunity to raise any issues that I may have had with any of them or their products. I am told that the lads back on station weren't convinced of my reasons for going, as they all thought that I was just using the show to have a jolly (to have a bit of fun). They couldn't comprehend that all my time spent at the show was about serious business, or the fact that I worked so hard at the show that I always returned to the island absolutely worn out.

To get the most for the IOMFRS from this important event, I always liked to take another member of personnel with me on this annual pilgrimage to Birmingham. Which member of staff accompanied me depended on what I was planning to spend the yearly equipment budget on, or sometimes it might be a member of another department within the Service, who realised that they could find anything they required at this huge event. For example, if we needed new line rescue gear, someone from the Line Rescue Team would accompany me; if it was a training package that was required, a member of the Training Department would come along. Occasionally, I would even convince a Senior Management Team member to attend, as I felt it was an ideal place for them to get a feel for the changes that were happening within the modern-day Fire Service. Nevertheless, no matter who it was that went, they all agreed on the value of attending and that it was an exhausting couple of days. But they all also added that they would love another invite to go back.

Meeting all my suppliers was always an enjoyable time, but I also made a point of speaking to all of their competitors, just to keep my suppliers on their toes. This meant that I would literally stroll around the two big arenas for hours, stopping to chat with anyone that carried equipment that was of any interest to the IOMFRS.

One year, as I was strolling around the show, I received a telephone call from Douglas Station. It was lunchtime and the duty Watch were watching the news, which was showing on the television. Apparently, as the news started, the broadcaster stated that later on in the programme they were going to have a look at the Fire Show being held in Birmingham, so someone had a bright idea of giving me a call. On answering my mobile, I was greeted by everyone shouting down the phone, and I was initially puzzled about what they were rabbiting on about. Eventually their giddiness settled down and they got to the point: they had called me with a challenge to get on the TV. Always one for a bit of fun, I accepted, and began running around the large halls, trying to locate where the BBC were doing the filming. I found them just in time, as my phone rang again with another call from the station, saying that the news piece had started.

I quickly positioned myself in the frame, and I could hear the lads on the phone absolutely killing themselves with laughter. As I stood behind the presenter's back, I gave a smile and a little wave to the camera, with the knowledge that the boys on station would be highly amused. I stood for a few more minutes, pretending to show an interest in the products that were on display, before throwing a few more waves at the camera, whilst thinking how ridiculous I must look to anyone that was passing. But no matter what others were thinking, the challenge had been accepted and achieved, so I smiled and waved one last time at the camera, before moving on to continue the reason I was there – work!

CHAPTER THIRTY

FIRE INVESTIGATION

My career in the IOMFRS was starting to flourish, and I was definitely in a role that was holding my interest. I was running various projects simultaneously, finding myself as busy as I had ever been, but extremely content in the knowledge that I was beavering away on subjects that I especially enjoyed. As if my daytime role wasn't enough to keep me engaged, I also had to fit in the duties of being the Lead ALP Instructor, overseeing the other six ALP Instructors and ensuring that all the initial training and any refresher training was being completed to the required standards. Added to this was my position as a Manual Handling Instructor where, along with other instructors, I would visit all the Retained Stations, making sure that all personnel were adequately trained in manual handling. But no matter how busy I was, the one thing that had always piqued my interest was fire. So when I was asked if I wanted to become a Fire Investigator (FI) for the Service, I jumped at the chance.

Along with a colleague, I left the island to attend a Fire and Explosives Investigators Course, being held by the reputable firm called Gardiners Associates. They supply Fire Investigation training to all Police and Fire Services, as well as the UK Forensic Science Laboratories and insurance companies. If you were to be trained as an FI, this was the place to be, as their training team included people like John DeHaan, an independent Fire Investigator and author of the books, *Kirk's Fire Investigation* and *Forensic Fire Investigation*. Also onboard was the owner of the company, John Gardiner – an ex-firefighter with masses of experience in the line of fire investigation. Every one of their team brought something to the party, so I knew it was going to be a great learning experience and felt confident that I would go on to pass the course to become a fully-fledged Fire Investigator.

Adding to the experience was the fact that the course was an inter-agency event. This meant that as well as fire officers on the course, we also had people from the Police, including scenes of crime officers, as well as a few forensic scientists. Everybody shared their knowledge, and explained what they were looking to achieve when faced with a suspicious fire. Having been in the Constabulary, I already had an awareness what Police and SOCO would be looking for, but it was still good to see them in action.

Various rooms and scenarios were set up, and a fire set within. Once the fire was extinguished, we would go in as a team and investigate the origin and source of the fire, hopefully coming to a correct conclusion once we had discussed our findings with each other. Everything was videoed, and we would watch the recording back as we debated the outcomes. It was a highly intense course, with a lot of studying required to pass the last exam, but I must add that I enjoyed every minute of it, ranking it as my favourite course attended during my time in the Service.

Being in that environment for the duration of the course brought back a load of memories of investigating all sorts of fires with my old Station Officer back in Tyne and Wear. The experience I gained then definitely assisted me during the course, with some scenarios being almost identical to real jobs that I had attended.

FIRST FI

Having passed the course with flying colours, I returned to the island to await my first turnout as a fully qualified Fire Investigator, and thankfully I didn't have to wait too long. It would be fair to say that, with it being my first FI on the island, I was feeling a bit apprehensive knowing my peers would all be watching, but I just hoped that I could find the right outcome. I arrived on scene to discover that it had fortunately only been a small fire, so I wouldn't have too much digging around to do. The fire had been in the lounge of a house, and the initial crew had extinguished it pretty sharpish, leaving only a modest amount of damage to deal with. The OIC of the crew had then tried to work out what had caused the fire, but he could not find a source of ignition, so automatically suspected that it may have been maliciously ignited, and requested an FI to attend.

It had been a hot and sunny day, and the fire had been discovered when the owner of the house returned from a shopping trip. She confirmed that no-one else had been in the house, and that she had been out for about three hours. I scratched and poked around the remains of the fire, considering, then rejecting, all obvious possibilities to the cause, until eventually the reason behind the fire became clear to me. About a metre away from what remained of the fire was an empty crystal vase, standing empty on the windowsill. I came to the conclusion that the sun had been shining directly through the vase, which literally acted like a magnifying glass, directing the sunlight onto some nearby material, which had then subsequently come to ignition point. The fire was noticed pretty quickly, and the damage caused was minimal, but I was confident with my conclusions. However, being a belts and braces type of guy, I did return to the house the next day just to confirm my findings. It was exactly 24 hours from when the fire had been discovered, and right enough, I found with the position of the sun that everything was as I had expected it to be. Accidental cause, case closed!

CONFLICTING RESULTS

I was confident in my ability as a FI, and tried to attend as many jobs as I could, in order to build up my overall knowledge and experience. This often brought me into conflict with other fire investigators when I disagreed with their findings. One such case was following a fire at a newly-built pizza parlour. I was asked to assist a Station Officer who had been allocated the job, and who was a fully qualified FI in his own right. I felt from an early stage that he was totally going down the wrong route, and tried to explain what I thought. But as I was a Leading Firefighter, which was two ranks below him, he was not prepared to listen to what I had to say and just shrugged off anything I suggested. I listened to his findings and knew he was wrong, but how was I going to convince him? We left the job, and he was still insisting that he was right, which left me mulling it over and over again in my head. I could feel myself getting wound up over the whole affair, so approached my line manager with my grievance, who then spoke to the CFO.

Later that same evening, I received a call from the Chief, ordering me to go back to the job the next morning and re-do the investigation. I attended with another Station Officer, who was also FI trained, and he totally agreed with my findings. I don't think the original Station Officer was too happy, but that was the last thing that I was bothered about. All I knew in my mind was that I wasn't prepared to put my name to something that wasn't right, even if it did mean stepping on a few toes.

Not too long after this incident, I was asked to assist another Station Officer who was investigating a blaze within a property on the South Quay, Douglas. There was a lot of damage, and it was proving to be a thought-provoking job, but I was really enjoying the challenge. It was a different Station Officer to the one that I had disagreed with, and I thought things were going well, but found myself flabbergasted when he decided that he was putting the fire down to an electrical fault on the ground floor. I had traced the origin to a small fire that had been set in the basement, so was heading along the line of it being caused deliberately. Again, he pulled rank and wouldn't listen.

I figured he didn't fancy having to attend court, as his last appearance there hadn't gone too well. So, pinning the incident on an electrical fault would have suited him just fine. However, I was fuming, and immediately by-passed my line manager and telephoned the CFO. He listened to my complaint and again instructed me to go back the next day and lead on the investigation. Another officer also attended with me, and agreed totally with my findings. I wrote the report up and submitted it, and a few weeks later my findings were proven to be correct, as the Police found and arrested the person who had set the fire.

From then on, I seemed to be the one who got the call to do any fire investigations that were required, especially if it was a fatal incident, or one that had caused a serious amount of damage. If, due to work load commitments, I was unable to lead on the investigation, then I would be asked to assist another FI that had been allocated to the job, leaving all the report writing to him.

SPONTANEOUS COMBUSTION

One of the more interesting jobs that I was asked to investigate was a fire at a property called Harold Tower. Situated on Fort Anne Road, Douglas, the property sat in its own 3-acre grounds, with access being via a small road that passed a coach house and separate bungalow. It was a huge building, built circa 1830, in the style of a gothic castle complete with its own tower, overlooking Douglas Bay. The property was owned by a multi-millionaire, who was having the house extensively renovated whilst he lived in the coach house.

The fire had been discovered when the contractors arrived early in the morning to continue their work. They immediately contacted the Fire Service, and two pumps were rapidly dispatched. I arrived on scene shortly after the blaze had been extinguished, having been requested by the OIC of the incident, who had recognised that a large insurance claim was likely to be involved. Apart from the two teams of BA wearers and the OIC himself, who had entered the building post-fire, access to the property was denied to all persons until my arrival. This helped contain any evidence that I may find, making my job a lot easier when it came to collecting statements.

I entered the front doors to find myself in a large hallway, and I could tell straight away that no expense was being spared with the refurbishment, but there had been a serious amount of smoke damage coming down from first floor level. I had been told that the main fire had been contained to a bedroom on the first floor and, on looking up, I could see the direction of travel that the thick black smoke had taken. I climbed the impressive stairwell and took notes on all the rooms. It was evident that almost every internal door had been in the open position during the fire, as smoke damage was extensive throughout the building. I also came to the conclusion that this fire had been burning for quite a while, although actual fire damage seemed to have been contained to a bedroom and the hallway adjacent to it, due to a lack of fuel loading within that area.

I entered the bedroom, and could see that the room had been relatively empty prior to the incident, but my attention was drawn to an area of flooring that had been severely damaged by the fire, eventually breaking through to the floor below. On investigation of this area, I came across what appeared to be lumps of charred cloth. I completed my initial survey and left the building to speak to the contractors who had been working in the building the previous day.

They explained that the bedroom had been used to store a lot of the materials that they were using in the renovation, adding that the last time they had been in the room was to have their afternoon tea break the day before. Following further questions about the cloths, they revealed that they were old used rags that had been bagged in bin liners, and that they had used them to sit on during their breaks. I asked for a full list of materials that they had stored in the room, and they came up with the following items.

- Genuine Turpentine (Highly flammable and can support spontaneous combustion)
- Liming Wax (Flammable with paraffin wax as a component)
- White Polish (Highly Flammable)
- Quick Drying Wax Polish (Flammable and can support spontaneous combustion)
- Methylated Spirit (Highly flammable)
- French Polish (Highly flammable)
- Two bags of used cotton rags

I returned to the Station, where I went about investigating the materials that the contractors had used on site. Before long, I was getting hit after hit of reported fires that had involved one or another of the same materials used, with the search engine also showing a number of case histories of fires in buildings under renovation, including a fair number in the USA. This was all good information, so I dug a little deeper to find out what the conditions had been like for fire to occur in these circumstances, while I pondered if the conditions at Harold Tower could have been similar to what I was reading. As luck would have it, two of the case studies that I had come across distinctively mentioned some of the materials causing rags to ignite, but only whilst the rags were under compression. This was even more evident if linseed oil was one of the components of the material used. Taking this information onboard, I consequently explored the breakdown of all the materials that the contractors used, finding – as I suspected – that a number of them had linseed oil as a major component.

This allowed me to come to the conclusion that the fire had been caused by spontaneous combustion of the used rags that had been contaminated with flammable products. The two bags of rags had been inadvertently compressed together by the contractors when they sat on them during their tea breaks. This had caused an exothermic reaction within the rags, that had finally broken into fire once the contractors had left the building.

I had ruled out malicious ignition as being the cause as, according to the contractors, they had secured the premises on leaving work the previous evening and they were still secure when they discovered the fire. This was in line with the fact that there were no obvious signs of any break-in when I completed a thorough check around the outside.

Electrical issues were also ruled out, as there were no electrical appliances or sockets in the vicinity of the point of origin, and the main fuse box had been switched off by the contractors the evening before.

The fire being caused by discarded smoking materials was also ruled out, as none of the contractors were smokers, and there was no evidence of any smoking materials throughout the premise.

I presented my findings to the CFO, and a copy was requested by the insurance company representing the owner of the house, as they planned to recover the claim against the insurance company of the contractors. There had been over one million pounds worth of damage, so the contractor wasn't going to accept responsibility without a fight.

Days later, the insurance company for the contractor sent a forensic scientist (specialising in fire) across to make his own report. I met with him at the premises and presented my findings. He was impressed at my research, and agreed totally with my findings. This was to the relief of the other insurance company, who asked me to consider leaving the Fire Service and joining their team of investigators, as I had, without a doubt, saved them from a big pay-out. I politely declined, as I already had the job of my dreams, although the offer did leave me feeling gratified that my skills had been recognised by an outside party.

CHAPTER THIRTY-ONE

RESHUFFLE

Before long, I found myself promoted to Sub Officer within the Corporate Services Department. The Senior Management Team had decided that I was working way above my pay-scale, due to handling the second biggest budget in the Service, so they were reshuffling my department to make my job a Sub Officer role. The promotion wasn't automatic, and I still had to apply for it. I was eventually pitched against another couple of Leading Firefighters, who were also trying to build their careers. But I had done the role for a few years and therefore had all the right answers at interview, which definitely helped me towards winning the promotion.

The promotion also meant that I now had line management responsibilities, as a new position of a Leading Firefighter was also to be placed into the department, with the intention of the recipient assisting with my ever-increasing workload. This job was given to Justin McMullin, who had served with me on the Red Watch. He was a handy man to have in the department, as his knowledge of the communications system was invaluable, so any issues that the Service had with comms went straight to him.

He was also a bit of a character who, for some reason, never lost an opportunity to take his clothes off for a laugh, even though he wasn't built like Adonis and was more, like I have already described, a large space hopper on legs. I just knew the department would be full of laughter and looked forward to working with him.

LAUNDRY

At this time, Douglas Station didn't have its own laundry facility, and dirty fire kit would be sent on a regular basis to Nobles

Hospital, where it would be laundered in their facility at a cost. However, we were noticing that some of the fire kit being returned was displaying signs of damage, which I figured had been caused by the kit being washed at too high a temperature. I therefore put together a business case to install an industrial washing machine and dryer of our own within an underused store room at the station. Approval was given and the Miele machines arrived, although panic almost set in when we realised that they wouldn't fit through the doorway to the store. Luckily, the room had a large skylight, and by using equipment from the station, the two machines were lowered into place with millimetres to spare around the skylight opening. Soon everything was up and running, and I returned to my office to get my line manager, Alan Gawne, to come down to view our new laundry facility.

We walked down to the facility, with me feeling chuffed that this was another improvement that I had instigated, and on arrival at the laundry, I proudly pulled open the door and gestured to Alan to enter. As Alan stepped forward, he suddenly stopped, and where I expected to see a congratulatory look showing on his face, all I saw was one of total shock. Trying to fathom out what was wrong, I looked around the door and there, sitting reading a newspaper, was Justin! He was totally naked, except for a pair of socks, whilst his clothes were tumbling around in the washing machine. Both Justin and I simultaneously burst out laughing, but Alan's face was one of disbelief. He was probably thinking that he was in for a nightmare trying to keep these two jokers under control within the department, so he just turned around, dropped his head, and walked back upstairs to the peace and quiet of his office.

A RELUCTANCE TO CHANGE

I was still attending the North West meetings, and one of the contracts that we bought into was to replace an old navy-blue fire kit that the Brigade had worn for a fair number of years, with a new gold PBI fire kit. It was a huge outlay for the IOMFRS, and one that didn't go down too well with a lot of firefighters on the island. They didn't like change, and thought the gold kit would get dirty too quickly, compared to the blue kit that they were used to.

What they were failing to see was that if the kit looked dirty, it was more than likely dirty, contaminated with anything from blood and body fluids to all the products of combustion. Therefore, this kit would require laundering to remove all these contaminates.

With the blue kit hiding the signs of dirt or staining, it became obvious that a lot of the guys were not washing their kit as often as they should have been, and were just content to wear it dirty. However, for their own health and safety, they should have been aware – especially as it was a well-documented fact – that a fair number of firefighters throughout the world die due to the effects of various cancers, with a lot of these cancers being put down to excessive exposure to highly carcinogenic pollutants found on used fire. It is, therefore, essential that in order to reduce the risk of exposure to any of these contaminants, all fire kit should be regularly laundered.

What they also hadn't appreciated was that I had been present at all the trials done on all the fire kits submitted for tender to the North West Consortium, where the PBI material had been proven to be the best available at that time. The PBI cloth was more expensive than other options available, but what had swung it for me was the burn test, in which the Gold PBI kit had excelled.

The various kits that were in the tender process had been sent to a scientific lab in Lancashire to be tested. Each of the kits was placed on a mannequin, before being placed into a burn chamber. The mannequin had sensors attached all over it, that recorded what heat would be penetrating through the fire kit, which in effect would reflect what the wearer would suffer on their bodies. Jets of flame were then turned on to where the chamber temperature reached areas in excess of 1000 degrees (representing the temperatures that are reached during a flashover). After an allocated time, the fire kits were brought out of the chamber, allowed to cool, and then examined. The kit that we were currently wearing did not perform as well as the new PBI cloth in this test, and it showed signs of failure in various areas of the tunic and leggings being tested. The Gold PBI, though, had maintained its full structure, with only charring observed on the outer material.

To make sure that this one-off test was not a fluke, I requested the test be redone using an old set of fire kit that I had brought with me from the Isle of Man. This kit had come from a recently retired firefighter, who had worn the kit over a period of four years, so it was compatible with what most of the island's firefighters were wearing. Allowing for the fact that the kit had been regularly washed, I had expected the kit to have lost some of its fire protection properties, but when the kit was examined following the chamber test, the results shocked even me. Parts of the outer layers of the kit were so badly burnt that the material broke up in your hands as if it was burnt cardboard and not a fire-resistant material, and the inner layers also showed massive charring, which told me that any firefighter wearing this in a flashover would have suffered serious burns to the body.

After the test, I asked if I could keep the burnt fire kit in order to show all the island's firefighters the difference between the Gold PBI and the kit that they were currently using. I returned to the island, carrying the fire kits that had been tested, and immediately reported the results to the Senior Management Team. I explained to them that my plan of action was to take the burnt kits out to each of the island's stations to demonstrate the difference between the materials, but this plan was rejected, as they decided that it wasn't in the best interests of the Service to show the firefighters the badly charred fire kit. This decision was purely down to the fact that we had initially only ordered enough PBI to replace one full set of fire kit for each firefighter, with their second kit to get replaced at the start of the new financial year. The CFO figured that if we showed them the 'burnt to a crisp' old kit, nobody would want to wear their blue kit, therefore leaving them without a change of fire kit if the need arose. To this day, I still think it was the wrong decision not to show them the difference in standard, as the majority of the Retained personnel across the island favoured wearing their one remaining blue kit, rather than the new Gold PBI – until, of course, they received their second PBI kit, and the old kit was taken off them. I believe that if the firefighters had seen the results of the burn test, they would not have shown such reluctance to the change, and would have appreciated that the aim of my department was to improve their safety.

BUDGETS

As I worked away in Corporate Services, trying to improve standards, it became noticeable that my annual budget was always being reduced in order to help the IOMFRS make the savings that the Government was demanding of them. Each year, the Isle of Man Government would try to squeeze and reduce all the budgets allocated to the various Departments, yet they still expected the same standard of service to be delivered. CFO Draper would go into battle with the politicians, trying to maintain the IOMFRS budgets to an acceptable level, and overall I think he did as good a job as any Chief could have done. Because of these financial pressures that the Service found itself facing, it became essential that I used my budget as wisely as I could in order to maintain the high standards set as well as, whenever possible, continuing to deliver any improvements to the Service that the budget would allow.

One philosophy I always stuck to was that I felt that the frontline firefighters were the most important people in the organisation, so therefore their safety with regard to PPE was paramount to any spending that I did. Since being in the Corporate Services role, I had changed the helmets, fire tunics and leggings, firefighting gloves, flash-hoods, fire boots, and numerous other bits of equipment that I deemed improved the safety of the frontline firefighters. I had also made smart changes to their working rig uniform, with better quality shirts, trousers, and an introduction of a dry wick t-shirt that could be worn under fire kit.

However, all these changes had a cost to purchase and maintain. The budget was only so big, so I had to make cuts elsewhere, and this didn't go down well with a lot of personnel. One of the cuts was to take away the undress uniform from all operational firefighters up to the rank of Station Officer. The undress uniform was mainly used at ceremonial occasions, such as the likes of funerals of retired members, and as we had a Ceremonial Colour Party to fulfil that role, I felt that savings could be made by withdrawing it. These savings could then be spent on more safety critical equipment to the benefit of our frontline firefighters. Besides, due to the fact that a lot of the undress uniform didn't fit the firefighters – due to weight gain, etc – those wearing it at various events looked scruffy and unprofessional, and were not setting a good image of the IOMFRS. Retained stations took the withdrawal of the undress uniform particularly to heart, letting me know their feelings every time I visited one of the stations. Nonetheless, I stuck to my decision, as I believed the savings allowed important improvements to be made.

IS IT A MONSTER?

Having mentioned the Ceremonial Colour Party, it would be unforgivable of me not to mention a certain funeral that they attended. It was a funeral of a retired member of the Service, and the family had requested that the Colour Party attend to give their loved one a send-off he deserved.

The ALP, adorned with wreaths and black bows, looked impressive, and the coffin, covered by a Manx flag, was secured to the deck for its journey to the cemetery. The Colour Party, dressed in their full regalia, took their positions, and escorted their lost comrade on his final journey. The ALP arrived at the gates of the cemetery and six of the Colour Party respectfully lifted the coffin onto their shoulders, to proceed the short march up to the church within the cemetery grounds. Although only a short march, the Colour Party knew they had to keep everything tight, as the path leading from the cemetery gates had a steady incline before dropping back down to the church entrance. But they had done this numerous times before, so didn't envisage any issues.

Leading Firefighter McMullin was one of the six dressed up in all his glory, and assigned to be a pall bearer. Unfortunately for Justin, he had not silenced his phone before placing it in his tunic pocket, and just as they were reaching the crest of the hill,

212

someone rang him. His ring tone was from the song called *Monster* by the band The Automatic, and the words 'what's that coming over the hill? Is it a monster?' blasted out across the silent graveyard. Justin was horrified, and his face glowed like a ripe tomato, but he couldn't do anything about his situation as he was tied up carrying the coffin. The call ceased just as they arrived at the doors of the church, with the vicar giving Justin a wry smile.

Justin never made the same mistake again, which is just as well, as I deliberately tried to ring him whenever he was part of a pall bearing party or at other ceremonial events that he attended, just to keep him on his toes!

PHOENIX

Back in the early 1800s, each town on the island ran its own Fire Brigade, and it wasn't until 1940 that a single Isle of Man Fire Brigade was established. Some Retained personnel resent that everything is run by the Wholetime staff at Douglas, and go out of their way to try and keep their individuality as a Station/ Brigade. So much so, that if you ask some members of staff where they are Retained, they will say Laxey Brigade or Peel Brigade. This humoured me, but I never let it get in the way of my decision making. Every now and again, though, I would have to pull someone up and remind them that we were all the same Service.

One day, I was at local supplier picking up some t-shirts that had been embroidered with the Brigade logo. Whilst there, he gave me a pack of ten other shirts and asked if I could drop them down to Laxey Station. I looked at them. They were definitely our work shirts, with the Brigade logo on the chest, so I asked why they were going to Laxey and not back to me at Douglas. He stated that a firefighter from Laxey had brought them in with the Brigade logo already on, but that they wanted an extra logo on the sleeve. I took a shirt out of the bag and, right enough, there on the sleeve was a huge Phoenix rising out of the flames, complete with Laxey Fire Brigade embroidered underneath.

I was fuming at the audacity that the Laxey firefighter would think he could get away with it. But rather than raising it to a disciplinary offence, I decided to deal with it myself. I attended Laxey Station that night, and on Parade I presented the firefighter with ten sleeves, complete with embroidery. I had cut the sleeves from the shirts, and reminded the Laxey personnel that we were one Brigade and that the shirts belonged to the IOMFRS. I told him that I was keeping the shirts, but as a gesture of goodwill, they were welcome to the embroidered patch that they had paid for. The firefighter glowed with embarrassment, as all his colleagues stood looking for a response. But he just stood staring in disbelief at the sleeves in his hands. So, having dealt with the issue I just bade them farewell, and left them to stew in their predicament of what to do with their Phoenix on a sleeve.

CHAPTER THIRTY-TWO

DEADLY ARSON ATTACK

In the early hours of Sunday 22nd March, 2009, an arsonist started a fire spree which sadly ended up with one man losing his life. The fires, all within a small radius of streets in lower Douglas, had started with a small fire in a back yard of a property in Bucks Road. The Fire Service attended and extinguished the blaze, before being re-directed to a property in nearby Peveril Street. The owner of the property had been awoken by their fire alarm activating, and found a small fire in the living room of the house. Luckily, the fire was extinguished before too much damage was done, but it was evident that the fire had been maliciously set. Less than thirty minutes later, the Fire Service responded to another property, just around the corner from Peveril Street, in a house in Clarke Street. Minimal damage was caused, but again it was deemed to be suspicious.

The arsonist was not finished yet, and a more serious blaze was set in the hallway of a block of flats in Demesne Road, literally a couple of minutes' walking distance from where the other fires had been set. This time the fire became established, and when I arrived on the back of the third pumping appliance, rescues were already being made by use of ladders. Five persons were rescued using the ladders, and others had escaped by another route, prior to the arrival of the Fire Service.

The fire was intense, and by the time it was brought under control there had been severe damage to the property. The premises had consisted of seven self-contained flats, covering three floors, all accessed by a communal stairwell. The top flat – a converted roof space on the third floor – had suffered a lot of structural damage, which resulted in the roof collapsing in. It was in this flat that the remains of a body could be seen, but only by the cage operator of the ALP in use.

Sadly, due to the extent of the damage, the casualty had to be left in situ until a scaffolding firm could erect scaffolding to help support the external structures. This delay meant that it wasn't until the Tuesday evening that a Line Rescue Team could safely enter the building to finally retrieve the body. By that time, police had flown in Steven Andrews, a fantastic Forensic Scientific Officer (FSO) from the UK, to lead the fire investigation. The Fire Service was asked if we could supply someone to assist Steven, and since I had worked with him on a previous incident, the CFO thought it would be best if I was that man.

We began the FI, and on entering the front door into the hallway, it was clearly evident that a severe and rapidly developing fire had taken place. The top pane of glass in the outer front vestibule door had been blown out. This had been witnessed by the crews of the first appliance in attendance, who stated that a flashover had occurred. The inner vestibule door had glass that had melted, which proved heat in excess of 850C within this area. This, and observation of the damage done throughout the building, led us to believe that temperatures in excess of 1000C would have been recorded on the floors above. This was evident in the scale of the damage caused within the premises.

It was going to be a challenge to locate the point of origin, but the FSO had a gut feeling that it may have started close to a back door to the premises, which was in a small lobby area next to the stairs. The door frame had been totally destroyed, so the FSO had started to dig in this area, while he asked me to investigate an alcove at the bottom of the stairs.

The alcove area seemed more promising to me, and it certainly looked as if there was a decent fire load in this area. I started to pull things out that had been stored under the stairs, and this included a frame of a bike and an empty beer keg. I then came across the remains of a few boxes, and slowly started to peel the layers back. As soon as I got to the bottom of the pile, I could smell the distinctive odour of an accelerant. I immediately called the FSO over, and when he observed and smelled what I had uncovered, his eyes lit up. I had found the point of origin and the remains of whatever accelerant that had been used. The area was photographed, and the evidence bagged, then we continued on our search, just in case there were any other areas of potential interest regarding where this blaze may have started.

We could see that the fire had spread rapidly to the floors above, using the stairs as a natural chimney. There was also plenty of oxygen to help nurture the fire, as a two-foot space beneath the floorboards drew in air from airbricks built into the external walls. This, along with a strong breeze that blew that night, had allowed the air to feed the accelerant-fuelled fire and whip it straight up the stairs.

This rapidly developing fire had prevented the deceased from escaping its grip. The autopsy report stated that the deceased, Terence Losh (aged 61), had been dressed and alive before he sadly succumbed to the fire. It is assumed that he may have heard the fire alarms ring out and had dressed to make his escape. Unfortunately, having opened his front door, he was faced with flames coming up his main escape route. He had returned to his bedroom, where he was then overcome by smoke, before the fire eventually broke through to engulf his room.

The evidence was gathered, and my job was done, but it was now down to the Police to use their investigative skills to bring the killer to justice. The initial feeling around Douglas Fire Station was that the job held the hallmark of Shadow – the serial arsonist that we had dealt with in the past – but this was proven to be untrue as Shadow was still in prison, serving time for another fire. The Police, though, did a fantastic job reviewing tons of CCTV footage, and eventually arrested a man called Simon Paul Leece, a 35-year-old local man. He appeared in court the following year, and despite his not guilty plea, was proven guilty of all charges and sentenced to life imprisonment. He was not a person that the Fire Service had come across before, and he could give no motive as to why he had gone out to commit this horrendous crime.

CHAPTER THIRTY-THREE

TT DUTIES

As I have previously mentioned, the Isle of Man is well known as the Road Race Capital of the World. Hosting the annual TT motorcycle racing event, the races are run around a 37.7- mile circuit, all on closed public roads. This, along with the fact that the island plays host to over 40,000 spectators who visit to watch the races and enjoy the event, creates a need for special procedures to be put in place by all the emergency services. This helps to ensure the safety and wellbeing of all that live on the island, and also all those extra visitors during this busy time of year.

During times when the roads are closed for races, the IOMFRS deploys its resources in such a way that they are still able to respond to any incidents that they are required to attend. This is aided by placing a Station Officer in the Emergency Services Joint Control Room to assist control room staff in choosing to mobilise the most appropriate station to any incident reported. In the worst-case scenarios, where the Fire Service have no option but to use the closed roads, the Station Officer in Control would immediately liaise directly with the race Control Tower to get the race red flagged (stopped). Once it was deemed safe, with all racing stopped, the appliances would enter the closed road at predetermined entry points. To ensure that every Service has an awareness of what's happening on the circuit, all the emergency services have representatives in the Race Control Tower, helping to keep them fully informed if any incident arises out on, or near, the race track.

As well as Control Room and Race Control Room duties, the IOMFRS also covers any incidents in the pit lane and the surrounding grandstand areas. A crew is dispatched to man the pit lane, and the races cannot start unless this crew is in place, dressed in suitable firefighting attire, with their equipment spaced out to enable a rapid response to any incident in that area.

DEVASTATION ON BRAY HILL

It had been a busy couple of weeks at the 2013 TT, and to be honest, I was looking forward to the end of the races, in the hope that the island could get back to some sense of normality. It was a bank holiday and the last day of racing, the sun was out, drawing masses of spectators to the circuit to watch the most prestigious of the races, the Senior TT.

I was allocated to ride a pumping appliance inside the course, which was positioned there as part of the TT procedures implemented during race periods. Douglas Fire Station sits outside the course, and as there is only a narrow access road to the inside, it was deemed best practice to have a pumping appliance in position on the inside of the course to allow the Service to attend any incidents without delay. We parked up at Brigade Headquarters, which also happens to be located on the inside of the course, and sat in the sun as we discussed the races, whilst listening out for any messages on the appliance radio.

We could feel the excitement building in the spectators as we watched groups of them hurrying past us to take up their viewing positions at the bottom of Bray Hill, which was literally a hundred metres from where we were parked up. Bray Hill is a very popular viewing area for the races, as it's a notoriously fast part of the circuit that the riders face just after leaving the start of the race at the Grandstand. The bikes often reach speeds in excess of 170mph as they come down the hill, before shooting off towards Quarterbridge, another favoured spectator site.

The appliance radio suddenly cackled into life to inform all mobiles that the Senior Race had started, although we didn't need telling. From our position, we could clearly hear the roar from the superbikes as they were unleashed down the hill. The noise was unmistakable, and the sound reverberated through the air, whilst the commentator on the radio speakers, positioned along the road, blasted out the names of which riders were next to leave the Grandstand.

Everything seemed to be going to plan until suddenly we heard an unusually loud bang, followed by the sound of people screaming. I jumped up, trying to figure out what had gone on, and within a minute, Control came on the radio to state that the race was being red-flagged due to an incident on Bray Hill. I instantly thought that it didn't sound good and that we should be mobilised to the incident, so we asked Control if they required us to attend, but were told to hold our position until they clarified what had happened.

Feeling frustrated at knowing we were only a hundred metres away and being denied permission to mobilise, we decided to make our way on foot to the bottom of Bray Hill, just to see if we could gather any further information for Control. We figured that it would be best to leave the appliance parked out of the way at HQ, as we assumed that ambulances would be requiring access, so the last thing we wanted to do was block the road with a fire engine that hadn't been officially mobilised. Grabbing all the essential medical equipment that we could carry, we hurried as fast as we could to the barrier that closed off the bottom of Bray Hill to vehicles coming from the side roads.

On arrival at the barrier, we collared a race marshal who was standing with his flag out, and asked him what had happened. He told us that a rider had come off his bike, and the bike had struck a load of spectators. Our liaison officer in the Race Control Tower then came on the radio to inform us that no further bikes would be coming down Bray Hill, and that a number of spectators had reportedly been injured. With no danger of any other bikes hurtling down the hill, we took the decision to enter the course to try and assist with those injured.

What we came across was a scene of utter devastation. About 20 metres up from the bottom of Bray Hill, we could see a mass of spectators, surrounded by race marshals and bits of a motorbike scattered right down to the bottom of the hill. All at once, help started to arrive in the form of ambulances and the Police. However, you could tell by the look on people's faces that there were some serious injuries to deal with. I started to evaluate the more seriously injured, and pointed the ambulance staff in their direction. One particular individual had a very serious leg injury, which I later found out needed to be amputated, but there were also others that obviously required urgent medical attention to treat their injuries. It was one of the worst crashes in TT history, made worse by the fact that it had involved so many spectators, who were there purely to enjoy watching the racing, but ended up being involved in a nightmare of an incident.

In all, ten spectators were injured in the crash, with seven needing operations on reaching hospital. The rider, Jonathon Howarth, suffered a minor fracture of his leg and the loss of some skin in his genital region, but overall had escaped relatively unharmed and had even staggered to his feet straight after the crash, despite the pain he must have suffered.

Jonathon had lost control of his Kawasaki ZX-10R due to a mechanical failure, whilst travelling at close to 170 miles per hour. He came off the bike and slid down to the bottom of the hill, where he came to an abrupt stop. His bike disintegrated as it also slid down the hill, before crashing into the scaffolded sitting area, where it caused the devastating injuries to the spectators in that location. The fuel tank, having been dislodged, flew down to the bottom of the hill and soared over the heads of another group of spectators. The front wheel bounced down the road and took off into the air, smashing through a first-floor window of a house looking onto the course. As luck would have it, two children who were watching the race from this viewpoint, had just left the room moments before to retrieve something from elsewhere in the house. Months after this incident, the house was put up for sale, and who could blame the parents after their miraculous escape?

FIREBALL

Having mentioned the Bray Hill incident, I feel it only right that I mention another TT incident which ended up requiring the attendance of the Fire Service.

In 2010, Guy Martin – a top TT rider and well-known television personality – was leading the Senior TT race as he entered the pit lane to be refuelled, before setting off on his third lap. He was pushing hard, willed on by most of the crowd watching, as the popular Guy had never won a TT race, despite coming close on a number of occasions.

As he entered a fast part of the circuit, called Ballagarey (nicknamed Balla-scarey by all the riders), he was reaching a speed in excess of 170mph. Suddenly, he lost control, smashing his Honda CBR1000RR into a stone wall. Guy was flung from the bike as its brimming fuel tank ruptured, causing a fireball that had never before been seen in a TT race. Guy bounced across the road and slammed into another wall, before coming to rest in the middle of the road.

The race was immediately red-flagged and, due to the fire that had engulfed hedges and bales of straw, the Fire Service were requested to attend.

Alan Gawne, my line manager, was the Station Officer in charge of the pump that day, and he described the drive out to the job as being a bit surreal. He says he received notice to go, and sat in the appliance to join the course at Quarterbridge, where they waited for the course inspection car which was going to lead them to the incident. The car, a Porsche, came flying down Bray Hill and took the right at Quarterbridge. The driver of the appliance put his foot down to follow, but there was no way he was going to keep pace with the Porsche, no matter how hard he tried, so Alan asked him to just take it steady and to make sure they all got there in one piece.

They passed Braddan Bridge and Braddan Church, which were packed with spectators, who cheered as they sped through, taking up both sides of the road, as if on a racing line. Alan said that all the way through Union Mills and in the fields leading to Glen Vine, people were waving and cheering them on as if they were part of the race.

They arrived at the scene and expected to see a blanket covering a body, as a rider had died in the same place the day before, and Alan expected the same result. But there was no sign of Guy Martin, so the boys got to work putting out the fires.

He stated that the whole area was a bit of a bomb site, looking like a scene that had been lifted straight out of a movie, with small fires spread across a large area, and a helicopter hovering overhead. Just then the lead travelling marshal (marshals who ride motorbikes placed around the circuit) arrived, and pointed out Guy Martin in the distance, being strapped to a stretcher, whilst talking away to the medics. Alan says that he walked up past the smouldering remains of the Honda and looked across at Guy, who appeared very alert and unbelievably calm as he was lifted to the helicopter to be transported to hospital.

Nobody at the scene could believe how Guy had survived such a big crash, especially with it being at such a high speed. On arrival at Nobles Hospital, it was found that Guy had only suffered bruising to both lungs and some minor fractures to his upper spine. He had lived to tell the tale, and said in a later interview that as he came off the bike, he had expected the worst to happen and that it would be the end of him. He said that he remembered bouncing off the walls, but was not aware of the fireball, and it wasn't until someone showed him the footage that he realised how lucky he had been.

The driver of the fire appliance, David Craine, stated afterwards that it was one of the highlights of his career driving to the job, with the amount of people cheering and waving him on. I must admit there is not one firefighter, including me, who would not have loved to have been in the driving seat, speeding along to that incident. The adrenalin rush must have been great, especially as they were hitting the bends at speed, with the knowledge that they could take the racing line without the worry of any oncoming traffic. Nevertheless, we hope an incident like that never occurs again, and that all the riders who come to race travel home safely.

CHAPTER THIRTY-FOUR

DUTY OFFICER AND THE LAST BIG JOBS

In late September 2011, my line manager Alan Gawne retired, and the Service looked at how best to fill his position. Initially, an Assistant Divisional Officer was put in place, until eventually, in July 2013, I took on the role of Station Officer in charge of the Corporate Services Department.

The promotion meant that I would no longer ride fire appliances to incidents, but would, whenever I was the Duty or Second Officer, travel to incidents in the Duty Officer car. These cars were engine-enhanced Ford Focus, which I later changed to enhanced Hyundai i30s. They were fully decaled up with Fire Service livery, and came complete with a full light bar on the roof, as well as an excellent audible warning system which penetrated the sound to a good distance. As a Station Officer, you were rostered to do Duty/Second Officer duties either a couple of days during the week, or for the weekend, starting on the Friday morning until Monday morning.

When on duty, you would be the first point of call for the Control room, who would ring you any time of day or night to inform you of an ongoing incident, or to check what they should mobilise to any unusual jobs. You were expected to make decisions immediately, even though you might have just been awoken from a deep sleep, where your mind would be working overtime to understand the gravity of the situation that Control would be describing to you, knowing that they required instant answers to their questions.

If you thought there was a need for you to attend the incident, you would swiftly dress, get in the car, and blue light it to anywhere on the island. The phone would ring, and your heart would pound at the thought of what incident was coming next, but I loved every minute of it and never let an opportunity go by that allowed me to book mobile in the car and to have an adrenalin-fuelled blue light drive. Even when I was off duty, my personal radio would always be switched on, allowing me to listen to any jobs that were happening on the island. If the job happened to be anything decent, I would listen to the radio traffic intently, whilst being slightly envious of the Duty Officer who was attending.

I found the whole system fun – as did my kids when they watched me pull off the house driveway, with blue lights flashing and horns blazing, mobile to an incident. It did, however, have a downside, where I would periodically leave a trolley full of shopping in the middle of a supermarket, or leave the wife and kids stranded on a beach on a sunny Sunday afternoon, whilst I disappeared for an unknown amount of time. But it was a fabulous experience, and I would do it all over again in the blink of an eye.

Most times, when you turned out to an incident, you knew the OIC in attendance would have had the job covered. I would still go to these kinds of jobs, not to undermine their decisions, but to offer any support or reassurance that they might need. Occasionally, if the job was going to escalate, only then would I take command of the incident. Fortunately, the need to take over was a very rare occurrence, as all the Retained Officers, as well as the Wholetime Officers, were well trained in incident command.

FISHERS HILL RTC

On Saturday, 5th October, 2013, I was Duty Officer for the weekend, and was sitting at home watching television when I received a call from the Emergency Services Joint Control Room. They stated that there had been a collision between a bus and a car at Fishers Hill, on the outskirts of Castletown. They said that they had mobilised Castletown's pumping appliance and Rescue Pump, as well as the Emergency Rescue Vehicle (ERV) with supporting pump from Douglas. I immediately booked mobile to incident.

I was just driving past the grandstand in Douglas when Jeff Howland, the OIC of the first appliance to arrive at scene, put back his initial informative message. He had assessed the situation and realised straight away that he needed extra assistance to deal with the enormity of the incident in front of him. However, in delivering his message, he was standing too close to the persons trapped in the vehicle, and the haunting sound of a child screaming was transmitted loud and harrowingly across the airwaves. It sent chills through my soul, and I put my foot to the metal and accelerated down Bray Hill to head south to Castletown.

I quickly caught the Douglas appliances on Richmond Hill, and they gave way to me as I sped past them, hurrying on towards the incident. Jeff had stated that there were a number of casualties, and requested enough ambulances to attend. As luck would have it, the Ambulance Service was having a team bonding day at a local adventure centre, and had ample personnel and vehicles available. They mobilised immediately on hearing of the incident, with even the Ambulance Chief Officer driving an ambulance to Fishers Hill that day.

I arrived at the scene and could see that a BMW had smashed into a single-decker Citaro bus, which in turn had crashed into a stone wall in an instinctive effort to try and avoid the collision. I observed that there were a number of people trapped in the wreckage of the BMW which, by looking at the damage caused, must have been travelling at some speed prior to hitting the bus. Jeff briefed me with what he had put in place, and pointed out six casualties that were walking wounded. He had placed them in a casualty holding area to await the arrival of the Ambulance Service. He reported that all four of the occupants of the car were in a bad way, but that it was a young girl that was causing him the most concern. The Douglas crews arrived, and I spoke to the OIC of the ERV, who just happened to be a highly trained Road Traffic Collision Instructor. I relayed Jeff's concerns, and asked him to formulate the best plan of action.

The crews on the ground worked extremely professionally, and despite the extraction being tremendously difficult, they eventually had all the trapped casualties cut out of the wreckage and transported by ambulances to hospital. Sadly, the young ten-year-old girl died before reaching hospital. Her young brother suffered serious injuries and was flown off the island that day, to be treated at a hospital in the UK, and the mother was also badly injured, but was able to be treated on the island at Nobles Hospital in Douglas.

The father, who was the driver, was in a critical condition, and was flown immediately off island to Walton Hospital in Liverpool. Following his recovery, he was charged with causing Death by Dangerous Driving as well as causing Serious Injury by Dangerous Driving. His defence was that he had fallen asleep at the wheel, having just returned from a trip to Ireland that morning. He was given a 12-month suspended prison sentence, but his bigger sentence is that he has to live the rest of his life knowing that he caused his daughter's death.

The bus driver, Donald Faragher, despite having a broken ankle, managed to evacuate his passengers and isolate the electrics on the bus, and he was praised by everyone who attended the scene. His calmness in alerting the emergency services and putting all his passengers' safety first, was appreciated by all those he dealt with that day. He never really recovered from the incident, though, and ultimately had to give up his job as a bus driver. The day after the incident, as a mark of my appreciation for his actions at that traumatic job, I dropped down a bottle of malt whisky to the bus company to pass onto him, with a note of my gratitude attached, sincerely wishing him 'the best' in whatever his future held.

As a side note, it is worth mentioning the performance of the Duty Officer's car that I drove that day. Unfortunately, on hearing the screams of the child when Jeff passed his informative message, I had driven the Ford Focus so hard getting there, that when I went to leave the scene, it refused to start. I had literally blown the engine, which resulted in it being recovered and eventually scrapped. It had given everything driving to its last incident, and it was sad that it couldn't be repaired, but at least the insurance pay-out allowed us to buy a new Hyundai i30 as a replacement.

COSTLY BLAZE

It was a bright and sunny autumn day on Thursday, 7th November, 2013 and I was rostered to be the Second Officer for the day, whilst my colleague, Station Officer John Bellis, was the Duty Officer. We were both working on Douglas Station, when a call came through for a confirmed fire at a large hotel called the Mount Murray Hotel and Country Club, located in Santon. A roofer doing some repair work had accidentally set fire to the roof, whilst trying to dry out some timber with a blow torch. Due to the nature of the call, it was obviously going to be a working job. So, as John jumped into the Duty Officer's car to mobilise to the incident, I proceeded to stand in the car park to ensure the crews responding to their alerters reacted swiftly when they arrived at the station.

I listened carefully to my radio and heard John booking his arrival on scene, where he immediately made-up pumps and requested both the Aerial appliances to attend. On hearing this, I thought it best if I headed up to the Emergency Services Joint Control Room, where I could monitor the job more closely. I guessed that this job was going to be a big one.

I figured Control would be the best place for me to be, as I knew that if the incident was going to escalate, I would be required to make important decisions on all our resources. I could ensure that not only would John receive all that he required to fight the blaze, but also that the rest of the island had sufficient fire cover to keep it safe.

The problem we have in firefighting on an island is that we cannot rely on support from neighbouring Brigades, as they do in the UK. Once all our resources are in use, that's it, no further help will be arriving quickly. Therefore it's vital that we monitor closely what is in use and what is going to be required. We do have agreements with Merseyside and other North West Brigades for them to send assistance, but in reality, that would take quite a few hours to sort out and to get them here.

Another factor is that if we are unable to have sufficient fire appliances available in the south of the island to assist the Airport

Fire Service in the event of an aircraft incident, then the airport
has to close down, refusing any aircraft permission to land or take
off. These are not decisions that can be made lightly, and if we got
to that stage, the muck really would have hit the proverbial fan.

I arrived in Control and set myself up at a free desk. The job
was escalating, and further pumps were being requested. The
ambulance and hospital were put on notice that there was a major
incident happening, but luckily only one man suffered minor
injuries the whole day. Information from John stated that the fire
was spreading throughout the roof of the accommodation block,
and that they were trying to get a stop on it before it reached the
restaurant and reception area of the hotel.

I wished I had been the Duty Officer watching the flames do
their dance, but I had a job to do in the Control room, and I was
watching carefully, monitoring what resources we were using,
whilst considering what was remaining in the event of another
incident happening elsewhere on the island. I had to ensure that
all our major risk areas still had sufficient resources if the need
arose, but things were getting tight, so I hoped that the boys at
Mount Murray would soon have a stop on the fire. However,
listening to the radio messages being passed from the fire ground,
I knew that the stop message was a long way off.

Just then, the Airport Fire Service came on to Control, offering
any assistance that they could. They would have been able to see
the smoke from the Airport Control Tower and would have had
concerns over the threat of closure to the airport if too many
pumps were pulled to the incident. They offered the use of an
airport Crash Tender that can deliver a huge amount of water
through a monitor mounted on top of the appliance. They also
advised that a couple of IOMFRS Retained personnel who worked
at the Airport Fire Service, were on duty and were willing to bring
the Crash Tender to the incident.

I tried to contact John, who was the OIC of the incident, but
due to the amount of radio traffic and the fact that he was as busy
as hell, I couldn't get through. I was becoming concerned over
the number of pumping appliances I had left to play with, so took
the decision out of John's hands and mobilised the Crash Tender.

I knew the Airport Fire Service did driver training in the Crash Tenders on public roads around the airport, so had no qualms about mobilising them, but I'm sure it must have been some sight watching it drive under blue light conditions from the airport to Santon.

The Crash Tender arrived on scene, and rapidly got to work with its monitor, although the driver must have been a bit overexcited, as he parked sideways on a huge grass slope leading up to the hotel. It wasn't a safe position, and that had been noticed by Divisional Officer Allan Bell who was on scene, so he promptly got the Tender repositioned and the fire fight recommenced. The airport boys were simply used to flat runways, and hadn't realised that the slope they were on had the potential to roll the truck. Lesson learned!

Eventually, the fire was brought under control, but not before it had caused £17million worth of damage. The business never recovered, and the hotel remained closed until 2016, when it was bought by another hotel group and renamed the Comis Hotel and Golf Resort. The roofer who started the blaze was prosecuted under Health and Safety Legislation, but was spared jail, and given 240 hours of community service, after being found guilty of three 'foreseeable' health and safety breaches.

A MIRACLE ON MARINE DRIVE

It was a cold bleak winter's night on Saturday, 23rd January, 2016, and I was sitting at home having an enjoyable meal with my wife, when the Duty Officer's phone rang. It was Control informing me that a car had been reported crashing over the cliffs on Marine Drive, Douglas. I confirmed the pre-determined attendance, and without delay jumped in the car to blue light it down to the scene.

Arriving at Marine Drive at the same time as the appliances from Douglas Station pulled up, I instantly started to survey the scene, trying to locate the vehicle that was reportedly involved. Scanning my eyes down the dark face of the cliffs, I struggled to pick out the shape of any wreckage. Nothing was obvious except the white foam of the waves as they smashed into the rocks below, causing a continuous rumble to fill the air.

We had been told that it was a black Subaru that had gone over the edge, and that one of the calls to the Emergency Services had come from a passenger in the vehicle. But as I continued to search over the cliff edge, I found it hard to believe that anyone could have survived the crash, never mind make phone calls. Eventually, with my eyes starting to adjust to the dark night, I could just make out the shape of a vehicle which had come to rest, jammed in a ravine, just metres from the raging sea below.

The occupants of a car following the Subaru had witnessed the crash, which was fortunate, as it enabled us to immediately pinpoint where the accident had occurred, instead of us having to search the whole coastline along the mile-long Marine Drive. Having located the vehicle, I asked the duty crew to set up as much lighting as they could, while I ordered on the Brigade's Line Rescue Team and requested the Coastguard to attend.

As I stood evaluating different plans of action in my head, I quickly came to the decision that plan 'A' would be to retrieve the casualties up the cliff face, but I needed a plan 'B' just in case things didn't work out. So I immediately requested for the Douglas Lifeboat to be launched. That would give me an alternative exit route, just in case we couldn't retrieve the casualties up the cliff face.

By that stage, I had been informed that the car contained three teenagers, and that they were all alive and had managed to crawl out of the wreckage, but they were stuck on the cliff face, unable to climb up the steep incline. How the three of them had survived the heavy impact into the ravine is still a mystery to me, but clearly someone up high was looking down on them that night.

The Line Rescue Team arrived and immediately got to work setting up their lines. After establishing good anchor points, they were just about ready to go down the cliff face, when the Coastguard arrived on scene. However, I was aware by their body language, as soon as they got out of their vehicle, that they were not a happy bunch. Their OIC rapidly approached me and expressed his thoughts that the incident should have been their job straight away, and that they were annoyed the Fire Service had been turned out first. Admittedly, the Coastguard are supposed to be called first to any incidents along the coastline, with the Fire Service being the first point of call for any incidents inland. But when the general public make their telephone call for assistance, a lot of the time they automatically ask for the Fire Service, especially when the incident isn't in the sea. It is a grey area which tends to upset the Coastguard, but the way I look at it is that it doesn't really matter which Service gets to the scene, as long as they respond quickly and do the job they are trained to do, and hopefully rescue any persons whose lives are deemed to be at risk.

Nevertheless, I reasoned that it wasn't the best time to get into an argument with another Service, so I tried my best to calm the situation and suggested they work alongside us, as we had already put our lines in place. They had no option but to agree, although I could feel the animosity towards us, as they whinged and complained about the position of our vehicles being in the way of them setting up their gear. I bowed to their demands and, to keep the peace, I got a couple of vehicles moved so that they could put their lines exactly where they wanted them. The lifeboat arrived and stood offshore to await further instruction, but as I have said, plan 'A' was to bring the youngsters up the cliff face. It was without doubt my preferred option, as the sea had turned a bit nasty and was being whipped up by the strong wind that seemed to be increasing by the minute.

While all the preparation for the rescues was taking place, I was presented with another small matter to deal with. Somehow – probably from a phone call by the youths themselves – a load of their relatives had turned up at the scene. Although they didn't cause any real issues, they obviously had concerns for their loved ones and wanted to know what was happening. This, along with the attitude of the Coastguard, was all I needed, so I insisted that the Police, who were in attendance, look after the relatives well outside the cordon we had set up. I wasn't being rude; I just had a job to do and could have done without the distractions.

Everything seemed to be in place to commence the rescue, and as the Line Rescue Teams began their descent, I realised that calling on the Lifeboat had been a great decision. The lighting the Lifeboat was able to produce from its strong searchlights, illuminated the whole bottom section of the cliff face, including the ravine where the wreckage was located, and that definitely made the job of the Line Rescue Teams a lot easier as they worked to bring the three casualties up the cliff. Slowly, one by one, the teenagers were safely rescued, and once at the top, immediately transported to hospital by ambulance.

To this day, whenever I walk along Marine Drive, I look down at the ravine and consider how things could have been a lot worse, especially if the three kids had been trapped by the wreckage. As it was, they all only received minor injuries, and for people who had driven off a 30-metre cliff, I believe this was 'A Miracle on Marine Drive'.

The driver, a 16-year-old boy, was prosecuted and charged with causing serious harm by driving without due care and attention. He received an 18-month driving ban, in which time I hoped he reflected on the incident and appreciated how lucky he and his friends had been. As for the car, what was left of the high-performance vehicle was eventually craned back to the top of the cliffs once the weather conditions permitted, and dispatched to its final resting place at the local scrapyard.

CHAPTER THIRTY-FIVE

RESPECT

Throughout my service, I always considered my promotions as a privilege, and hoped that I used my rank in the correct way. I tried to treat those working in ranks below me fairly, and always attempted to ensure that my passion for the job always shone through. I had constantly striven to make the job better for all and to put the Service first, even if it was to the detriment of my own ambitions. I, therefore, fully expected the same from those in ranks above me.

One man who I felt had shown the same passion for the job as me was CFO Draper. I had enjoyed working for him, and hoped he would be in post until after I had retired. But in 2013, CFO Draper took the decision to leave the Service and retire. I liked and respected Brian, as I felt that he had the Fire Service at heart and had always done his best in fighting the politicians to ensure the Service received as fair a budget as possible, which then enabled us to maintain the high standard that we delivered to the people of the Isle of Man.

Brian had been the fifth Chief Fire Officer that I had served with during my time in the Fire Service, and of course I had also served under two Chief Constables during my short stint in the Police. In my eyes, he had proven himself to be a fantastic Chief, who was well respected by everyone that dealt with him. It was sad news to hear that he was leaving, but life has to move on, and I waited in anticipation on the announcement of his successor.

Within a short period of time, it was announced that CFO Draper's replacement and my sixth Chief would be the person who had served as Brian's Deputy Chief. In that role, he had tended to concentrate on Fire Safety issues, and although he oversaw the Corporate Service Department's annual budget,

I really hadn't had that much to do with him. He tended to leave us alone to get on with our jobs, which suited me fine. But his reputation worried me as he was known to be a bit egotistical, which obviously made me wonder whether he had the capability of putting the Fire Service before his own needs and desires. I hoped that I would be wrong, and that as the CFO he would put up the same fight as Brian had, in trying to maintain all our allocated budgets. If he didn't, I was sure that the Service would suffer, because the politicians were still determined to cut government spending and we needed a leader who would fight tooth and nail to prevent it.

The change at the top happened, and I respected the rank as I tried to adapt to the new Chief and his way of running the Service. One of his first duties was to appoint a new Deputy to fill his old job, and this was given to a likeable character, who had spent a big chunk of his career serving with the new CFO in the Fire Safety Department. It was a big change in role for the new Deputy, and it clearly showed. In my view, he appeared at a loss to what his responsibilities should be, and initially struggled to find his way. During this period, for some unknown reason, he tended to interfere with everything Corporate Services were trying to do, which came across as showing a total lack of respect for everything my Department had achieved and were still achieving.

This came to a head when I had prepared a business case to replace all the life jackets within the Service, as the old ones were coming to the end of their recommended life span. I had sourced a credible supplier that most of the North West Brigades were using, and got a reasonable quote to complete the purchase. However, I had to put a stop to the deal at the last minute, as the Deputy said he could get a better price. I handed over the project and, to be fair to the Deputy, he did get a tremendous price for the new jackets. Unfortunately, after we had paid for them and the jackets arrived, it was discovered they were fake Chinese copies and not fit for purpose. The move had just cost the service thousands of pounds, and an awful lot of time to sort the mess out. It was at this time that I first thought it might be a good time to retire. I had little faith in the Deputy leaving me to get on with my job, and

I was certainly struggling to respect the new Chief Fire Officer, who seemed to lack the desire to fight the politicians while our Service continued to suffer more budgetary cuts.

ON THE PANEL

Unfortunately, I still had a few years to do before I had the maximum time served in order to retire, so I just had to put my head down and crack on doing the job, even if it meant dealing with the Deputy's continuous interference.

One of the duties that I did enjoy during this period, was sitting on a panel to interview potential new recruits. Having got through the various recruitment stages, the potential recruits would finally face a three-person interview panel, which was made up of two Fire Service personnel of Station Officer rank and above, and a person from the Human Resources Department. I always found it a joy to sit and listen to the passion shown by some of the potential recruits, but I was also dismayed by some of them, who obviously thought the Fire Service would just be an easy number, and showed no real hunger for the job. Those who had the passion always got my full attention.

As I sat on my first panel, I thought back all those years to my interview with Tyne and Wear Metropolitan Fire Brigade and could remember how nervous I had felt. I had empathy with the candidates, and tried to make them feel at ease as soon as they entered the room. Humour has always been my go-to thing whenever I am nervous, so I tried to make the candidates smile with some witty comment that would help them relax into their situation. It seemed to work, and at times I had the HR person on the panel giggling away as well.

On one panel, a young lady called Amber Carridge came in for interview, having already successfully come through all the processes to this final stage. She was exceptional, and nailed every question that was asked of her, showing a passion which shone through right from the first question asked. There was no doubt in my mind that she was by far the best candidate that had come to interview that day. Following discussions with the other two on the panel, they had no option but to agree that Amber should be the first choice for the only job that was available. But there was an obstacle: the IOMFRS had never had a Wholetime female firefighter, and the station was not designed to take one. They had taken on a couple of females in the role of Retained Officers, but they didn't require sleeping quarters. Nonetheless, Amber had proved to us that she was the best candidate and deserved to be recruited, so we fought her corner to be given the opportunity.

The Senior Management Team were left with little option but to endorse the selection, and allowed us to invite Amber to join the IOMFRS. I was delighted for her, and while she spent her time away at training school, alterations were made to the station to accommodate a female sleeping and shower area, in order that everything would be in place when she returned to take her place on a Watch.

As it happened, the choice of Amber was proven to be a good one, as she went on to win the Silver Axe at training school. This award is only given to the candidate who the Instructors decide was the best recruit throughout the course. In winning the award, Amber had outshone the other 13 recruits on the course, from five other Brigades.

On returning to the island, Amber has gone on to be a fully competent firefighter, and I would expect her to climb through the ranks whenever she desires. She has become an ambassador to any females out there wanting to join the Fire Service, and I truly wish her all best for the rest of her career.

THE LAST JAPE

One of my last duties before retirement was to buy a couple of new cars for the Service. One was going to be the Chief's personal car, and one was going to be used for the Senior Officers whenever they were on duty in the role of Brigade Officer. I personally hadn't felt we should be buying these vehicles, as I wanted to spend the money on a new minibus to transport firefighters to incidents. The old minibus was well past its best and needed continual maintenance, so I believed that a replacement would be the best use of monies allocated for vehicle replacement within that year's budget. I also felt that both the Chief's current car and the Brigade Officers' car still had a couple of years left to run, but the Chief overruled me.

As a token of my disgust at the decision, I initially informed the CFO that I was going to get the vehicles fully decaled up, with reflective strips on the sides and the Brigade logo on the bonnet, along with a large lightbar across the roof. The Chief told me I would be on a discipline charge if I did, and that he wanted a plain silver car with no decals, and the blue lights had to be covertly hidden in the front grill.

The Chief was known to be a bit anal with his vehicles, and always had to have them spotlessly clean. He was forever down at Douglas Station, washing the car and polishing it with a chamois leather. So, before I left, I thought I would treat him to a car that he would love to polish. I ordered the vehicles and, as he had desired, they were to be left plain, with blue lights discreetly hidden in the grill. I had arranged for the delivery of the vehicles to be after my final retirement date, and left it at that.

I retired, and the cars arrived on schedule, to be proudly parked on the forecourt of the station to await inspection by the Chief. He arrived from Headquarters to take possession of his new vehicle, but when he arrived it was obvious to all that he wasn't a very happy bunny, and initially refused to give up his old car for what stood before him.

He had asked for the new car to be silver, so I intended to order moondust silver. However, in my haste to complete the order, I must have ordered the colour Shadow by mistake, in homage to the serial arsonist that we often dealt with. I hadn't realised my mistake until after the cars arrived, but had to raise a wry smile as I drove past the station and saw the newly arrived cars looking slightly dusty from their travels. The colour 'Shadow' just happened to be a lovely shade of black. And as everyone is aware, a black car is the hardest to keep clean. No matter how often they are polished, the dust off the road seems to stick to the bodywork like mud to a stick! What an unfortunate mistake to make! *But*, I thought, *at least the CFO enjoys polishing cars...* It appeared that the last jape was mine!

MANX CHARACTERS

In an earlier chapter of the book, I described some of the firefighters that I worked with in Tyne and Wear. I feel it is only fair that I give the same exposure to the characters I worked with on the Isle of Man, although I am sure most of them would rather I had just got on that boat!

John 'Degsy' Bellis, who was the Duty Officer in charge of the Mount Murray Hotel fire, almost had another claim to fame. Whilst doing secondary employment as a taxi driver, John had picked up a film producer, called Britt Allcroft, from the airport on the island and chatted to her on the way to her hotel. She loved his Liverpudlian accent and thought it would be ideal for the voiceover for *Thomas the Tank Engine*, the movie that she was planning. John, never one to miss an opportunity, agreed to do some demo takes, and before he knew it, he was being whisked away to Los Angeles to a professional studio. He arrived back on the island only to receive a telephone call from Britt saying they had put the demo tapes out to an American audience, but the feedback was that they couldn't understand a word he was saying in his strong Scouse accent. He had enjoyed the experience, but was swiftly replaced with someone who could speak the Queen's English. Personally, I think a Geordie accent would have worked wonders!

Paul 'Rothy' Rothwell, a firefighter I served with on Red Watch. Rothy was a fireman on the steam trains before joining the Fire Service, feeding the fuel into the fire alongside the train driver. On his retirement from the service, he returned to once again feed the flames on the trains, leaving him with a legacy of being the only man I know who was a 'Fireman, who became a Fireman, who then became a Fireman'.

Howard 'Tick Tock' Davies, a firefighter with a razor-sharp wit, who became a legend with all he served with. Howard never liked to wear breathing apparatus and never drove the appliances, but still managed to fulfil a 30-year career, despite Senior Management trying to get rid of him throughout that time. His family owned a local watch repair shop, and Howard always loved to tinker with watches, so received the name of Tick Tock. He was always hungry and would eat absolutely anything, although he came a cropper once when he retrieved some chicken skins from the kitchen bin and downed them in one, only to suffer the worst case of diarrhoea that the boys on station have ever witnessed. A taxi was called, and Howard was shipped off home to lose plenty of his body weight down the toilet.

Tony Duncan, a Station Officer within the Fire Service. Tony also heads up the travelling marshals for the TT and other motorcycle events, such as the Festival of Motorcycling and the Southern 100. Tony is an established motorcycle rider himself, having previously won the Manx Grand Prix, which is run on the same circuit as the TT but for amateur riders.

Richard 'Dick' Harvey, who was the Station Officer in charge of Health and Safety within the IOMFRS. Dick is a huge character who once drove back from a job late at night, thinking that there was a fantastic full moon glowing in the midnight sky. But just after passing under a footbridge, he realised that it wasn't a full moon but that he had left the appliance light mast up. With an almighty crunch, the mast hit the footbridge, sadly bringing Dick's full moon crashing down to earth. He also had, to the annoyance of the Senior Management Team, a terrible habit of falling asleep in meetings, where he would have to be prodded awake. Once awake, he would then crunch on mint imperials like a cart horse enjoying a snack, making such a noise that never failed to put a disgruntled look on the faces of the Senior Officers.

Gary Hinds, who I almost arrested in my last week of policing, went on to become a competent Sub Officer, before retiring to run a cycle shop. Gary has a heart of gold, and although it has been broken on numerous occasions, he would do anything for anyone. As a strange coincidence, Gary and his lad used to put up firefighters from my old Brigade in Tyne and Wear, whenever they visited the Island for the TT races. This started well before I came to the island, and when he talked of these firefighters, I realised I knew them all from Station Kilo. It's a small world!

Steven Brearley, a former tank commander, who joined the IOMFRS at the same time as me. Steve drove fire engines like he drove a tank, and once got a Pinzgauer, which had a reputation as being able to drive anywhere, stuck on its side in a narrow track. He also had a reputation for reversing appliances into the appliance room ceiling. Some of the bays at Douglas were situated where you needed to reverse in carefully to avoid hitting the sloping ceiling at the back of the appliance room. Steve had asked me to be a banksman and watch him back in. I did watch him until he hit the ceiling, and then I said stop. The shock on his face as I walked away smiling was a picture to be seen. He never asked me to be his banksman ever again!

Paul 'Big H' Hunt. Although I have already mentioned Paul, I think it fair to comment that he was also a travelling marshal, having spent a number of years riding in the TT. Being a past Manx Grand Prix winner, he was a competent rider, but unfortunately came off his bike in wet conditions as he rode back down the mountain following a cancellation of a TT practice session. He received life-changing injuries, but it hasn't affected his sense of humour, and we meet for lunch regularly to reminisce over old jobs, or to listen to him tell stories of his racing career. Being out with H is like dining out with royalty. Everyone on the island seems to know him, and they cannot pass him without stopping to tell one tale or another. One story that he tells is how, when he was a firefighter on Watch, the now CFO (a Sub Officer then) threw H's newspaper out of the first-floor window of the station. H grabbed him by the ankles and dangled him out of the window until he apologised and promised to replace the newspaper. There have been a number of people who have said that the Service would be in a much better place had only H let go of his grip!

Other characters include the Brothers Grim – Keith and Trevor Moore, two brothers who were both firefighters on Douglas Station, although on different Watches. They, along with another retired firefighter, Keith Lund, are members of the world-famous Purple Helmets – a motorcycle comedy stunt group, who have entertained millions of people all over the world, with their daring stunts and unbelievable acts. If you ever get to see the Helmets, you can understand when I say they must all be nuts.

EPILOGUE

Like I said in earlier chapters, the Fire Service is full of all sorts of strange and wonderful characters, all with a story or two to tell. I have worked with some amazing people who, like me, have lived the dream, doing a job that we loved. However, not everyone joining the Fire Service, or the Police, will love what they are doing; both jobs can be physically and mentally draining, and that doesn't suit everyone. Some people join and leave after a short period of time, and I can fully appreciate and respect that. Nevertheless, for those who stay and make a full career out of it, one thing is for certain – you join as an individual, but you leave as a team member, with friendships that will last a lifetime. You are told when you join either Service that you are joining an extended family. After a while, you come to realise that this is so true, even down to those who are like grumpy grandads and spiteful aunties. But you also get brothers and sisters who will always have your back in times of trouble, and it's them you will always warmheartedly remember!

The Fire Service has changed dramatically over the years, even down to the rank structure in the UK. When I first joined TWMFB, the rank structure was as described, from Leading Firefighter to Chief Fire Officer. It changed just after I left, to Crew Managers and Watch Managers up to Chief Fire Officer. I still don't understand the reasons behind this change, but was glad to find that when I arrived at the IOMFRS, they still maintained the old rank structure. And rumour has it that the UK may revert to the old system. However, no matter how many changes are made, be it to rank structures or procedures, one thing you can rely on is that once those bells go down, those firefighters climbing onto those appliances will do their utmost to help anyone in need!